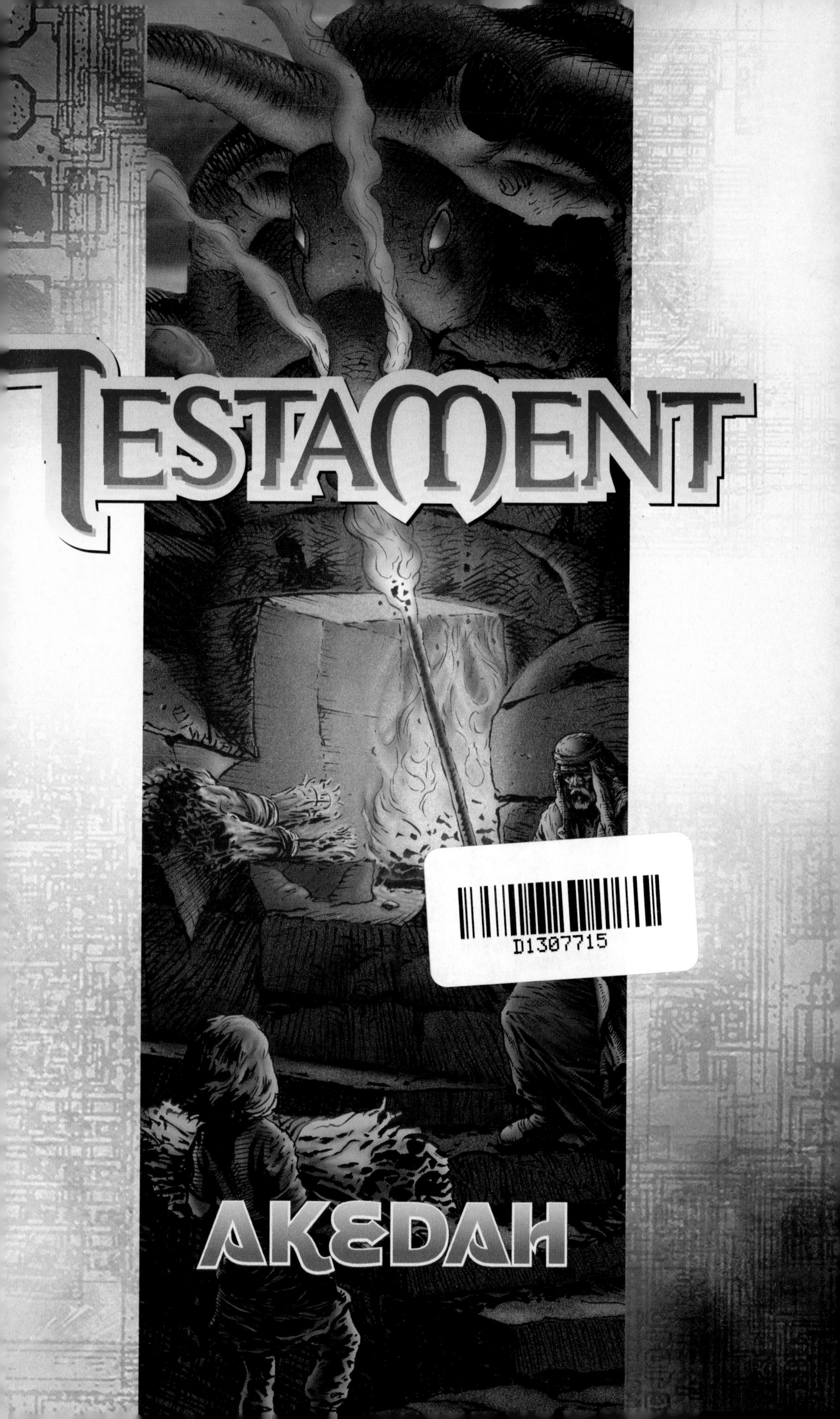
TESTAMENT
AKEDAH

"TESTAMENT IS DEFINITELY ONE OF THOSE SPECIAL READS THAT COMES ALONG TO THE WORLD OF COMICS ONCE IN A RARE WHILE."

—AIN'T IT COOL NEWS

"RUSHKOFF PROVES A NIMBLE YARN-SPINNER WITH THIS DYSTOPIAN SERIAL."

—ENTERTAINMENT WEEKLY

"TESTAMENT IS A GREAT COMIC BOOK, BUT MORE SIGNIFICANTLY, IT'S AN IMPORTANT ONE."

—COLUMBUS ALIVE!

"A STUNNING, RICHLY ENTERTAINING BOOK."

—ROBERT ANTON WILSON
CO-AUTHOR THE ILLUMINATUS! TRILOGY

"BIBLE SCHOLAR BRAINS MEET CYBERPUNK-SUPERHERO BRAWN! EXPLOSIVE!"

—GEOFF KLOCK
AUTHOR OF "HOW TO READ SUPERHERO COMICS AND WHY"

"THE MOST ASSURED AND ORIGINAL PROJECT TO EMERGE FROM VERTIGO SINCE SANDMAN."

—COMICS BUYER'S GUIDE

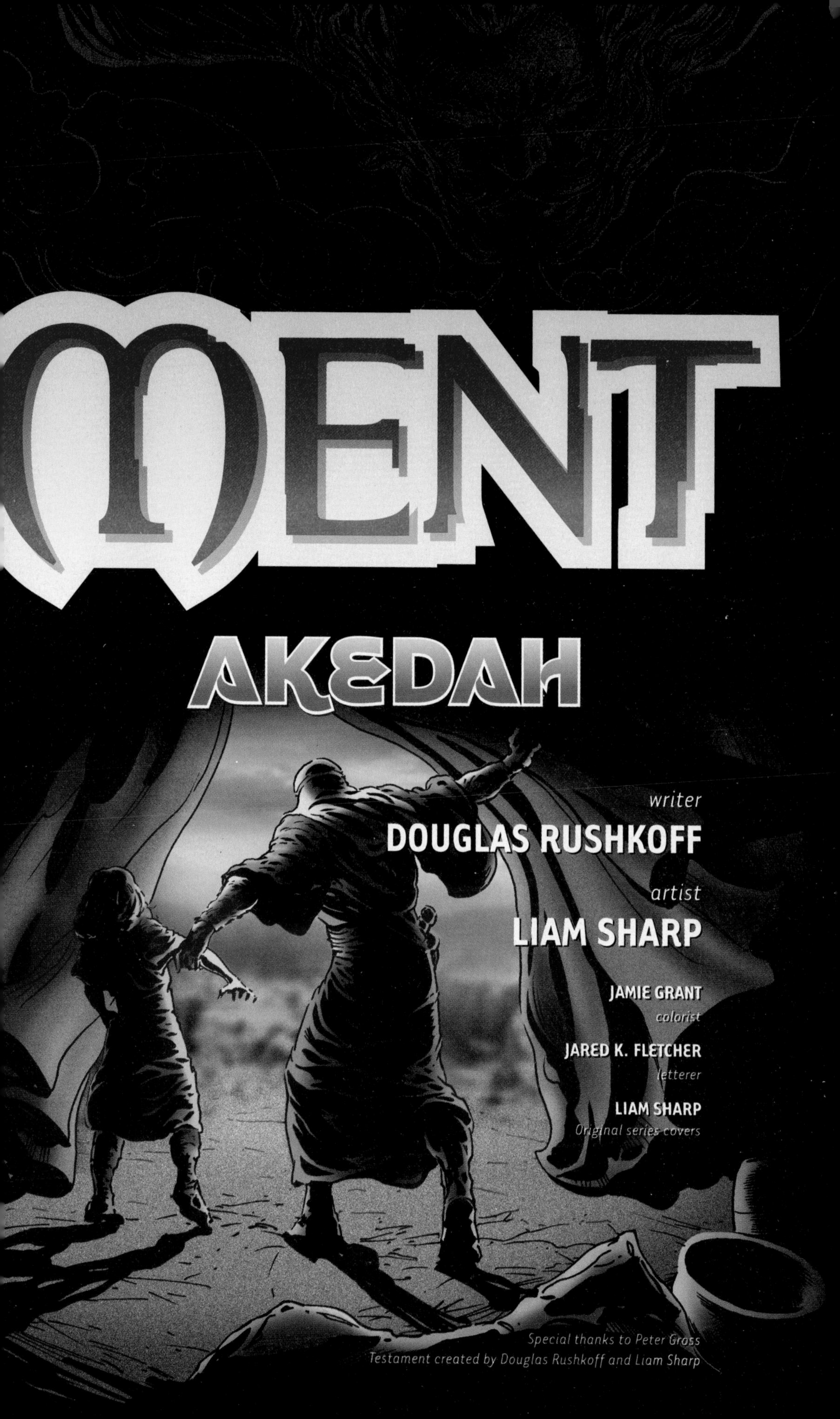

MENT

AKEDAH

writer

DOUGLAS RUSHKOFF

artist

LIAM SHARP

JAMIE GRANT
colorist

JARED K. FLETCHER
letterer

LIAM SHARP
Original series covers

Special thanks to Peter Gross
Testament created by Douglas Rushkoff and Liam Sharp

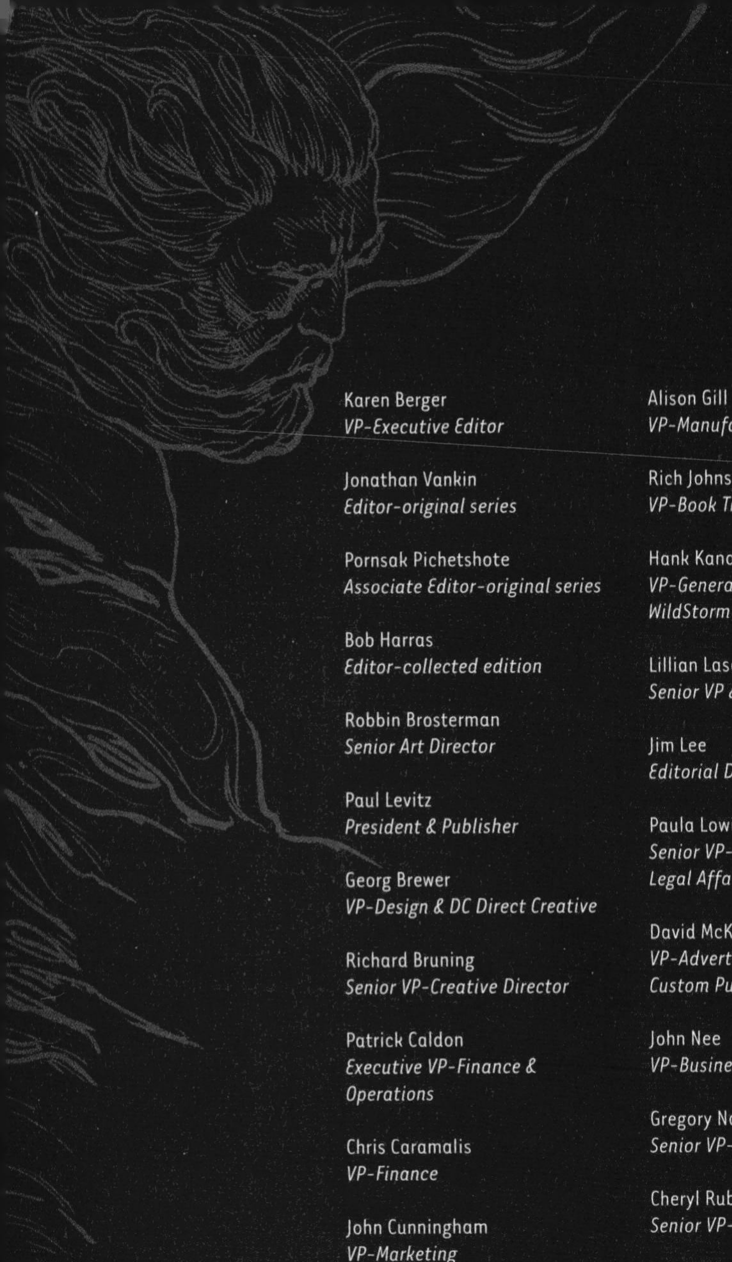

TESTAMENT: AKEDAH
Published by DC Comics. Cover, introduction and compilation copyright © 2006 DC Comics. All Rights Reserved.

Originally published in single magazine form as TESTAMENT 1-5. Copyright © 2006 Douglas Rushkoff and Liam Sharp. All Rights Reserved. All characters, their distinctive like-
nesses and related elements featured in this publication are trademarks of Douglas Rushkoff and Liam Sharp . The stories, characters and incidents featured in this publication are entirely fictional. DC Comics does not read or accept unsolicited submissions of ideas, stories or artwork.

DC Comics, 1700 Broadway, New York, NY 10019
A Warner Bros. Entertainment Company.
Printed in Canada. First Printing.
ISBN: 1-4012-1063-5. ISBN 13: 978-1-4012-1063-2.
Cover illustration by Liam Sharp.
Logo and publication design by Brainchild Studios/NYC.

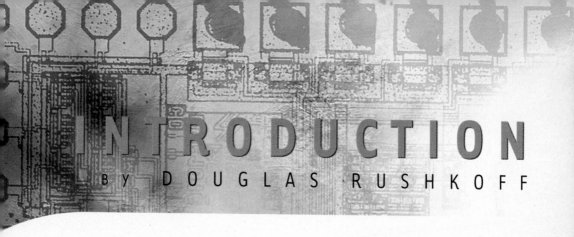

INTRODUCTION
BY DOUGLAS RUSHKOFF

THE BIBLE MAY HAVE ACTUALLY BEEN BETTER OFF AS A COMIC BOOK.

I'm saying this in my day-job persona as a halfway respectable media theorist — a guy who has written books and novels, taught university classes and made documentaries about the impact of new technology on the way we relate to stories. And particularly to those stories we happen to really believe in.

If anything, working in this field has taught me that our relationship to mythical narratives is stuck in a dangerous place. No, there's no great harm in watching TV or a movie and imagining ourselves as the characters on the screen. But we have lost access to the gaps in these stories. We're either afraid or forbidden to inhabit the places where temporality, interpretation and sequence are up for grabs. We just get lost in the seamless reality and get taken along for a ride. It's fun, even comforting on some level to be gently and unthreateningly entertained. We get a good night's sleep, and so do our stories' sponsors. As a general rule, that's how stories work — and how populations are kept in control.

Any time a new medium comes along, however, it challenges this little arrangement. The invention of text broke the monopoly that priests had on the collective story. Armed with a 22-letter alphabet, a ragtag bunch of Hebrew slaves went out into the desert and rewrote their reality from the beginning — along with a new set of laws based on living ethics instead of falsely promised rewards in the afterlife. It was an open source proposition — an ongoing conversation called Torah that eventually grew into what we now call the Bible.

Likewise, the invention of the printing press turned that sacred document into a mass-produced book. No longer dependent on a centralized priesthood for the holy word, people read the Bible for themselves, developed their own opinions and reinvented Christianity as Protestantism. And today, the emergence of interactive technologies like the computer has revived the open source tradition, providing the opportunity to again challenge unquestioned laws and beliefs and engage with our foundation myths as participatory narratives, as stories still in the making.

I've found some less than receptive audiences for these observations. When I wrote a book presenting the Bible as an "open source" collaboration, I was blacklisted by fundamentalists of more than one religion. They just didn't want their story messed with — even though I had been able to prove it was written with that very intent!

Yet these so-called men of God and the phony politicians they support are the very forces the Bible was written to warn us about! These scripture-thumping mind controllers are the last ones who want us to connect with the real power in these myths. I'm not bashing the Bible at all. I'm actually attempting to restore its integrity as perhaps the most transcendent narrative ever developed. If just a few people would truly read these stories, we wouldn't be led around like zombies anymore. We couldn't. It'd be like returning to normal after an intense psychedelic trip; it's just too late to go back.

Business people, religious people, educators and publishers are all equally threatened and confounded by the idea that human existence itself — the births, deaths, joys and sorrows, the repression and exaltation of real people — is actually occurring in the gaps between the moments that pass for history. We all could use the kind of wake-up call that a good dose of Bible could provide.

Now don't get the wrong idea. The Bible has been intentionally framed as a dry and sanctimonious tome just to keep thinking people from getting near it. In reality, it's powerfully dangerous stuff: the ultimate handbook for psychic revolt. It's filled with sex, temple prostitutes, incantations, incest, travel to other dimensions, conversations with aliens, wars with giants and, on more than one occasion, ritualized anal rape (if you don't believe that one, take a look at Genesis 19:5). Think you're an accomplished magician? Check out the source code on reality hacking, and see if you can handle it.

That's why the perfect place to tell what I've come to believe is the "real" story of the Bible may not be that leather-bound tome the Gideons put in hotel dresser drawers, but comics.

A comic is camouflage for me to expose the essential mythic battle underlying Western Civilization, and sequential narrative is a perfect way to tell a story that takes place in multiple universes at the same time — including our own.

For by insisting we "believe" that the Bible happened at some moment in distant history, the keepers of religion prevent us from realizing that the Bible is happening right now, in every moment. That's right: We still engage in child sacrifice — every time we send our youngest citizens off to another war. We still practice idolatry through our worship of the almighty dollar (in God we trust). And we're still victims of mental slavery courtesy of Madison Avenue's latest techniques of behavioral control. Technology and media are our magicks and mysteries, making hackers today's equivalent of the Hebrews.

That's why "Testament" follows a band of cyber-alchemist revolutionaries, wrestling against the pretty immense challenges of a future just a day after tomorrow — when the draft is reinstated and global currency takes the form of an insidiously promoted mind virus. It also takes place in Bible time — exposing how these sagas and their underlying themes have been recurring for centuries. And both story arcs are played out by the same set of characters who — for the time being anyway — are unaware of each other's existence.

Overseeing all this action — from beyond the confines of either narrative line — are the gods. They live outside sequential time and, accordingly, are always depicted beyond the panels. If they try to interfere in the linear action by reaching into a panel, their arm or breath transforms into an element like water or fire. Try to pull that one off in a book, a movie or on TV. Like I said, this kind of story was "born" to be a comic.

So please do me the honor of taking a look at a version of the Bible that I'll venture provides an experience a bit closer to what its original writers may have had in mind. The Bible's narrative and its power transcend time. All we need is access and will. Here's the access part. The rest is up to you.

For if we choose to take up the Bible's challenge together, reality itself will be at our disposal, and then *we'll* be the superheroes.

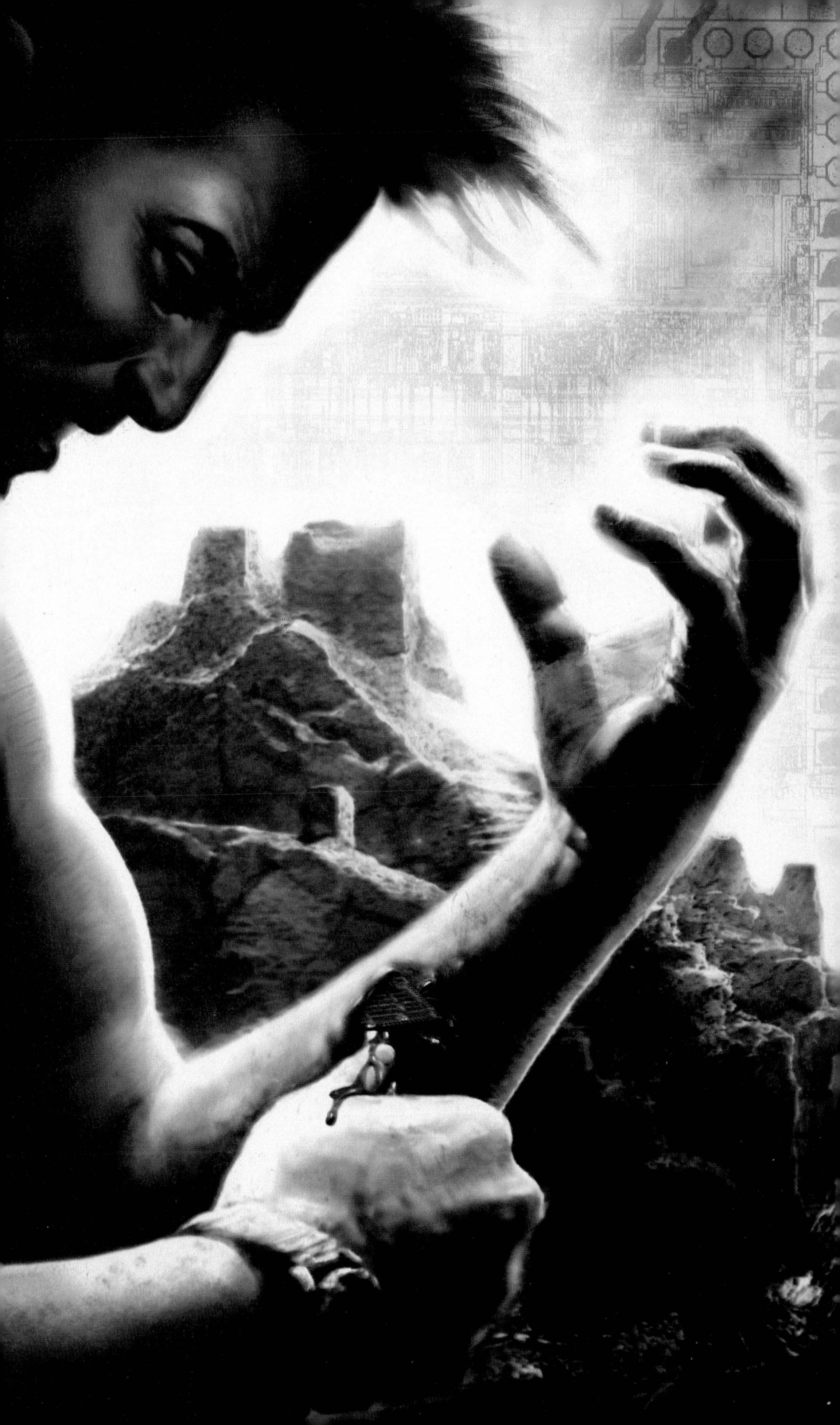

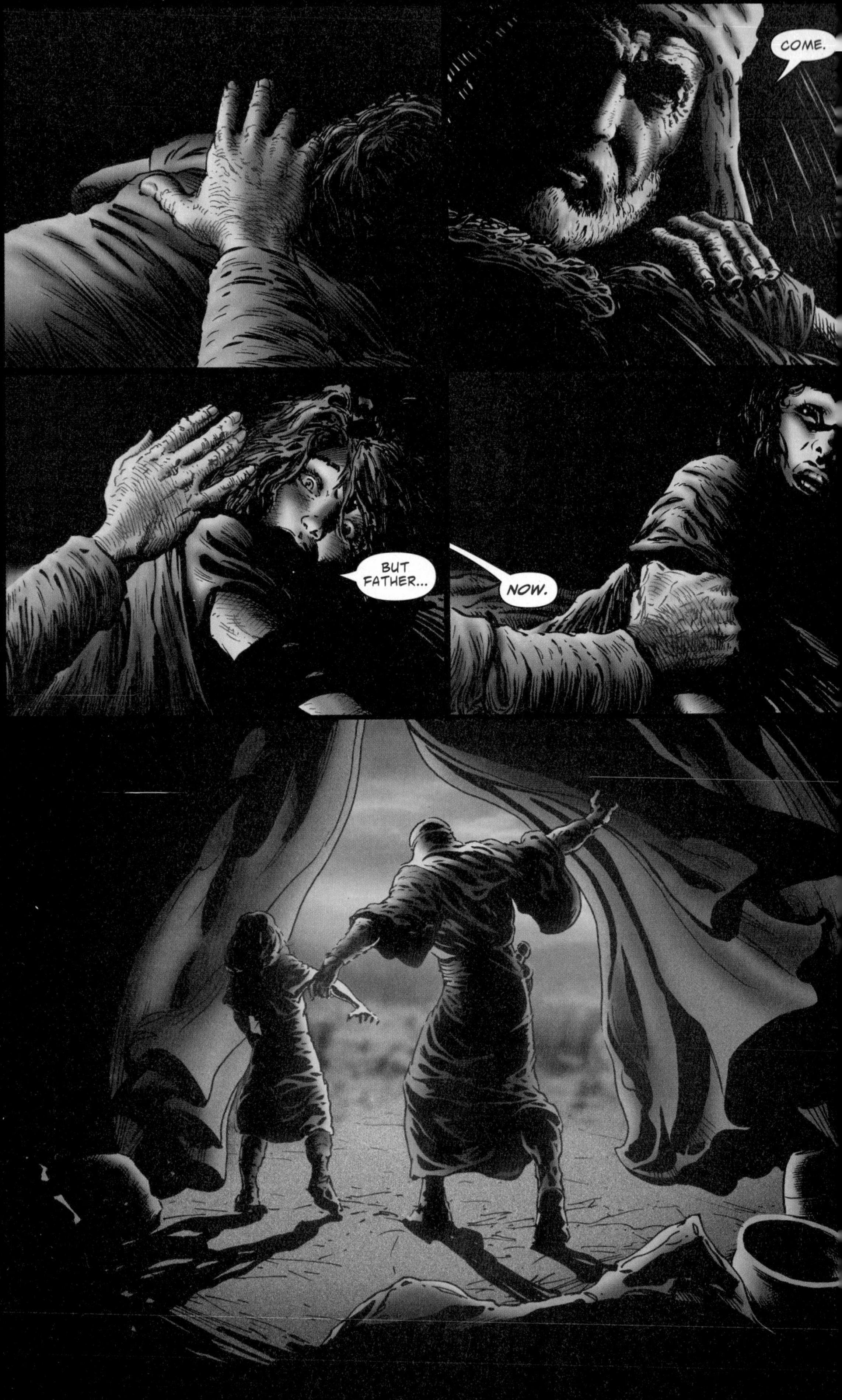
COME.
BUT FATHER...
NOW.

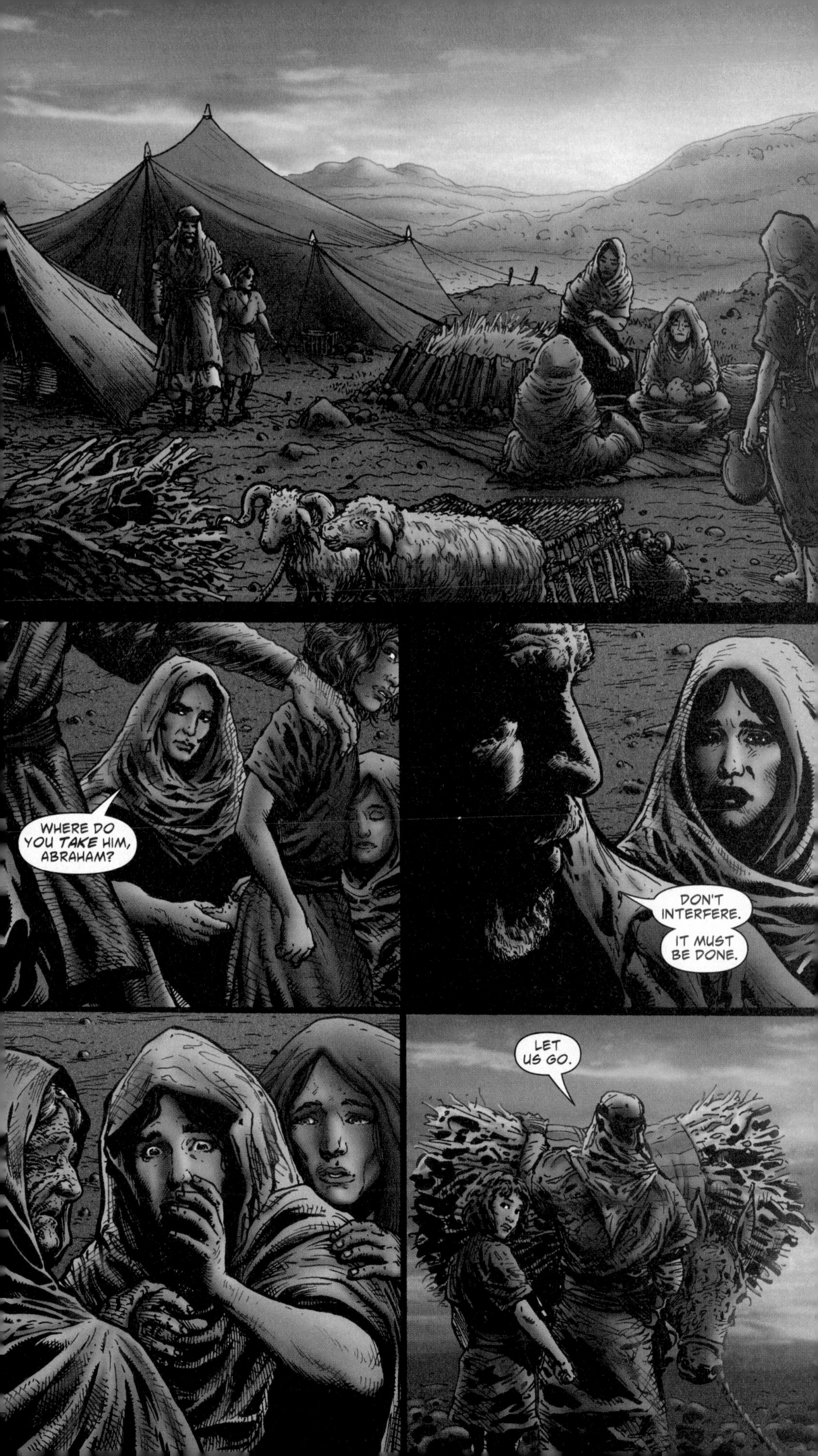
WHERE DO YOU TAKE HIM, ABRAHAM?
DON'T INTERFERE.
IT MUST BE DONE.
LET US GO.

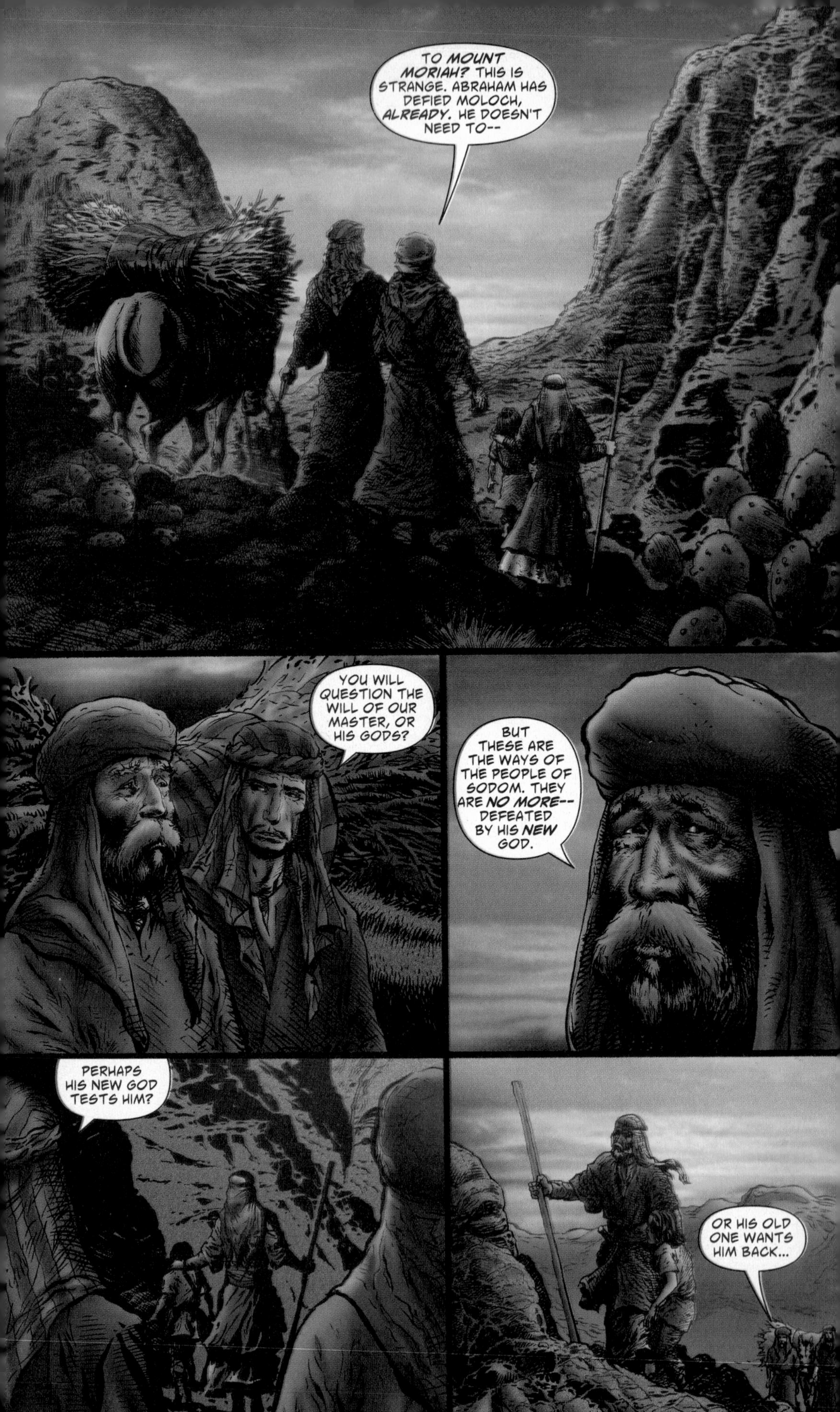
TO MOUNT MORIAH? THIS IS STRANGE. ABRAHAM HAS DEFIED MOLOCH, ALREADY. HE DOESN'T NEED TO--
YOU WILL QUESTION THE WILL OF OUR MASTER, OR HIS GODS?
BUT THESE ARE THE WAYS OF THE PEOPLE OF SODOM. THEY ARE NO MORE-- DEFEATED BY HIS NEW GOD.
PERHAPS HIS NEW GOD TESTS HIM?
OR HIS OLD ONE WANTS HIM BACK...

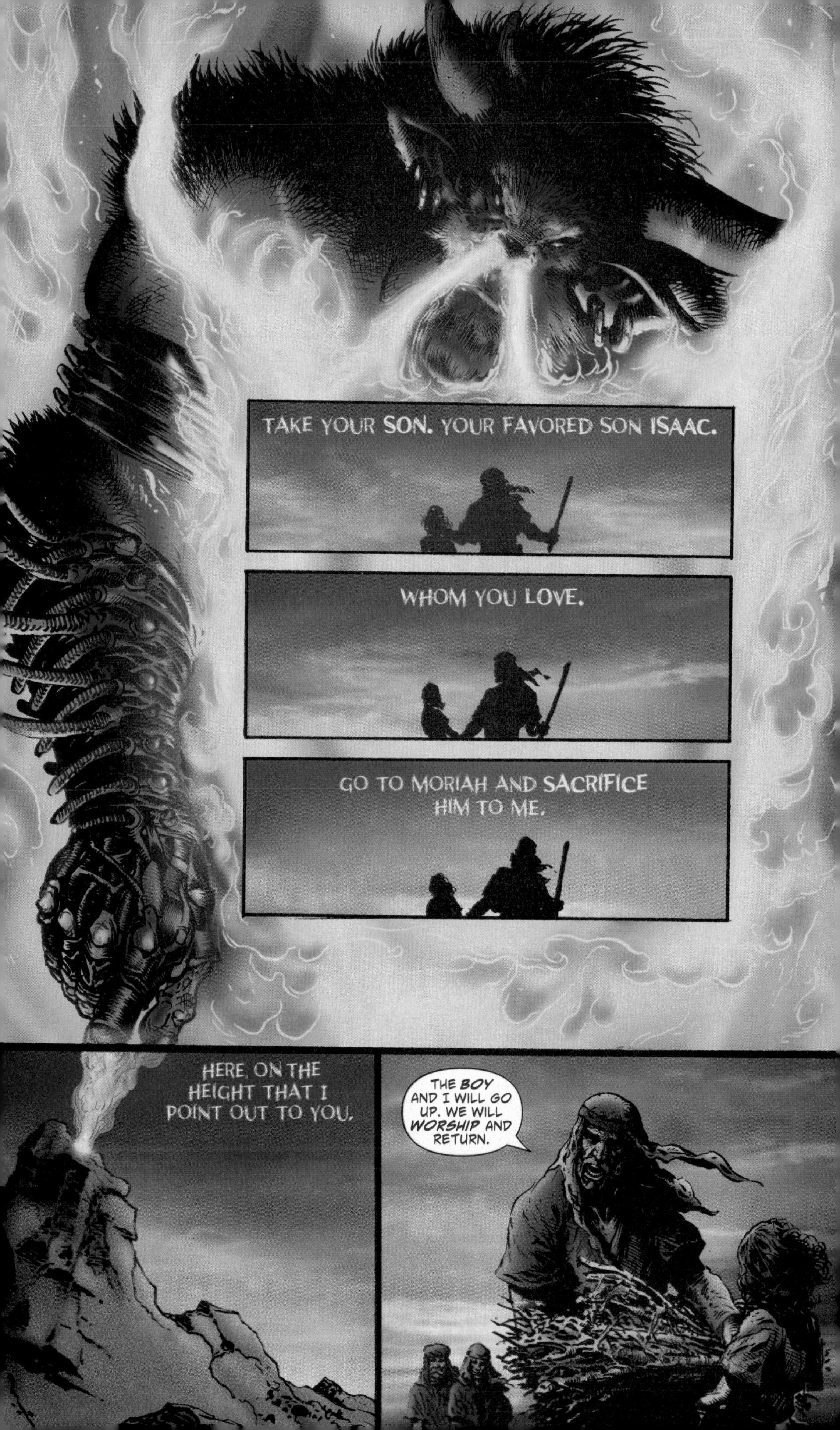
TAKE YOUR SON. YOUR FAVORED SON ISAAC.
WHOM YOU LOVE.
GO TO MORIAH AND SACRIFICE HIM TO ME.
HERE, ON THE HEIGHT THAT I POINT OUT TO YOU.
THE BOY AND I WILL GO UP. WE WILL WORSHIP AND RETURN.

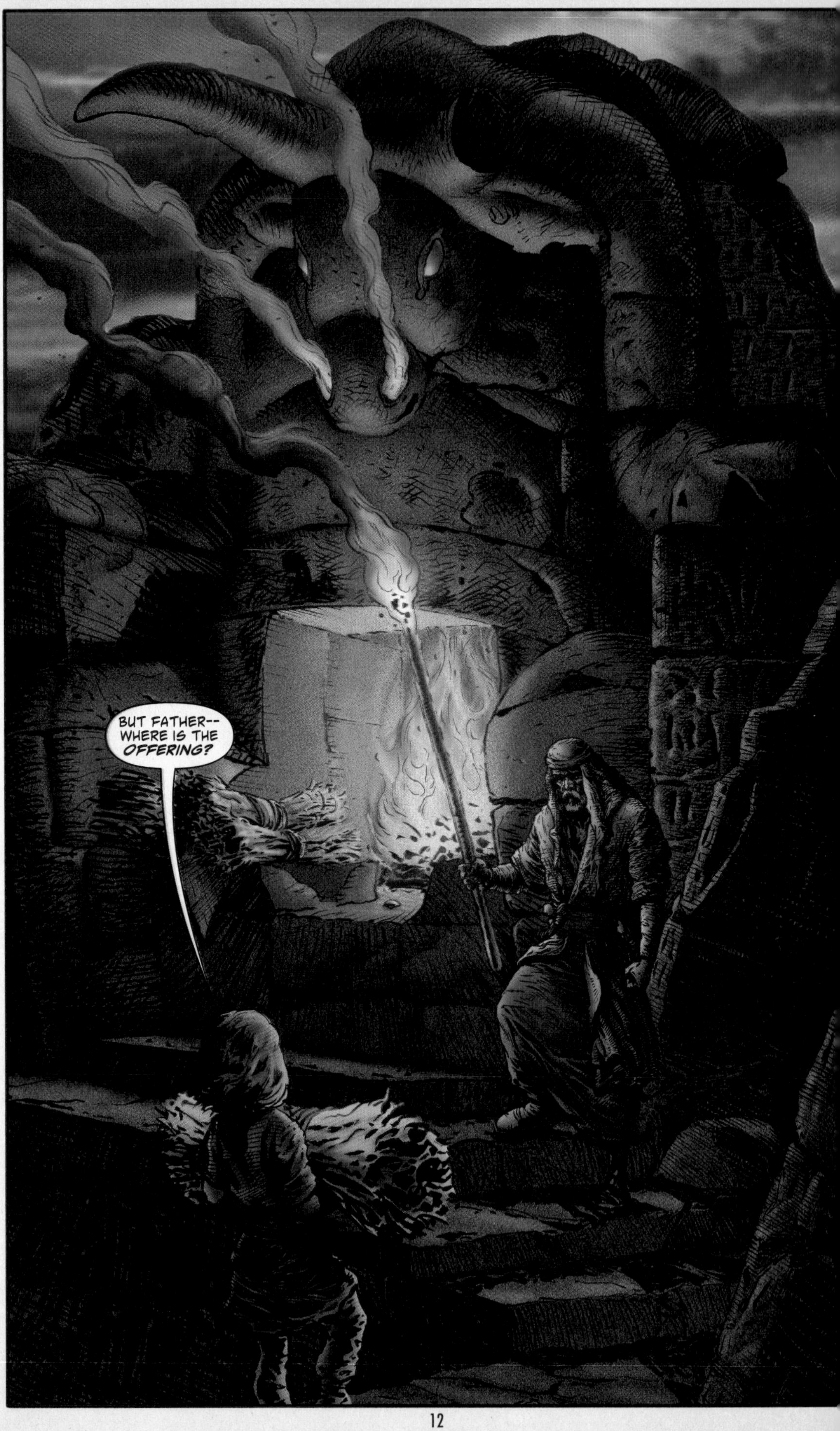
BUT FATHER--
WHERE IS THE
OFFERING?

COME ON.

YOU OKAY?

YEAH, I JUST...

WE DON'T HAVE A LOT OF *TIME*. IT'S GONNA BE A HARD DAY, WE MAY AS WELL GET *ON* WITH IT.

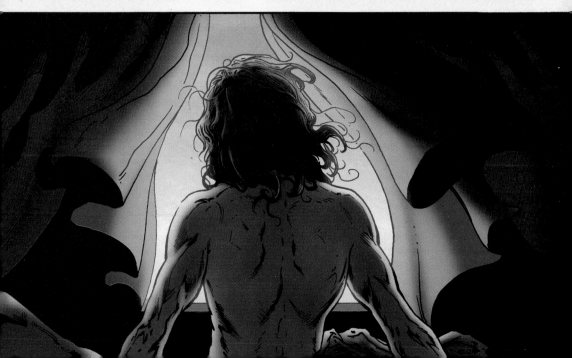

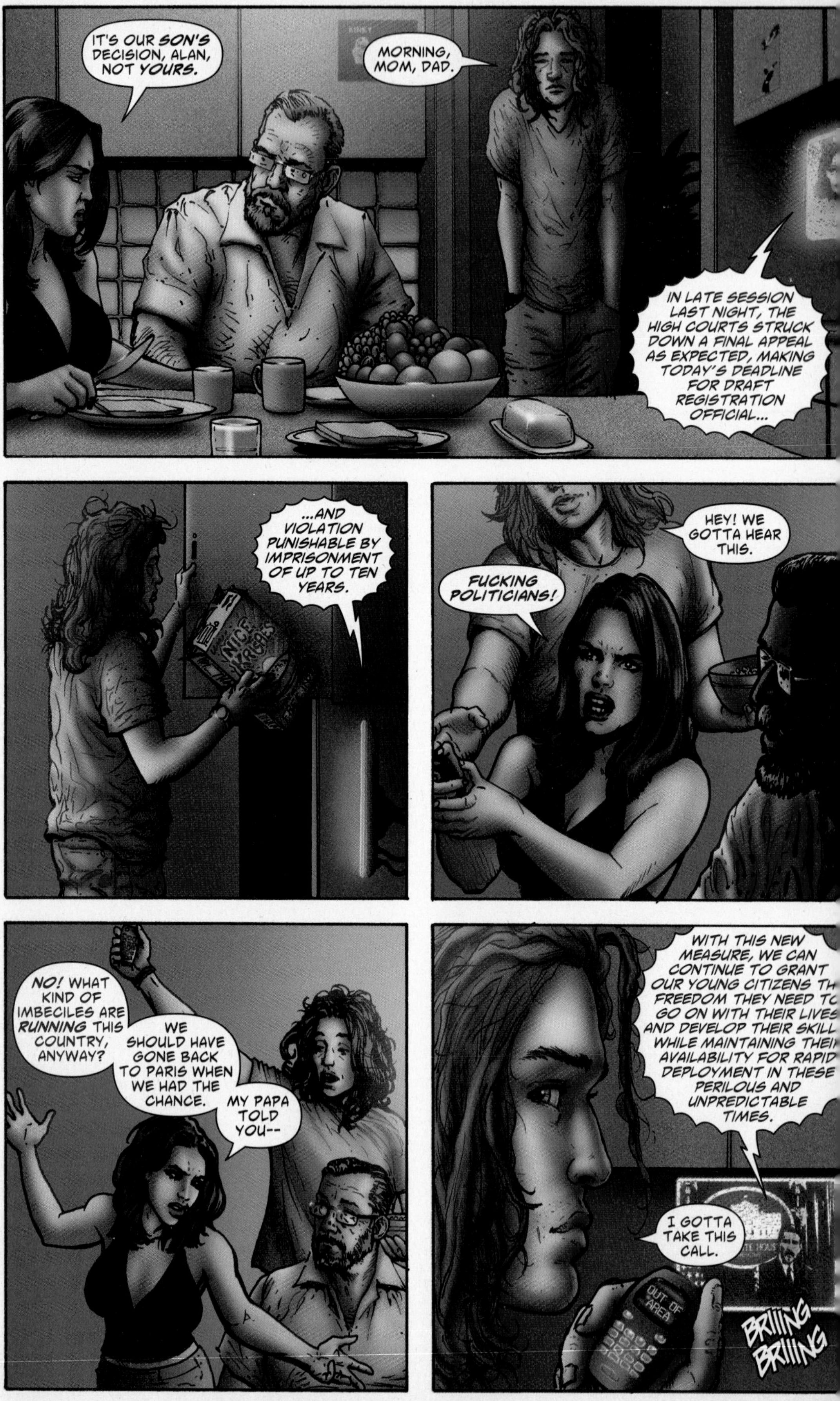
IT'S OUR SON'S DECISION, ALAN, NOT YOURS.
MORNING, MOM, DAD.
IN LATE SESSION LAST NIGHT, THE HIGH COURTS STRUCK DOWN A FINAL APPEAL AS EXPECTED, MAKING TODAY'S DEADLINE FOR DRAFT REGISTRATION OFFICIAL...
...AND VIOLATION PUNISHABLE BY IMPRISONMENT OF UP TO TEN YEARS.
HEY! WE GOTTA HEAR THIS.
FUCKING POLITICIANS!
NO! WHAT KIND OF IMBECILES ARE RUNNING THIS COUNTRY, ANYWAY?
WE SHOULD HAVE GONE BACK TO PARIS WHEN WE HAD THE CHANCE.
MY PAPA TOLD YOU--
WITH THIS NEW MEASURE, WE CAN CONTINUE TO GRANT OUR YOUNG CITIZENS TH FREEDOM THEY NEED TO GO ON WITH THEIR LIVES AND DEVELOP THEIR SKILL WHILE MAINTAINING THEI AVAILABILITY FOR RAPID DEPLOYMENT IN THESE PERILOUS AND UNPREDICTABLE TIMES.
I GOTTA TAKE THIS CALL.
OUT OF AREA
BRIIING BRIIING

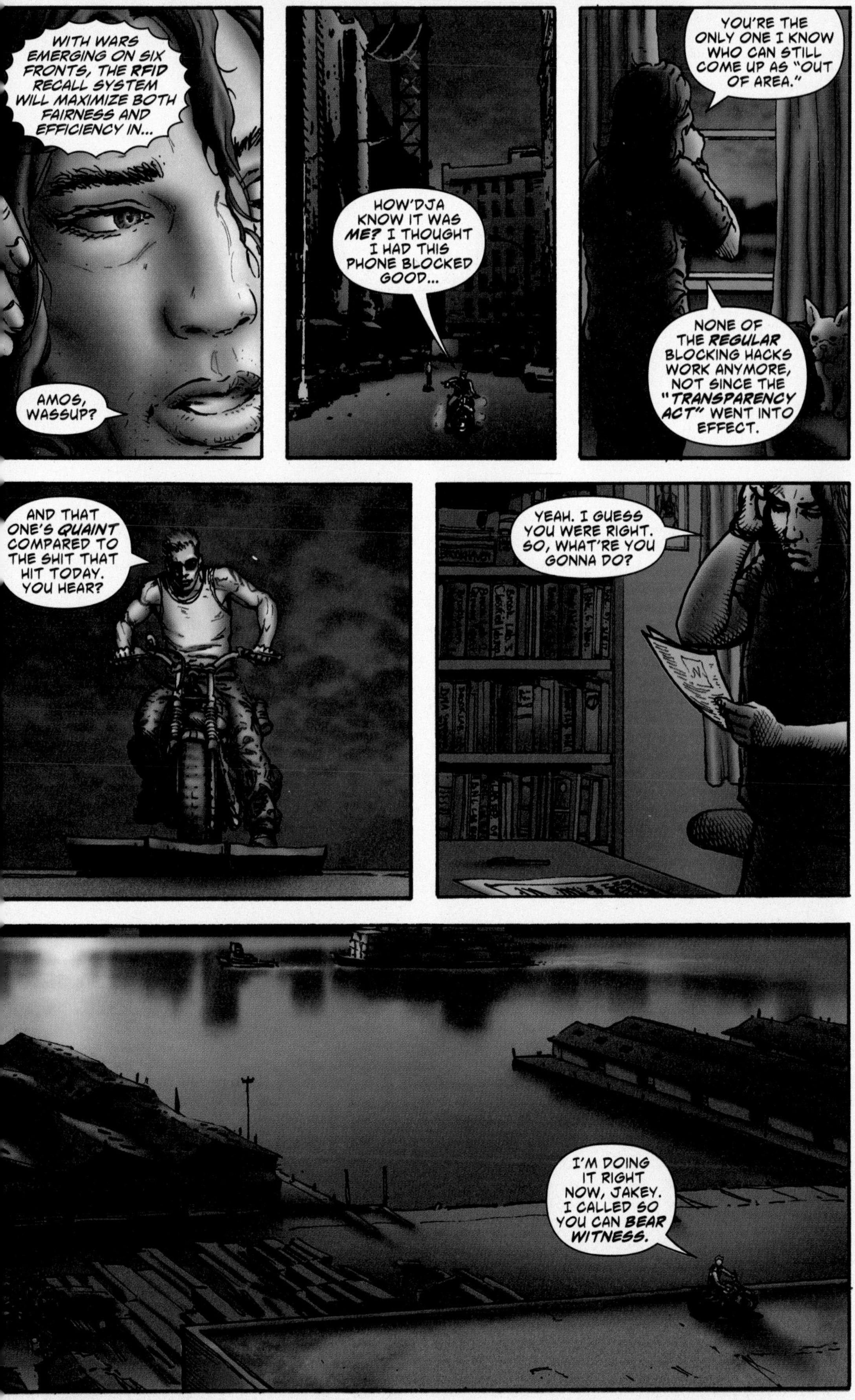

WITH WARS EMERGING ON SIX FRONTS, THE RFID RECALL SYSTEM WILL MAXIMIZE BOTH FAIRNESS AND EFFICIENCY IN...
AMOS, WASSUP?
HOW'DJA KNOW IT WAS ME? I THOUGHT I HAD THIS PHONE BLOCKED GOOD...
YOU'RE THE ONLY ONE I KNOW WHO CAN STILL COME UP AS "OUT OF AREA."
NONE OF THE REGULAR BLOCKING HACKS WORK ANYMORE, NOT SINCE THE "TRANSPARENCY ACT" WENT INTO EFFECT.
AND THAT ONE'S QUAINT COMPARED TO THE SHIT THAT HIT TODAY. YOU HEAR?
YEAH. I GUESS YOU WERE RIGHT. SO, WHAT'RE YOU GONNA DO?
I'M DOING IT RIGHT NOW, JAKEY. I CALLED SO YOU CAN BEAR WITNESS.

WHAT? WHAT'RE YOU DOING?
SETTING MYSELF FREE, JAKE.
BUT THEY DIDN'T CALL YOU UP, AMOS. THEY DIDN'T CALL ANYONE UP YET.
ARRRHHF
NOT YET. BUT BELIEVE ME, JAKE, THE SPACE BETWEEN "NOT YET" AND "TOO LATE" IS SHRINKING EVERY DAY.
'BYE KID. YOU KNOW HOW TO FIND ME. WE ALREADY SET UP SHOP. THERE'S OTHERS. IT'S ALL COOL.

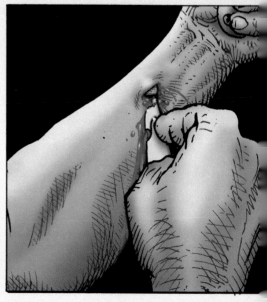

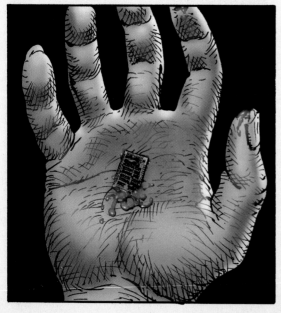

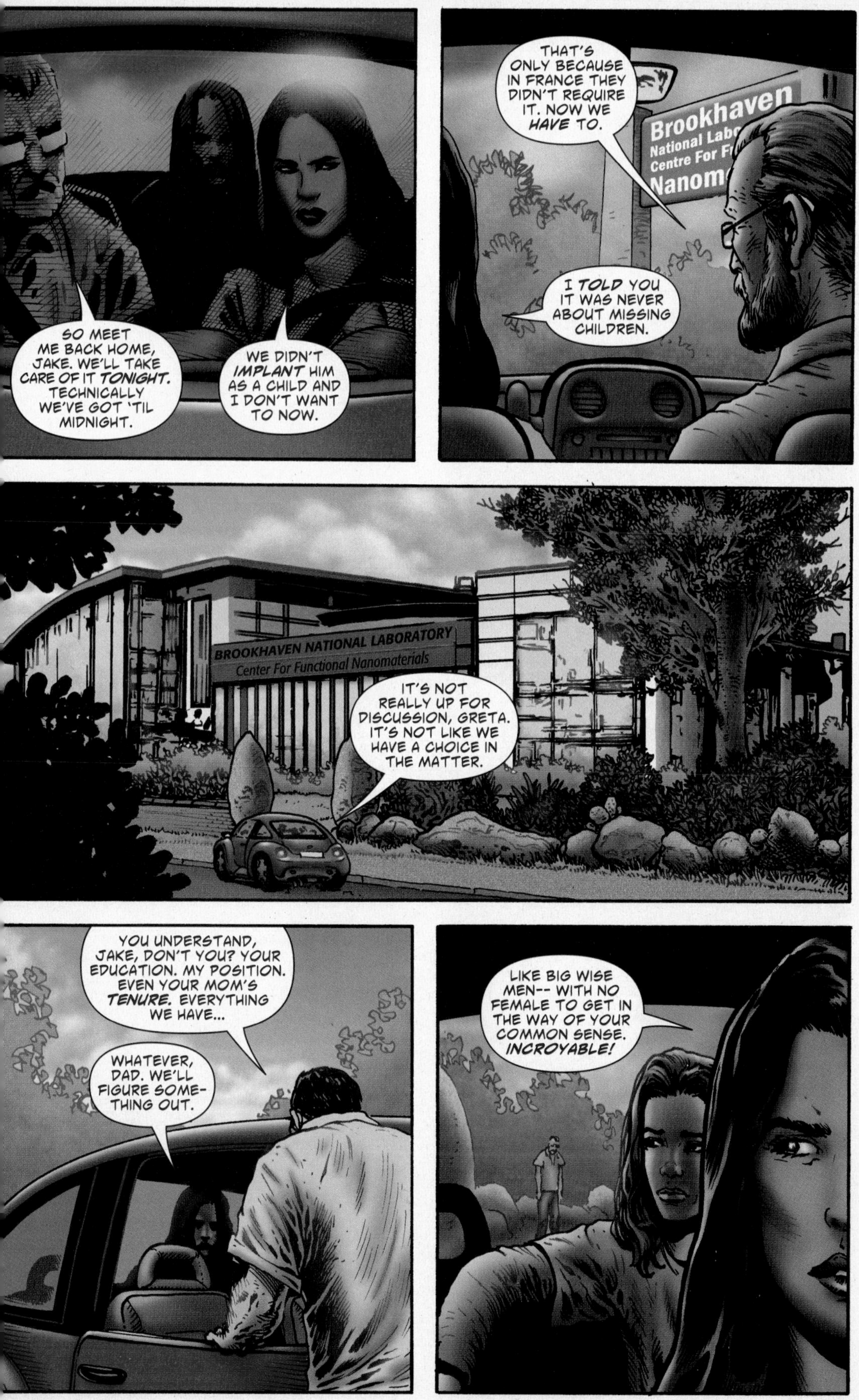
SO MEET ME BACK HOME, JAKE. WE'LL TAKE CARE OF IT *TONIGHT*. TECHNICALLY WE'VE GOT 'TIL MIDNIGHT.
WE DIDN'T *IMPLANT* HIM AS A CHILD AND I DON'T WANT TO NOW.
THAT'S ONLY BECAUSE IN FRANCE THEY DIDN'T REQUIRE IT. NOW WE *HAVE* TO.
Brookhaven
I *TOLD* YOU IT WAS NEVER ABOUT MISSING CHILDREN.
BROOKHAVEN NATIONAL LABORATORY
Center For Functional Nanomaterials
IT'S NOT REALLY UP FOR DISCUSSION, GRETA. IT'S NOT LIKE WE HAVE A CHOICE IN THE MATTER.
YOU UNDERSTAND, JAKE, DON'T YOU? YOUR EDUCATION. MY POSITION. EVEN YOUR MOM'S *TENURE*. EVERYTHING WE HAVE...
WHATEVER, DAD. WE'LL FIGURE SOME-THING OUT.
LIKE BIG WISE MEN-- WITH NO FEMALE TO GET IN THE WAY OF YOUR COMMON SENSE. *INCROYABLE!*

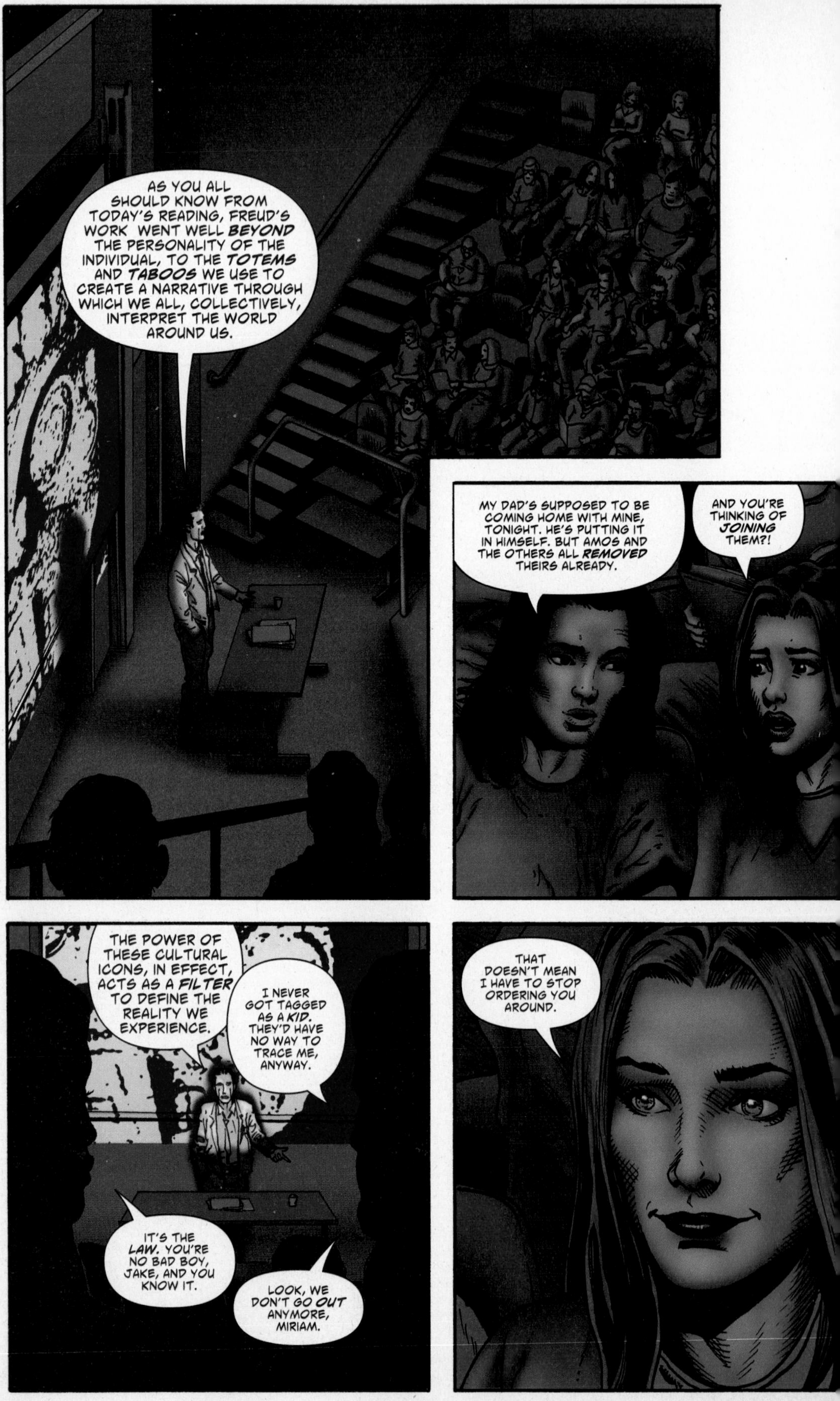
AS YOU ALL SHOULD KNOW FROM TODAY'S READING, FREUD'S WORK WENT WELL BEYOND THE PERSONALITY OF THE INDIVIDUAL, TO THE TOTEMS AND TABOOS WE USE TO CREATE A NARRATIVE THROUGH WHICH WE ALL, COLLECTIVELY, INTERPRET THE WORLD AROUND US.
MY DAD'S SUPPOSED TO BE COMING HOME WITH MINE, TONIGHT. HE'S PUTTING IT IN HIMSELF. BUT AMOS AND THE OTHERS ALL REMOVED THEIRS ALREADY.
AND YOU'RE THINKING OF JOINING THEM?!
THE POWER OF THESE CULTURAL ICONS, IN EFFECT, ACTS AS A FILTER TO DEFINE THE REALITY WE EXPERIENCE.
I NEVER GOT TAGGED AS A KID. THEY'D HAVE NO WAY TO TRACE ME, ANYWAY.
IT'S THE LAW. YOU'RE NO BAD BOY, JAKE, AND YOU KNOW IT.
LOOK, WE DON'T GO OUT ANYMORE, MIRIAM.
THAT DOESN'T MEAN I HAVE TO STOP ORDERING YOU AROUND.

I'M NOT GOING TO WATCH YOU THROW YOUR CAREER AWAY FOR *NOTHING*. IT'S NOT LIKE THEY'RE ACTUALLY CALLING PEOPLE UP... STAY *LEGAL*, AND YOU CAN WORK AGAINST THIS FROM OUT IN THE OPEN, LIKE *ME*.

YOU'LL FIND STRIKINGLY *SIMILAR* ARCHETYPES ACROSS THE GLOBE AND THROUGHOUT HISTORY.

THEY DISAPPEAR, SUBMERGED IN WHAT JUNG WOULD LATER CALL THE "COLLECTIVE UNCONSCIOUS" FOR *CENTURIES*, EVEN MILLENNIA...

ALL YOUR ACTIVISM MEETINGS AND JUDICIAL HEARINGS JUST GIVE THEM MORE POWER. WE'RE PRACTICALLY IN *FASCISM* HERE.

JUST DON'T DO ANYTHING *STUPID*, JAKE. I DON'T WANT TO LOSE--

--YOU.

...'EN TO *ME!*

...THING HER WIL...

AND THEN THEY RECUR *AGAIN*--

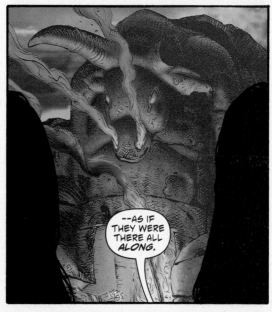

--AS IF THEY WERE THERE ALL ALONG.

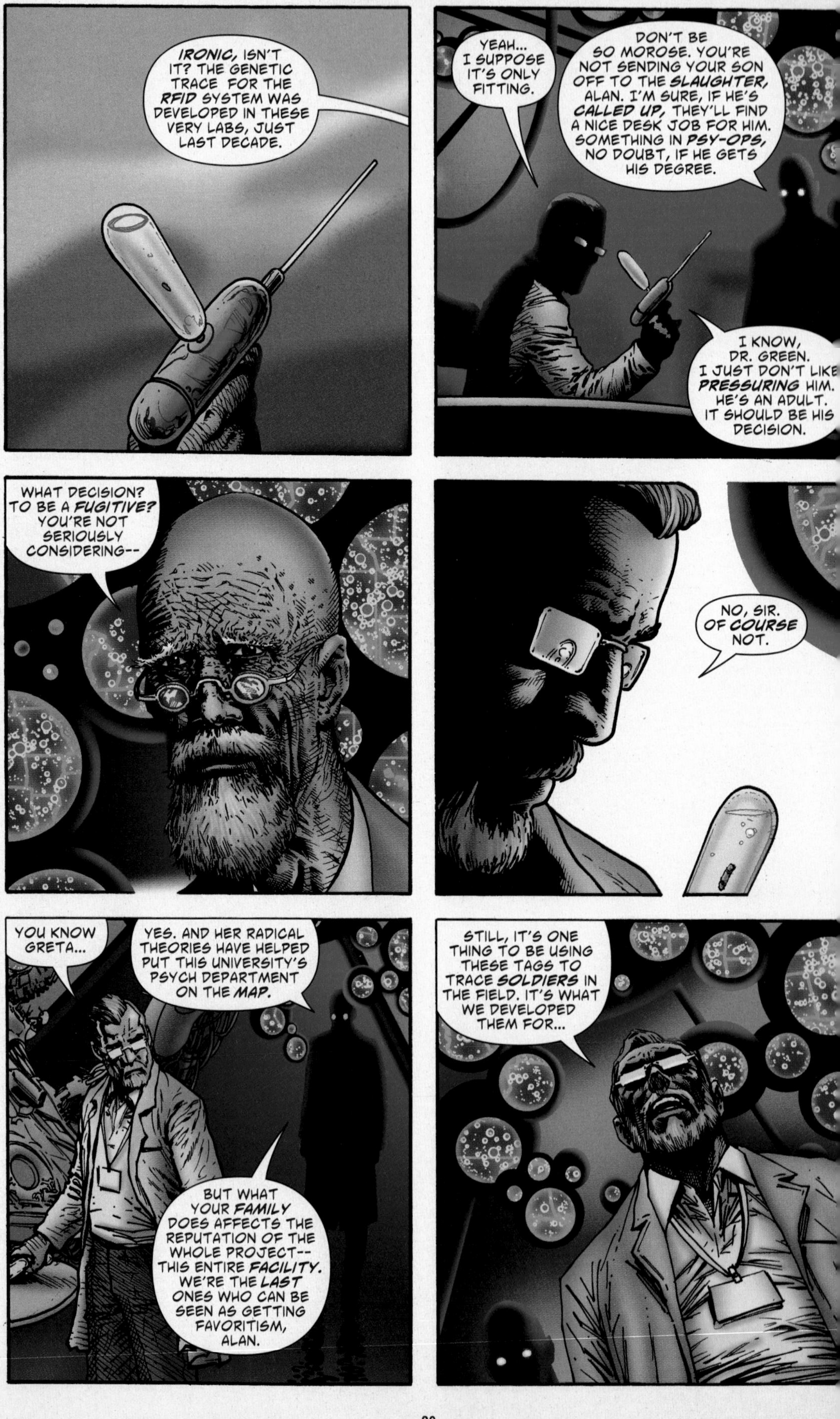
IRONIC, ISN'T IT? THE GENETIC TRACE FOR THE RFID SYSTEM WAS DEVELOPED IN THESE VERY LABS, JUST LAST DECADE.
YEAH... I SUPPOSE IT'S ONLY FITTING.
DON'T BE SO MOROSE. YOU'RE NOT SENDING YOUR SON OFF TO THE SLAUGHTER, ALAN. I'M SURE, IF HE'S CALLED UP, THEY'LL FIND A NICE DESK JOB FOR HIM. SOMETHING IN PSY-OPS, NO DOUBT, IF HE GETS HIS DEGREE.
I KNOW, DR. GREEN. I JUST DON'T LIKE PRESSURING HIM. HE'S AN ADULT. IT SHOULD BE HIS DECISION.
WHAT DECISION? TO BE A FUGITIVE? YOU'RE NOT SERIOUSLY CONSIDERING--
NO, SIR. OF COURSE NOT.
YOU KNOW GRETA...
YES. AND HER RADICAL THEORIES HAVE HELPED PUT THIS UNIVERSITY'S PSYCH DEPARTMENT ON THE MAP.
BUT WHAT YOUR FAMILY DOES AFFECTS THE REPUTATION OF THE WHOLE PROJECT-- THIS ENTIRE FACILITY. WE'RE THE LAST ONES WHO CAN BE SEEN AS GETTING FAVORITISM, ALAN.
STILL, IT'S ONE THING TO BE USING THESE TAGS TO TRACE SOLDIERS IN THE FIELD. IT'S WHAT WE DEVELOPED THEM FOR...

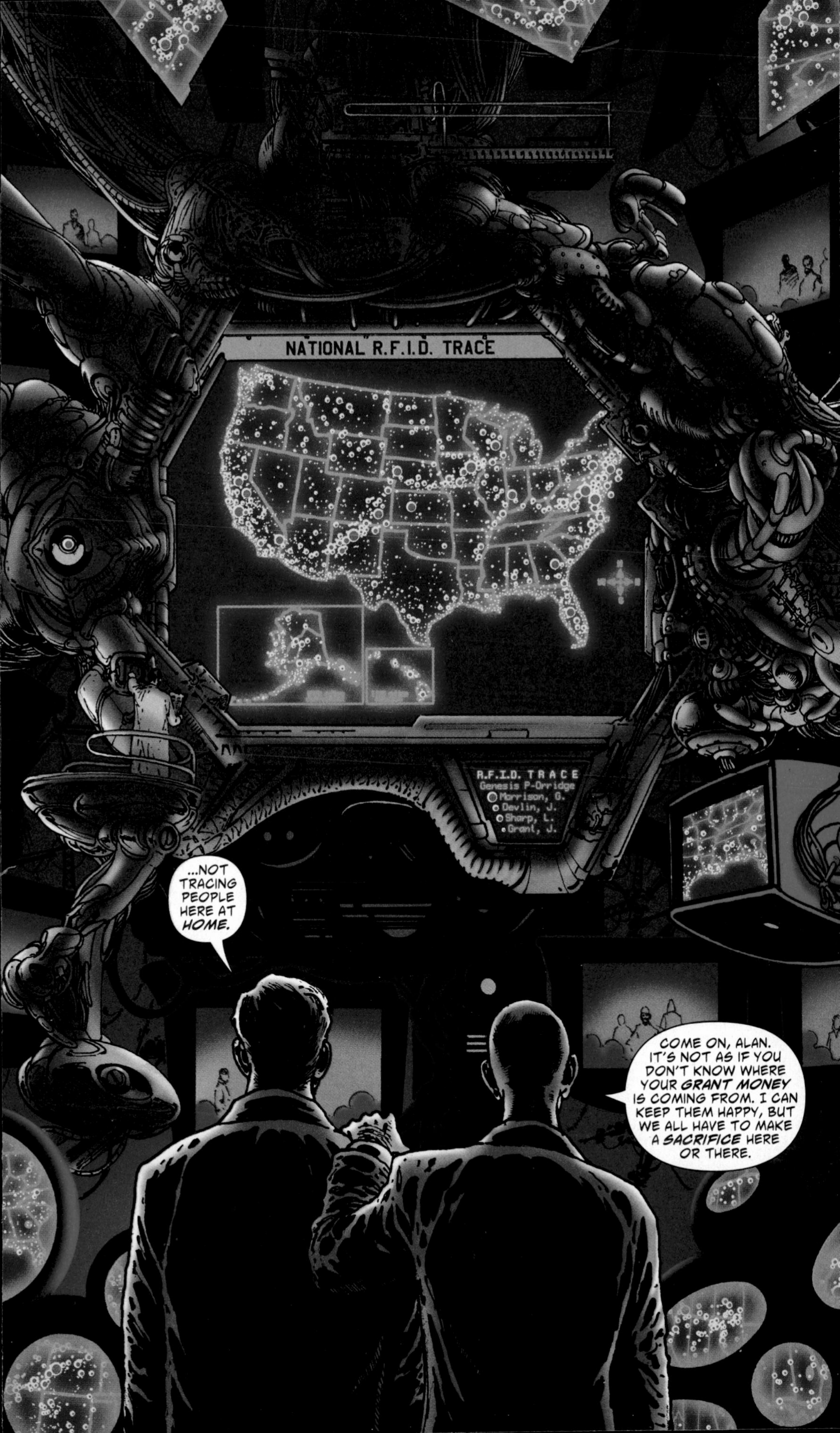
NATIONAL R.F.I.D. TRACE
R.F.I.D. TRACE
Genesis P-Orridge
Morrison, G.
Devlin, J.
Sharp, L.
Grant, J.
...NOT TRACING PEOPLE HERE AT *HOME.*
COME ON, ALAN. IT'S NOT AS IF YOU DON'T KNOW WHERE YOUR *GRANT MONEY* IS COMING FROM. I CAN KEEP THEM HAPPY, BUT WE ALL HAVE TO MAKE A *SACRIFICE* HERE OR THERE.

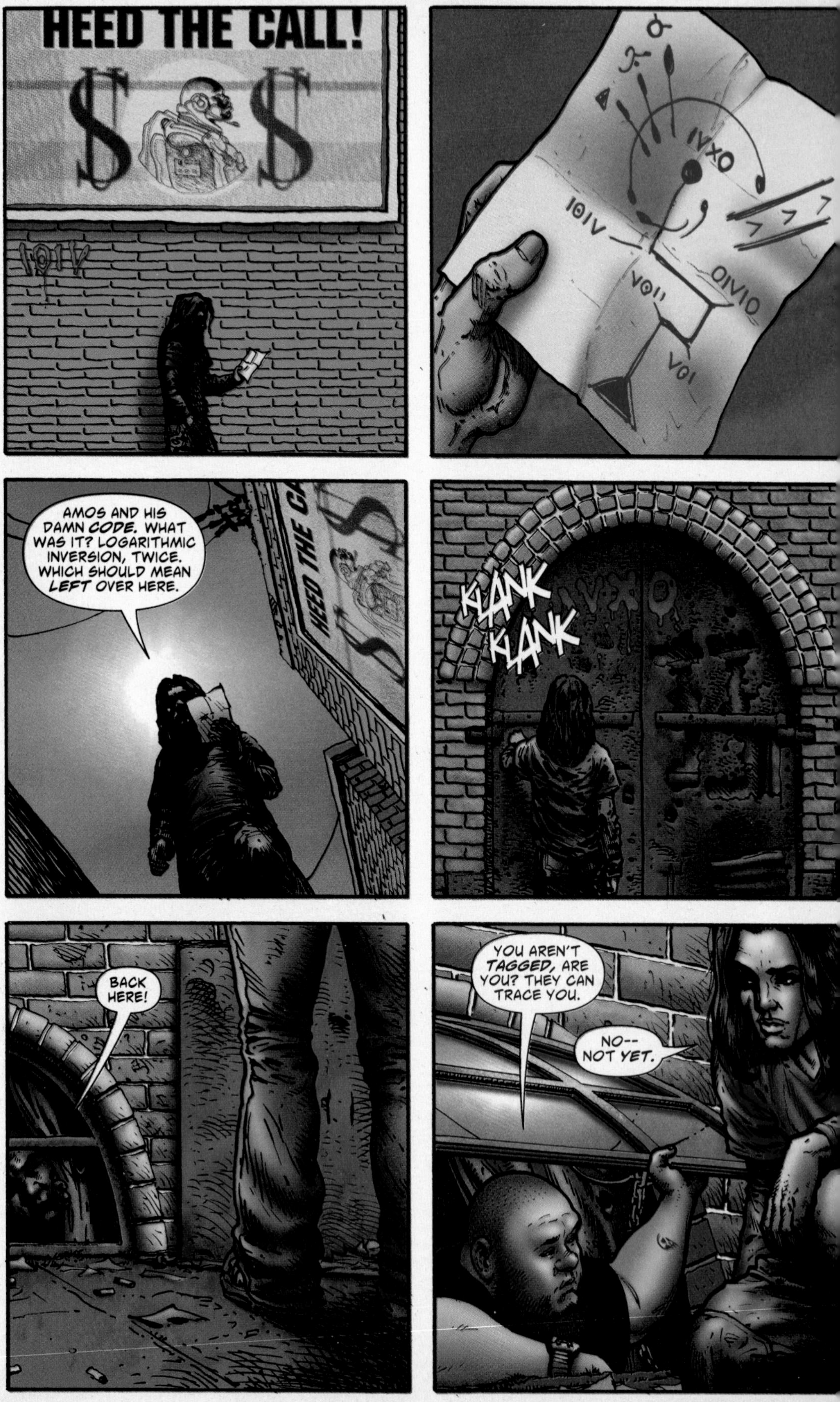
HEED THE CALL!
IOIV
IVXO
IOIV
VOII
OIVIO
VOI
AMOS AND HIS DAMN CODE. WHAT WAS IT? LOGARITHMIC INVERSION, TWICE. WHICH SHOULD MEAN LEFT OVER HERE.
HEED THE CA
KLANK KLANK
IVXO
BACK HERE!
YOU AREN'T TAGGED, ARE YOU? THEY CAN TRACE YOU.
NO-- NOT YET.

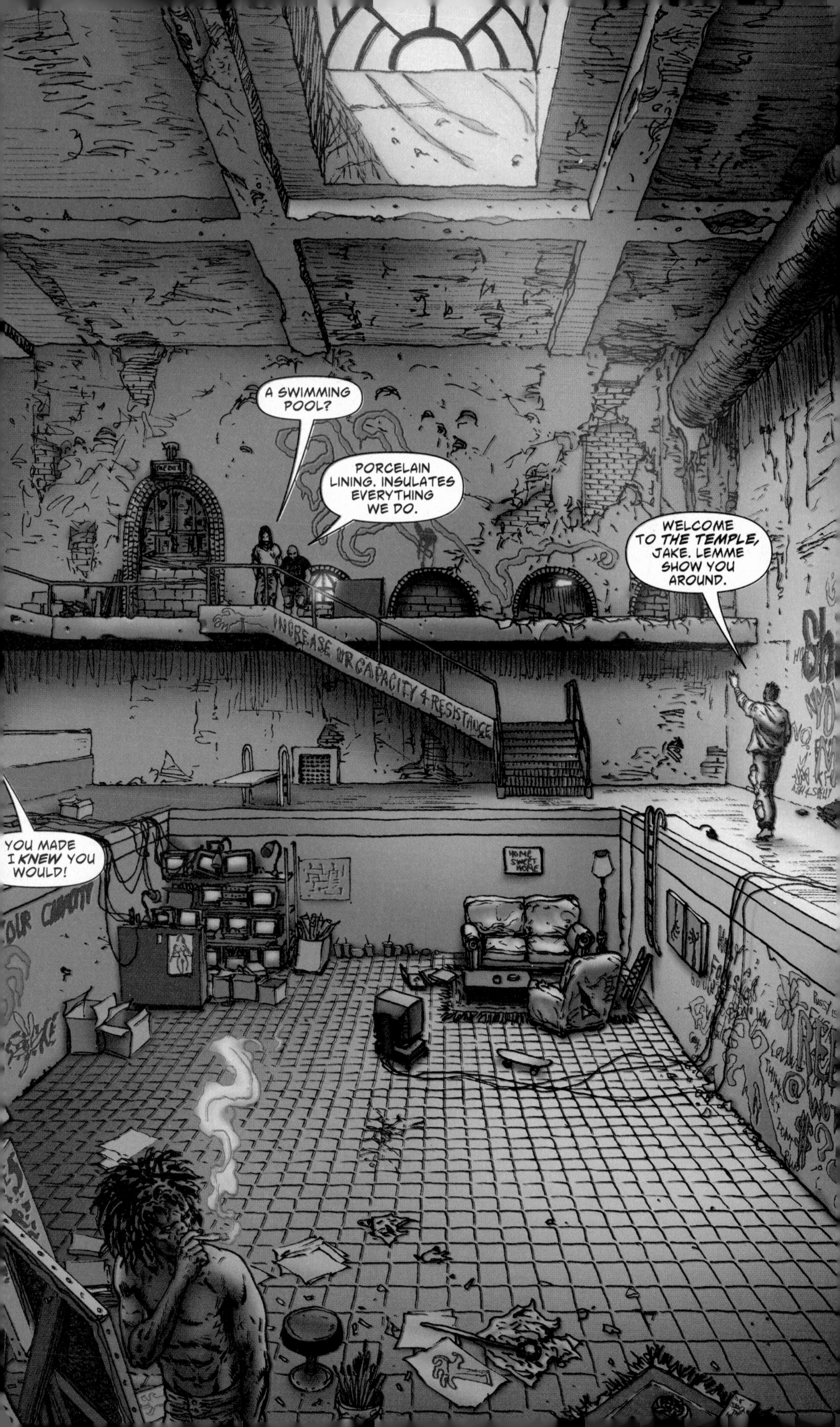

A SWIMMING POOL?
PORCELAIN LINING. INSULATES EVERYTHING WE DO.
WELCOME TO *THE TEMPLE,* JAKE. LEMME SHOW YOU AROUND.
INCREASE UR CAPACITY 4 RESISTANCE
HOME SWEET HOME
YOU MADE I *KNEW* YOU WOULD!

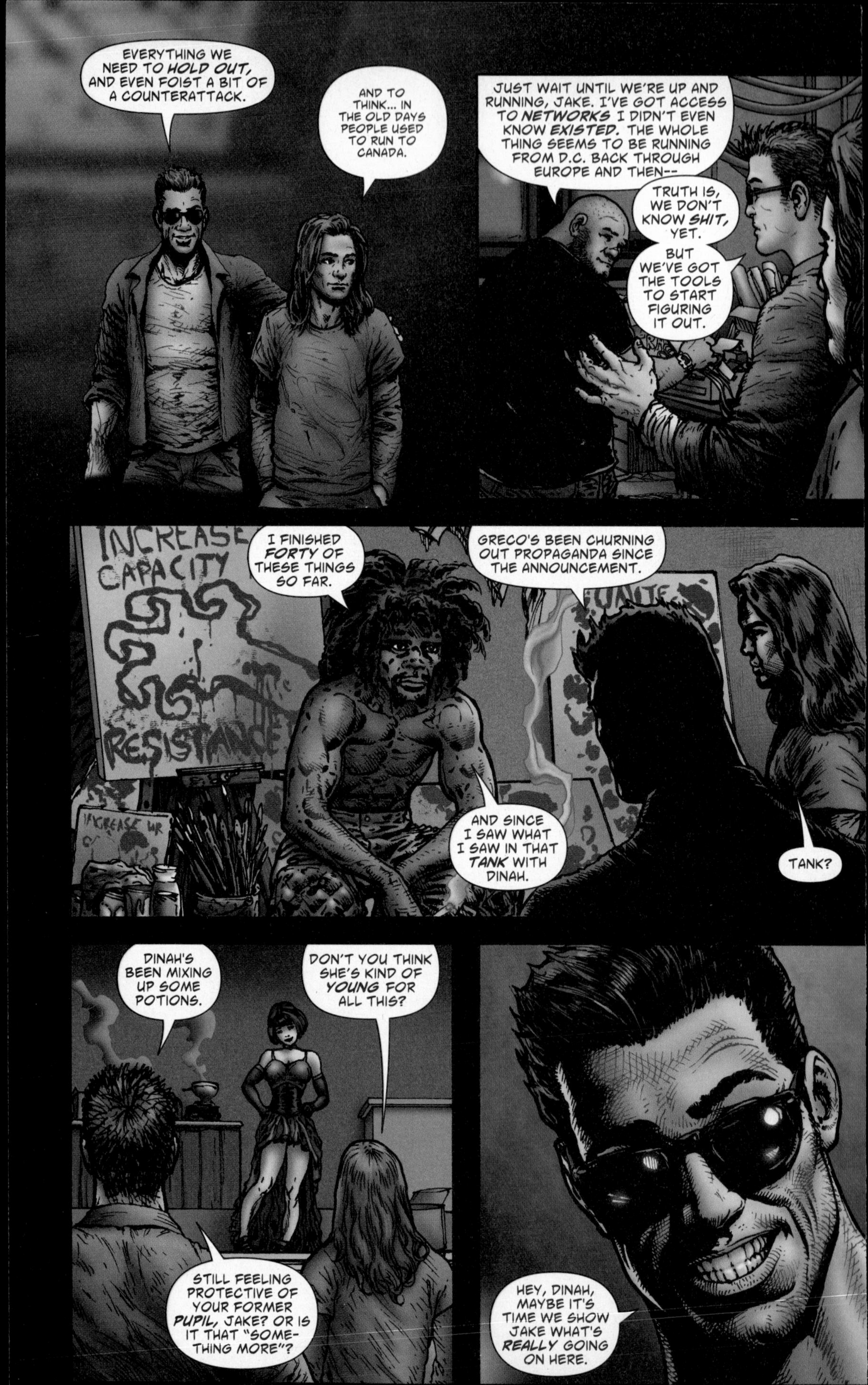
EVERYTHING WE NEED TO HOLD OUT, AND EVEN FOIST A BIT OF A COUNTERATTACK.
AND TO THINK... IN THE OLD DAYS PEOPLE USED TO RUN TO CANADA.
JUST WAIT UNTIL WE'RE UP AND RUNNING, JAKE. I'VE GOT ACCESS TO NETWORKS I DIDN'T EVEN KNOW EXISTED. THE WHOLE THING SEEMS TO BE RUNNING FROM D.C. BACK THROUGH EUROPE AND THEN--
TRUTH IS, WE DON'T KNOW SHIT, YET.
BUT WE'VE GOT THE TOOLS TO START FIGURING IT OUT.
INCREASE CAPACITY
RESISTANCE
I FINISHED FORTY OF THESE THINGS SO FAR.
GRECO'S BEEN CHURNING OUT PROPAGANDA SINCE THE ANNOUNCEMENT.
AND SINCE I SAW WHAT I SAW IN THAT TANK WITH DINAH.
TANK?
DINAH'S BEEN MIXING UP SOME POTIONS.
DON'T YOU THINK SHE'S KIND OF YOUNG FOR ALL THIS?
STILL FEELING PROTECTIVE OF YOUR FORMER PUPIL, JAKE? OR IS IT THAT "SOMETHING MORE"?
HEY, DINAH, MAYBE IT'S TIME WE SHOW JAKE WHAT'S REALLY GOING ON HERE.

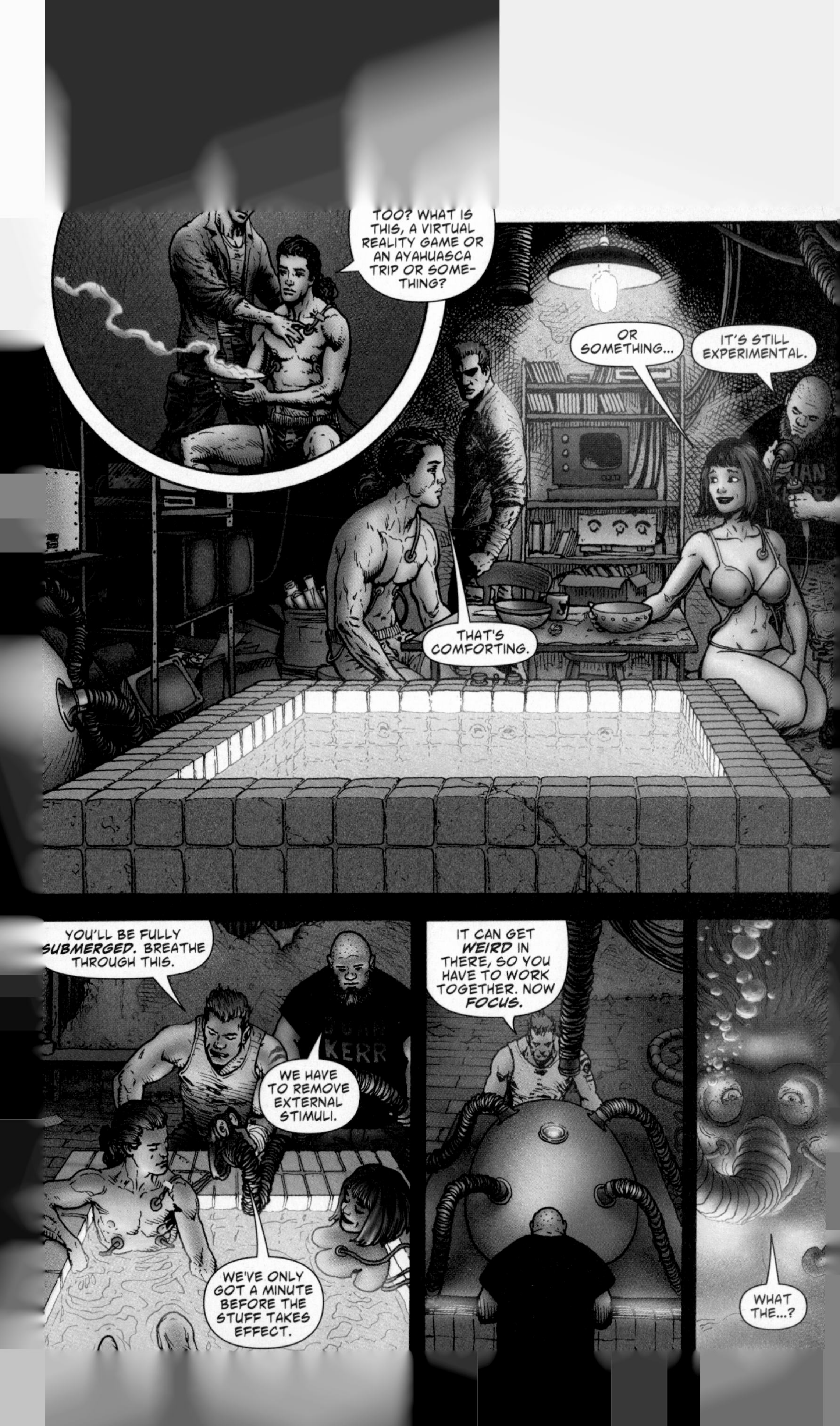
TOO? WHAT IS THIS, A VIRTUAL REALITY GAME OR AN AYAHUASCA TRIP OR SOME-THING?
OR SOMETHING...
IT'S STILL EXPERIMENTAL.
THAT'S COMFORTING.
YOU'LL BE FULLY *SUBMERGED*. BREATHE THROUGH THIS.
KERR
WE HAVE TO REMOVE EXTERNAL STIMULI.
WE'VE ONLY GOT A MINUTE BEFORE THE STUFF TAKES EFFECT.
IT CAN GET *WEIRD* IN THERE, SO YOU HAVE TO WORK TOGETHER. NOW *FOCUS*.
WHAT THE...?

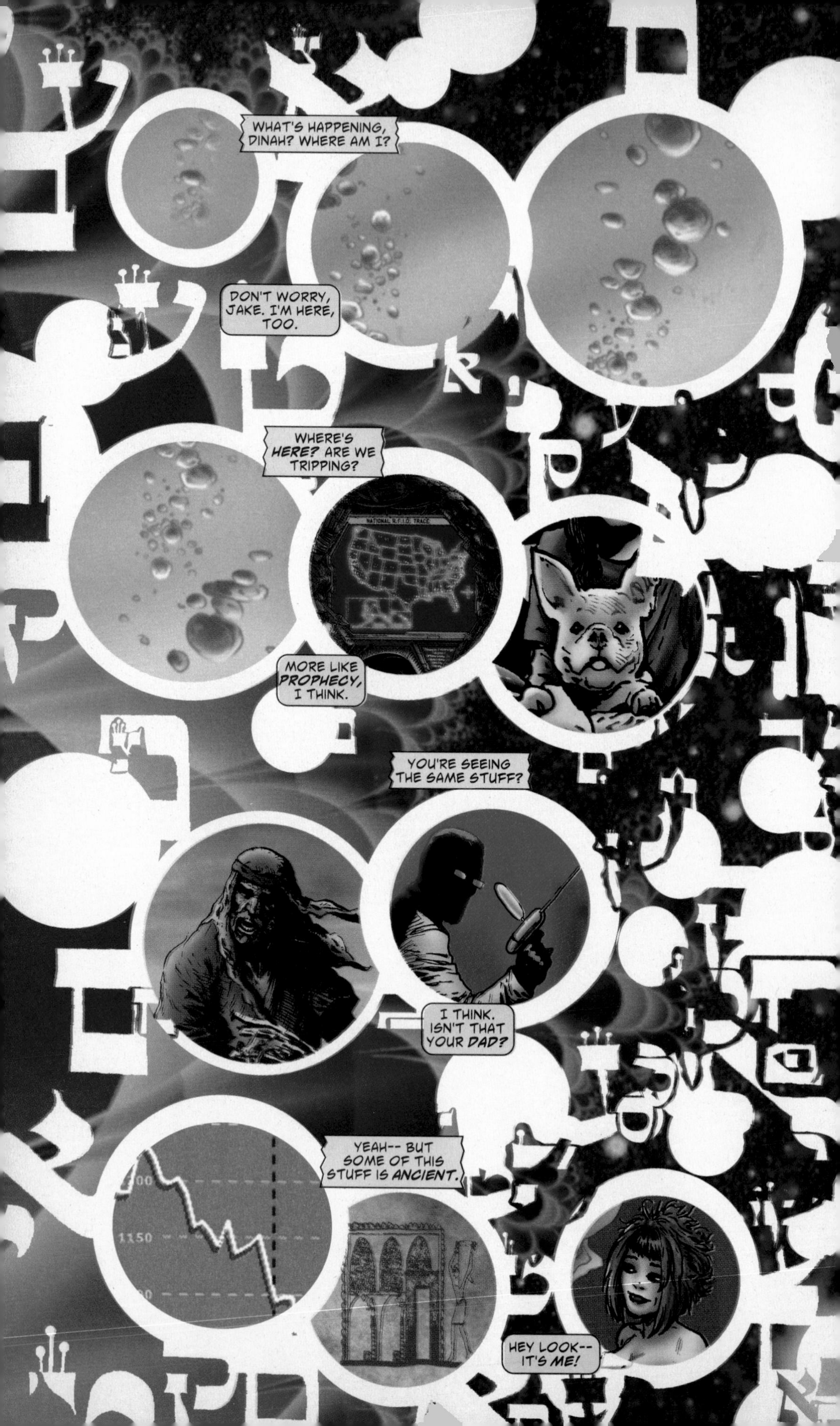
WHAT'S HAPPENING, DINAH? WHERE AM I?
DON'T WORRY, JAKE. I'M HERE, TOO.
WHERE'S *HERE?* ARE WE TRIPPING?
NATIONAL R.F.I.D. TRACE
MORE LIKE *PROPHECY,* I THINK.
YOU'RE SEEING THE SAME STUFF?
I THINK. ISN'T THAT YOUR *DAD?*
YEAH-- BUT SOME OF THIS STUFF IS *ANCIENT.*
1150
HEY LOOK-- IT'S *ME!*

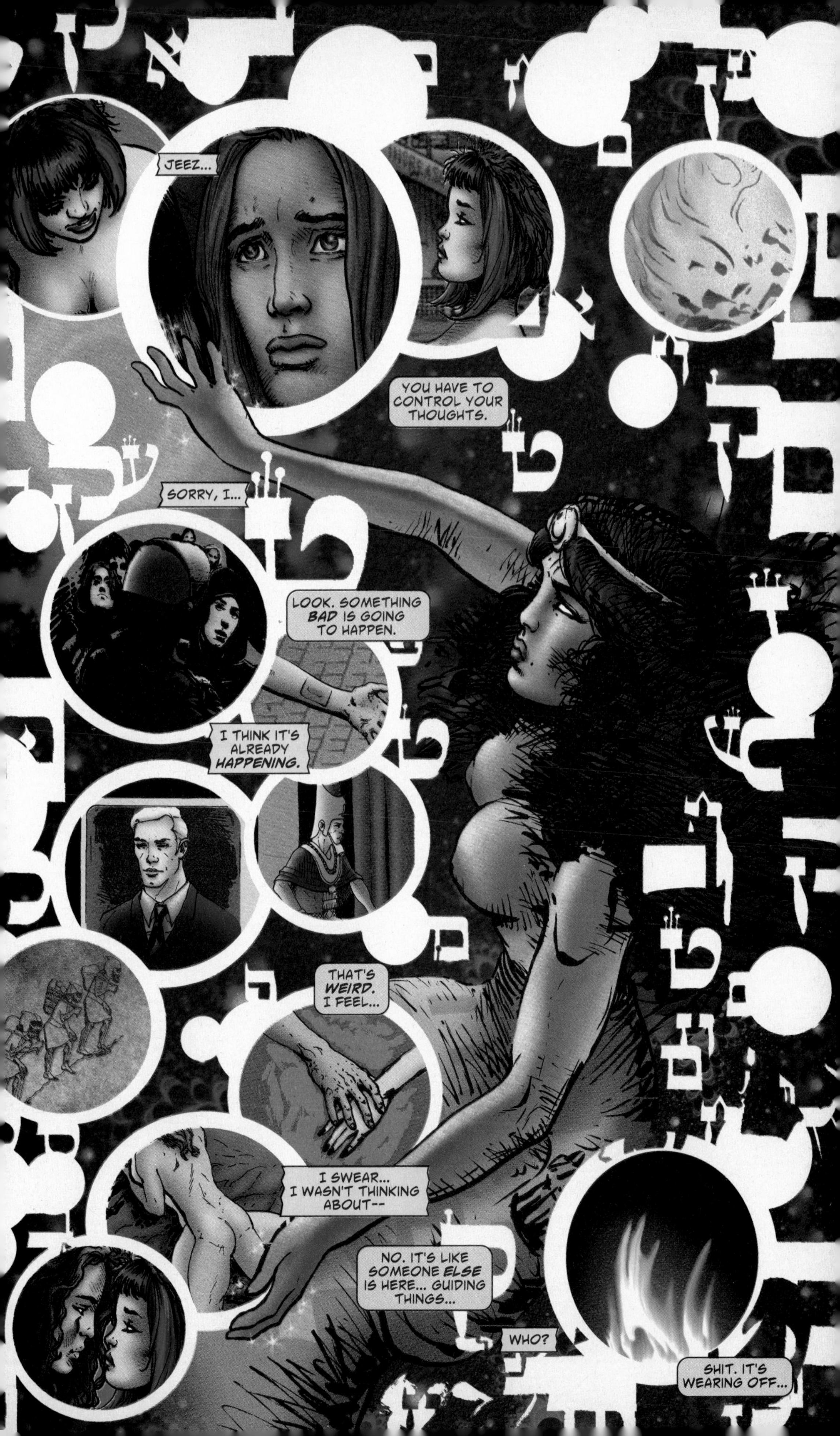
JEEZ...
YOU HAVE TO CONTROL YOUR THOUGHTS.
SORRY, I...
LOOK. SOMETHING *BAD* IS GOING TO HAPPEN.
I THINK IT'S ALREADY *HAPPENING*.
THAT'S *WEIRD*. I FEEL...
I SWEAR... I WASN'T THINKING ABOUT--
NO. IT'S LIKE SOMEONE *ELSE* IS HERE... GUIDING THINGS...
WHO?
SHIT. IT'S WEARING OFF...

THIS IS HEAVY STUFF THEY'RE MESSING WITH, DINAH. YOU'RE JUST A *KID*.

THAT'S NOT HOW YOU SAW ME IN *THERE*... BESIDES, I'LL BE EIGHTEEN NEXT MONTH.

EXACTLY. YOU CAN STILL ENROLL IN *COLLEGE*. BUY A FEW YEARS. SEE IF THIS WHOLE THING GOES AWAY.

FAR AS I'M CONCERNED, IT'S *GONE*.

SHIT, DINAH. I DUNNO... YOUR PARENTS HIRED ME AS YOUR *S.A.T. TUTOR*. I SHOULD'VE--

IT'S NOT YOUR FAULT, JAKE. YOU DIDN'T *CORRUPT* ME BY INTRODUCING ME TO YOUR FRIENDS, OKAY? THIS WAS ALL MY *CHOICE*.

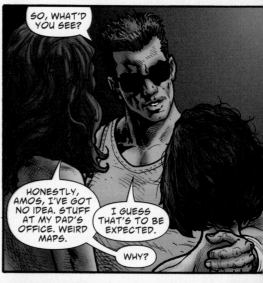

SO, WHAT'D YOU SEE?

HONESTLY, AMOS, I'VE GOT NO IDEA. STUFF AT MY DAD'S OFFICE. WEIRD MAPS.

I GUESS THAT'S TO BE EXPECTED.

WHY?

WE'RE USING THE *RFID* TAGS WE PULLED AS A REFERENCE. UPLINKING THROUGH THEM TO THE TRACKING SERVER.

IT'S AN OPEN WINDOW TO THEIR WHOLE NETWORK. THEIR SECURITY SUCKS.

BUT THE STUFF WE SAW-- IT WAS *ANCIENT*.

IS *THAT* WHAT YOU REMEMBER MOST?

WE'VE GOT TO LEARN HOW TO DISCIPLINE OUR MINDS A BIT. STEER THIS THING.

DINAH'S THE BEST, SO FAR. IT WAS HER IDEA TO DO THE POTION. MAKE IT MORE OF A RITUAL.

SHE'S A REAL ASSET, JAKE.

YEAH, WELL, YOU *REMEMBER* THAT.

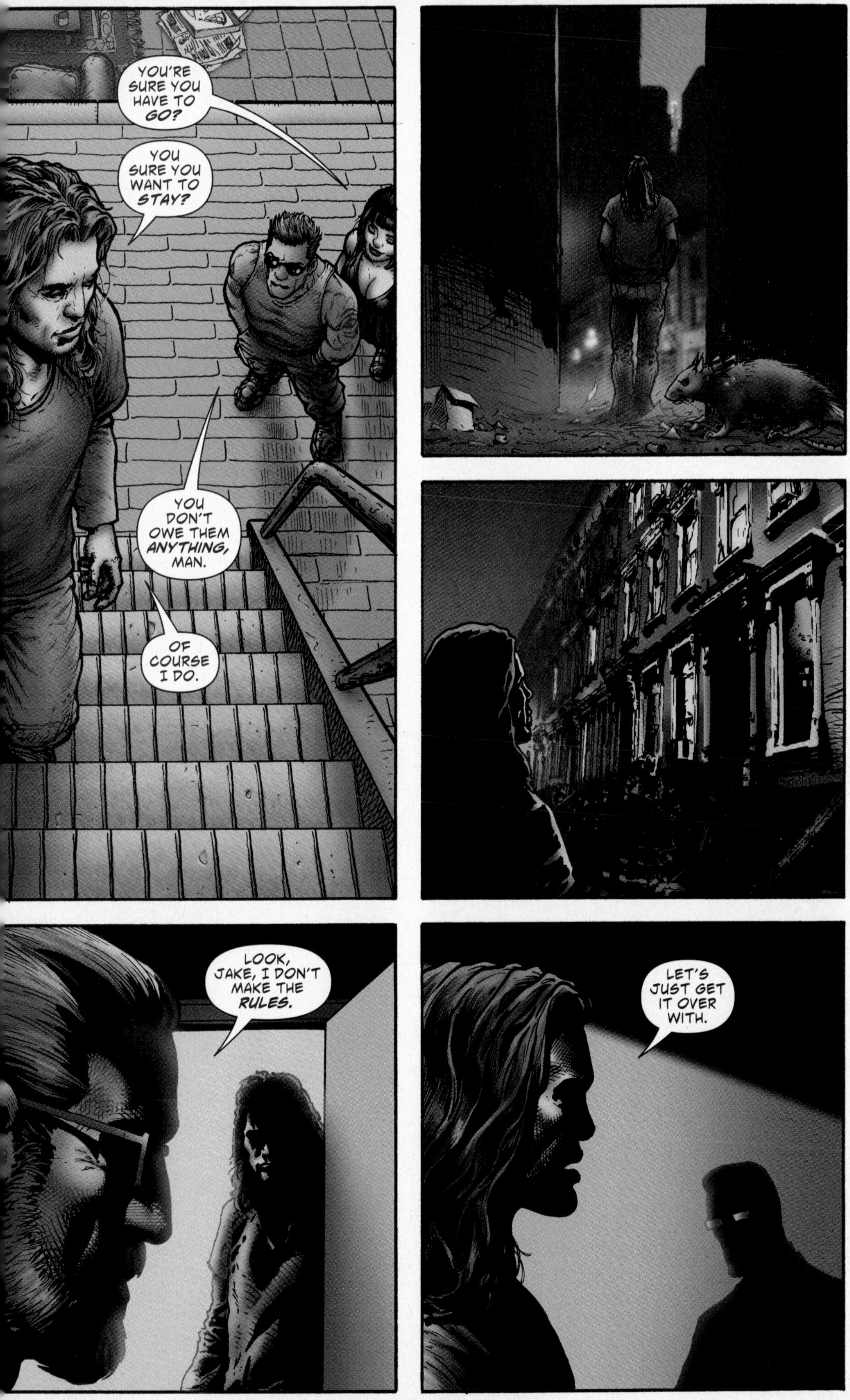
YOU'RE SURE YOU HAVE TO GO?
YOU SURE YOU WANT TO STAY?
YOU DON'T OWE THEM ANYTHING, MAN.
OF COURSE I DO.
LOOK, JAKE, I DON'T MAKE THE RULES.
LET'S JUST GET IT OVER WITH.

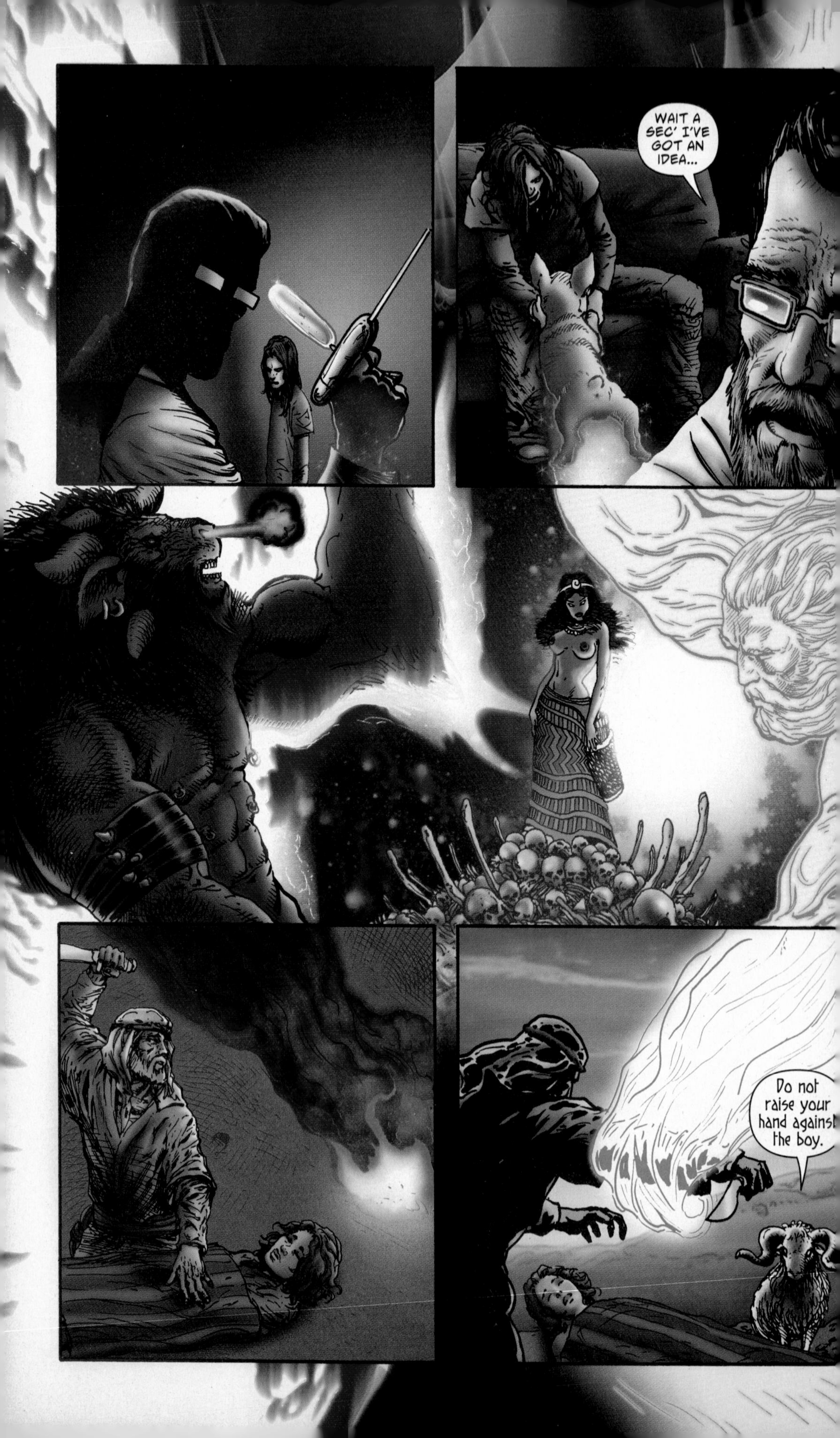
WAIT A SEC' I'VE GOT AN IDEA...
Do not raise your hand against the boy.

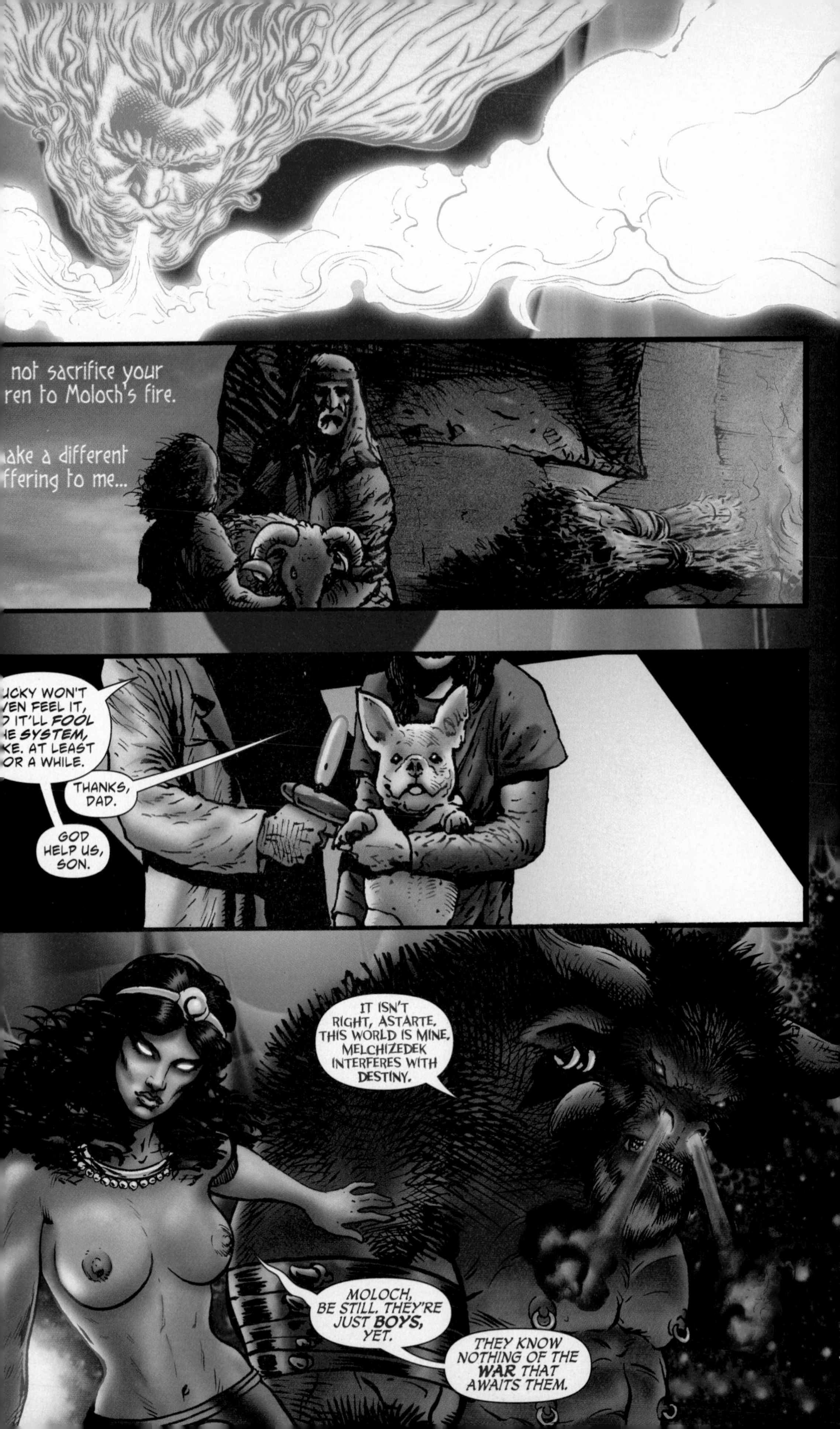

not sacrifice your
ren to Moloch's fire.
ake a different
ffering to me...
UCKY WON'T
VEN FEEL IT,
D IT'LL FOOL
HE SYSTEM,
KE. AT LEAST
OR A WHILE.
THANKS, DAD.
GOD HELP US, SON.
IT ISN'T RIGHT, ASTARTE. THIS WORLD IS MINE. MELCHIZEDEK INTERFERES WITH DESTINY.
MOLOCH, BE STILL. THEY'RE JUST BOYS, YET.
THEY KNOW NOTHING OF THE WAR THAT AWAITS THEM.

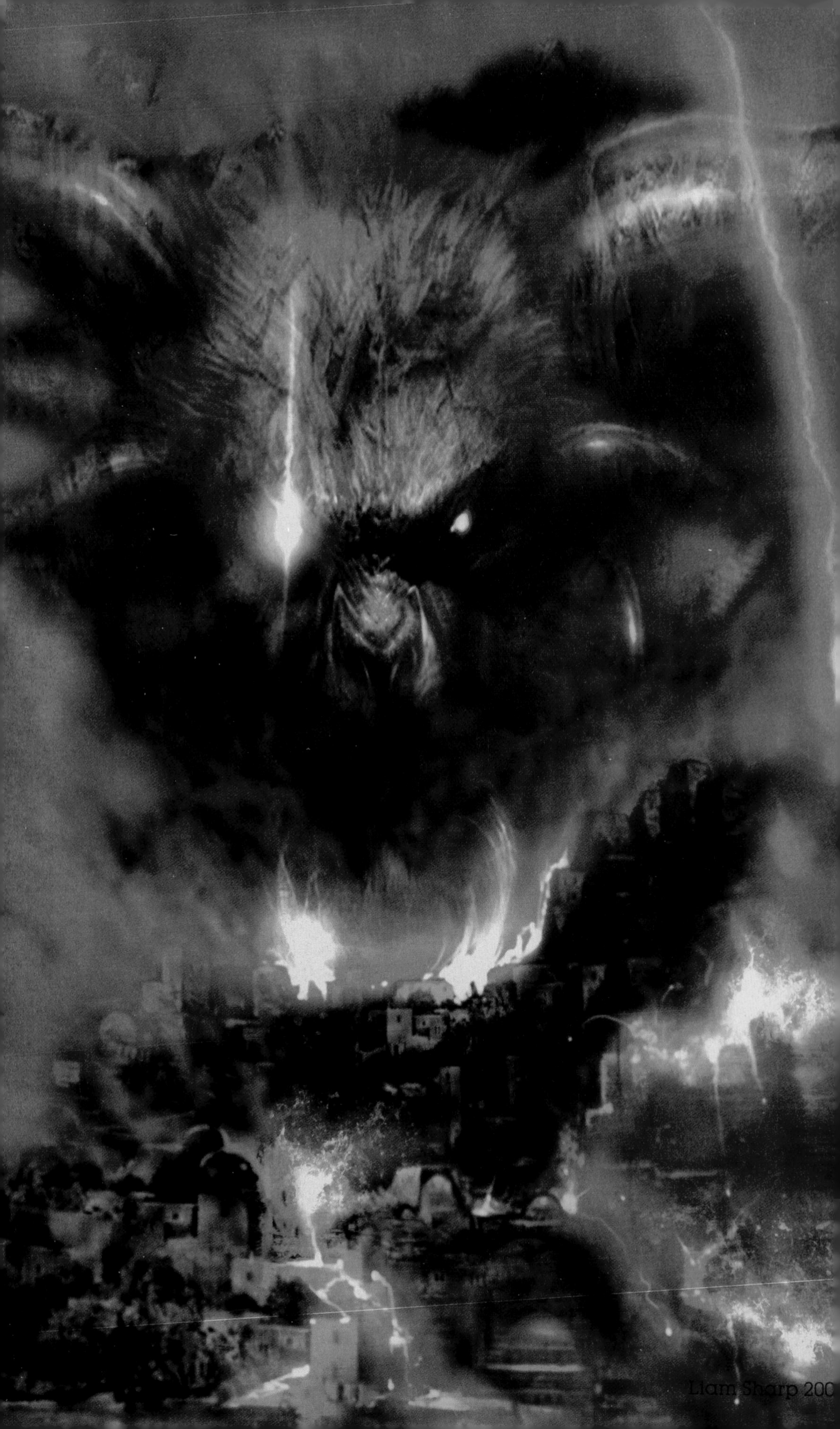
Liam Sharp 200

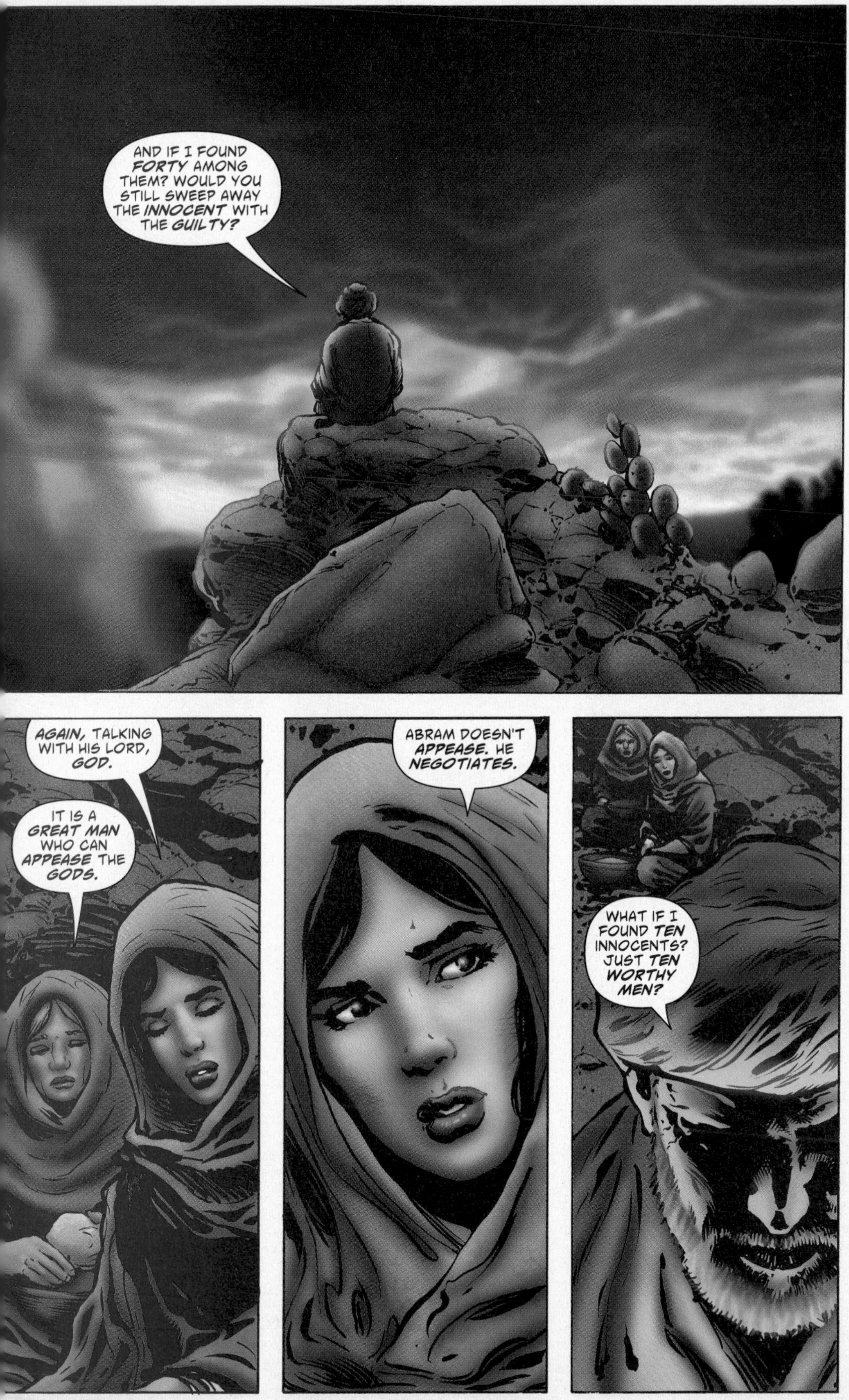
AND IF I FOUND FORTY AMONG THEM? WOULD YOU STILL SWEEP AWAY THE INNOCENT WITH THE GUILTY?
AGAIN, TALKING WITH HIS LORD, GOD.
IT IS A GREAT MAN WHO CAN APPEASE THE GODS.
ABRAM DOESN'T APPEASE. HE NEGOTIATES.
WHAT IF I FOUND TEN INNOCENTS? JUST TEN WORTHY MEN?

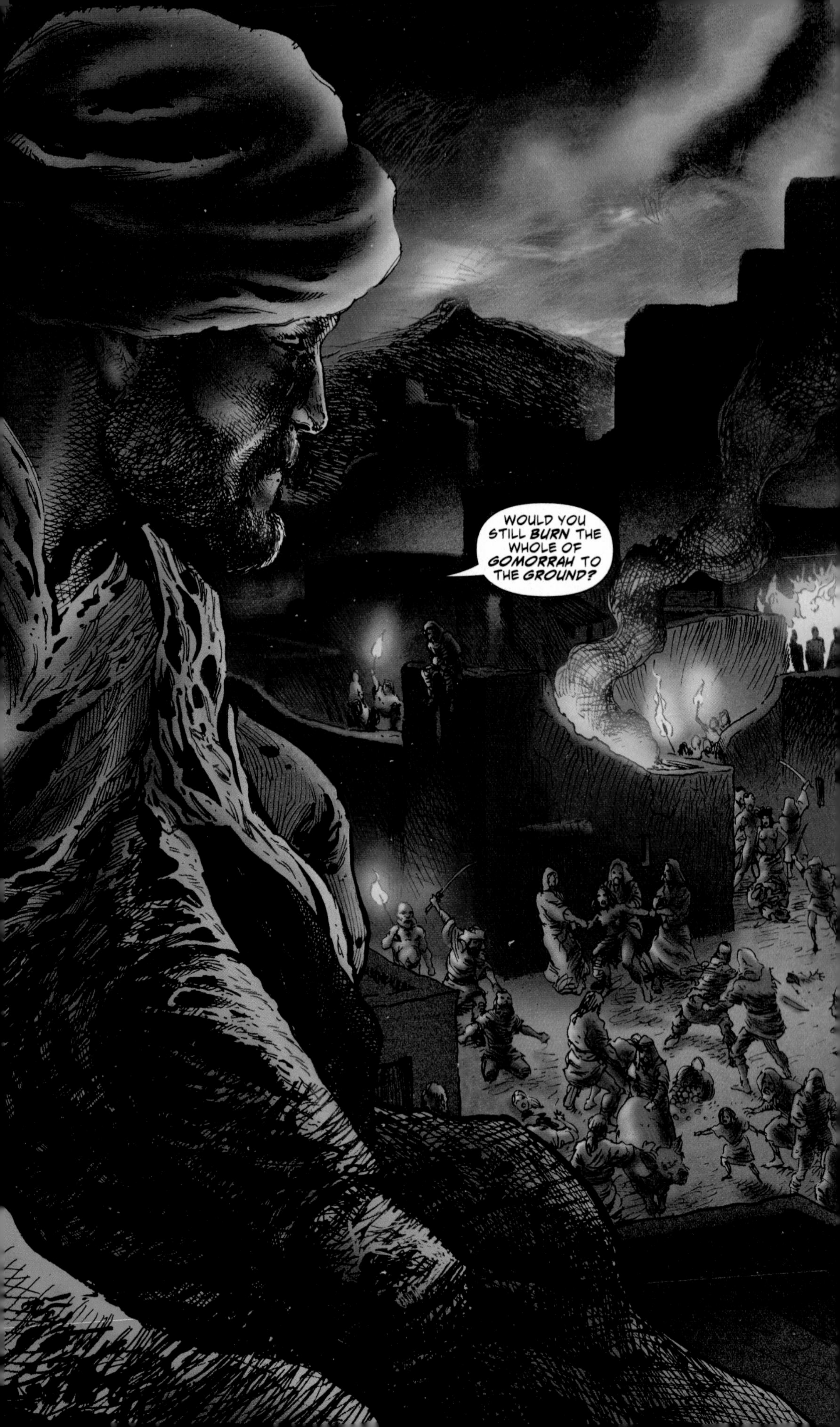
WOULD YOU STILL BURN THE WHOLE OF GOMORRAH TO THE GROUND?

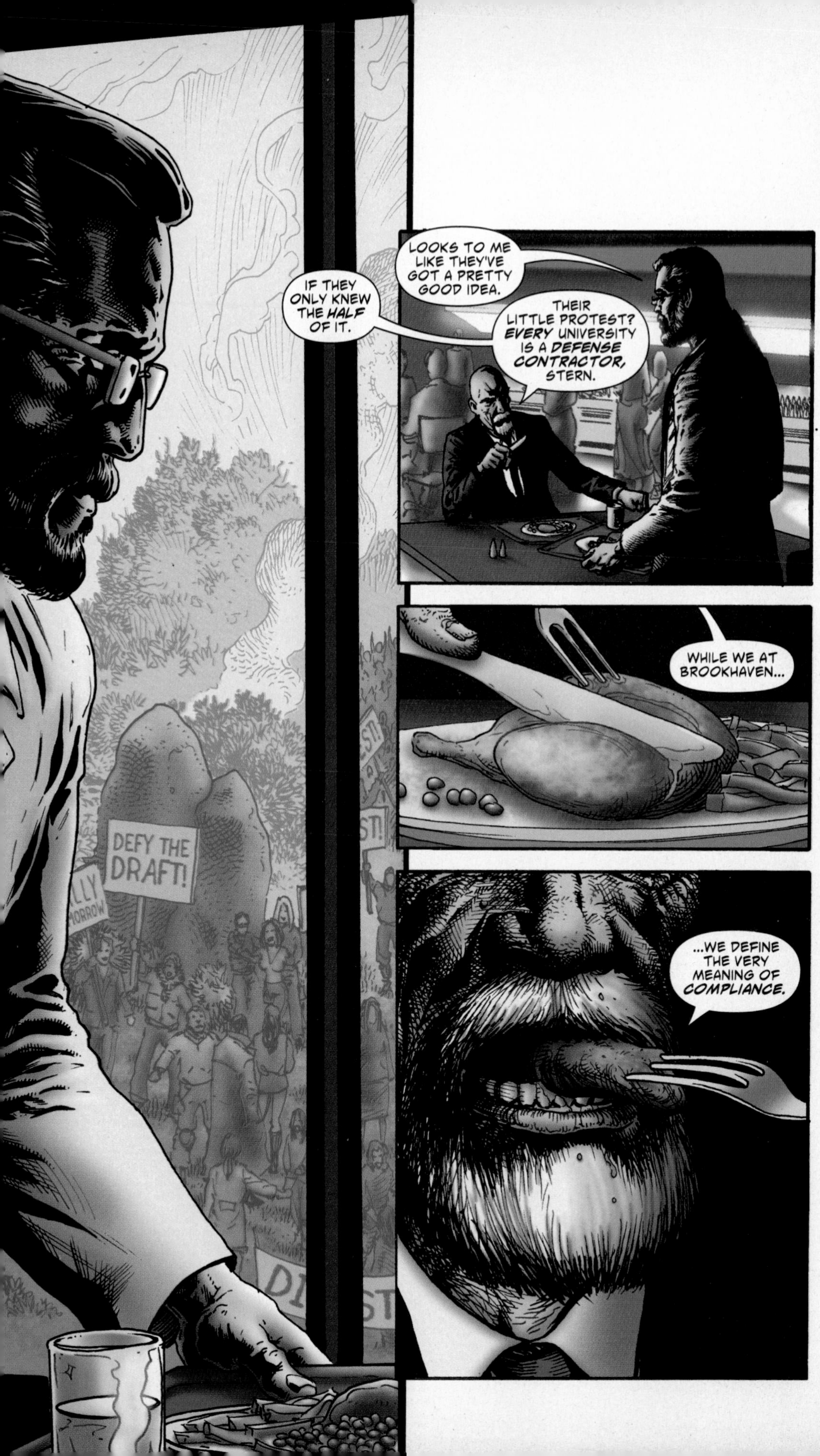
LOOKS TO ME LIKE THEY'VE GOT A PRETTY GOOD IDEA.
IF THEY ONLY KNEW THE HALF OF IT.
THEIR LITTLE PROTEST? EVERY UNIVERSITY IS A DEFENSE CONTRACTOR, STERN.
WHILE WE AT BROOKHAVEN...
...WE DEFINE THE VERY MEANING OF COMPLIANCE.
DEFY THE DRAFT!

YOU'RE NOT THINKING OF EXPLOITING ALL THE CAPABILITIES OF THOSE *RFID TAGS IN THEIR WRISTS*, DR. GREEN, ARE YOU?

WHAT BETTER *TEST SAMPLE* DO YOU THINK WE'LL EVER FIND?

BUT WE HAVE A RESPONSIBILITY, AS *SCIENTISTS*, OVER HOW OUR RESEARCH IS ULTIMATELY *USED*.

IT'S ONE THING TO TRACK THE PROTESTERS, *IDENTIFY* THEM. IT'S ANOTHER TO...

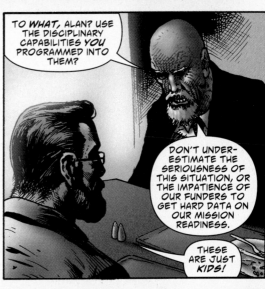

TO *WHAT*, ALAN? USE THE DISCIPLINARY CAPABILITIES *YOU* PROGRAMMED INTO THEM?

DON'T UNDER-ESTIMATE THE SERIOUSNESS OF THIS SITUATION, OR THE IMPATIENCE OF OUR FUNDERS TO GET HARD DATA ON OUR MISSION READINESS.

THESE ARE JUST *KIDS!*

THESE "KIDS" ARE IN LEAGUE WITH THE *NEONATIONALISTS*, ALAN. AND THE *NATS* ARE ESSENTIALLY *TERRORISTS*.

BUT SOME OF THE PROTESTERS ARE JUST *STUDENTS*. *PEACENIKS*. ANTI-WAR TYPES... IMAGINE HOW WE'D FEEL IF JUST *TEN INNOCENT KIDS* WERE INJURED BY THE PULSE.

IF YOU'RE REALLY WORRIED, STERN, THEN I'D SUGGEST YOU TELL *YOUR SON* NOT TO BE THERE.

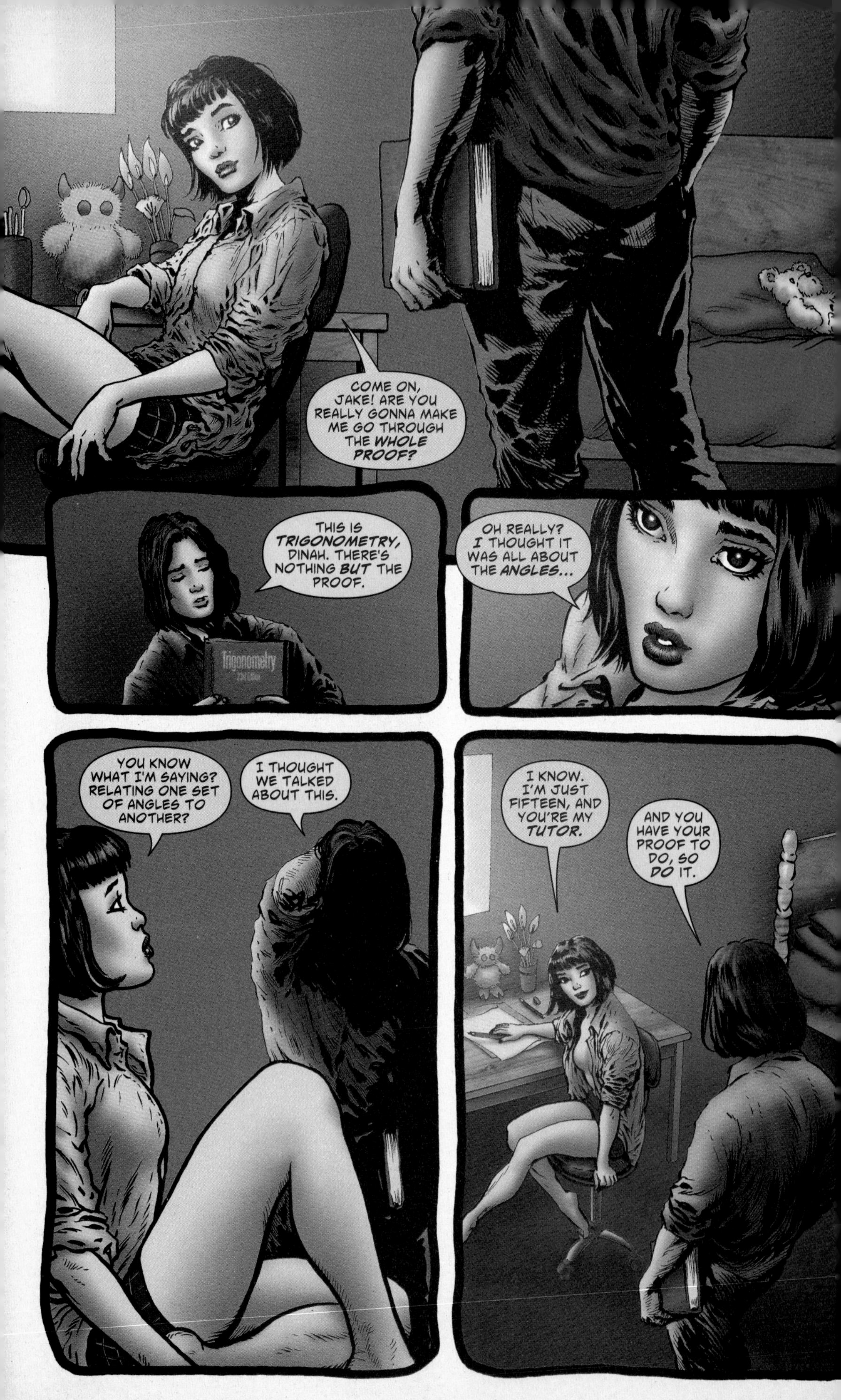
COME ON, JAKE! ARE YOU REALLY GONNA MAKE ME GO THROUGH THE *WHOLE PROOF?*
THIS IS *TRIGONOMETRY,* DINAH. THERE'S NOTHING *BUT* THE PROOF.
Trigonometry
OH REALLY? I THOUGHT IT WAS ALL ABOUT THE *ANGLES...*
YOU KNOW WHAT I'M *SAYING?* RELATING ONE SET OF ANGLES TO ANOTHER?
I THOUGHT WE TALKED ABOUT THIS.
I KNOW. I'M JUST FIFTEEN, AND YOU'RE MY *TUTOR.*
AND YOU HAVE YOUR PROOF TO DO, SO *DO* IT.

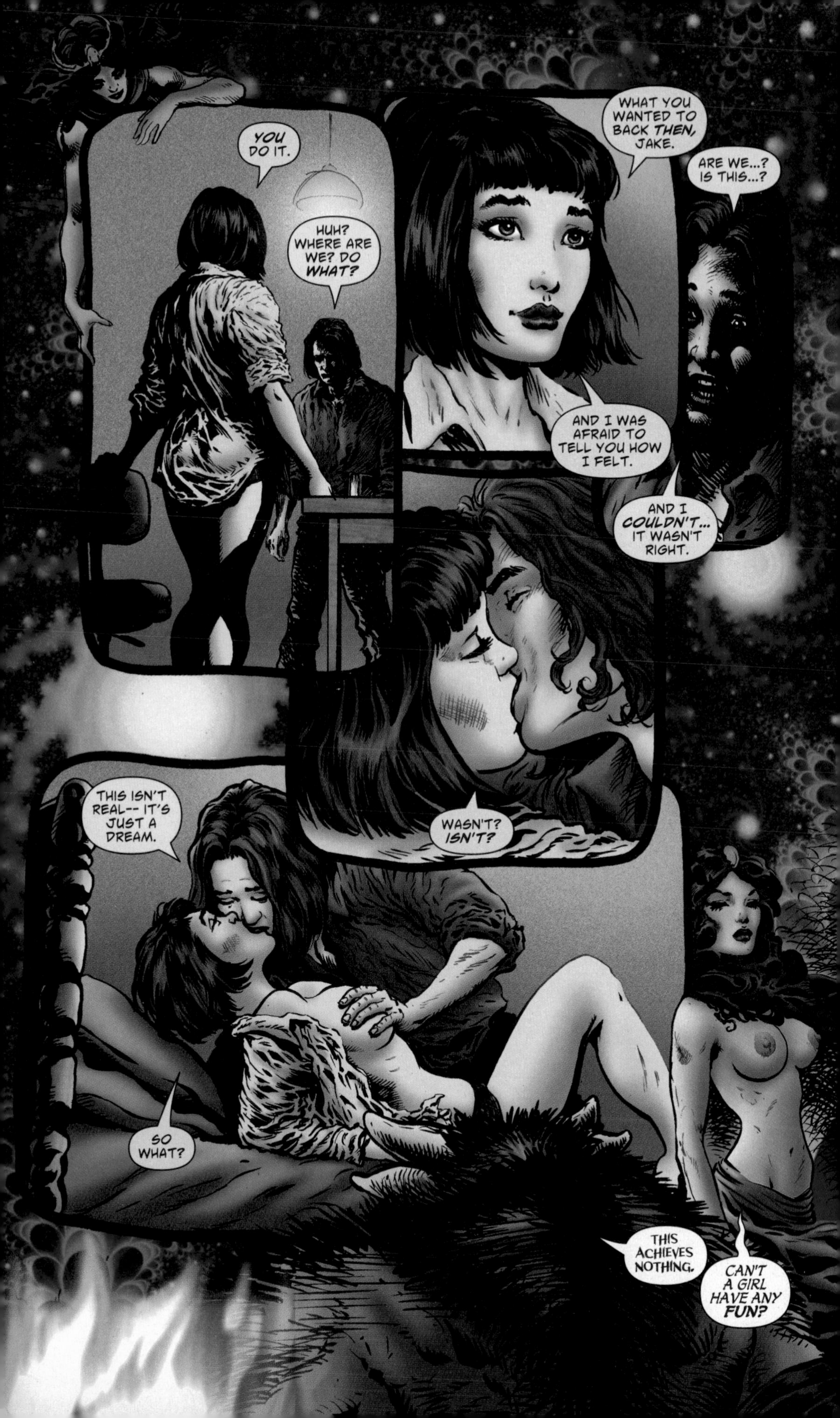
YOU DO IT.
HUH? WHERE ARE WE? DO WHAT?
WHAT YOU WANTED TO BACK THEN, JAKE.
ARE WE...? IS THIS...?
AND I WAS AFRAID TO TELL YOU HOW I FELT.
AND I COULDN'T... IT WASN'T RIGHT.
WASN'T? ISN'T?
THIS ISN'T REAL-- IT'S JUST A DREAM.
SO WHAT?
THIS ACHIEVES NOTHING.
CAN'T A GIRL HAVE ANY FUN?

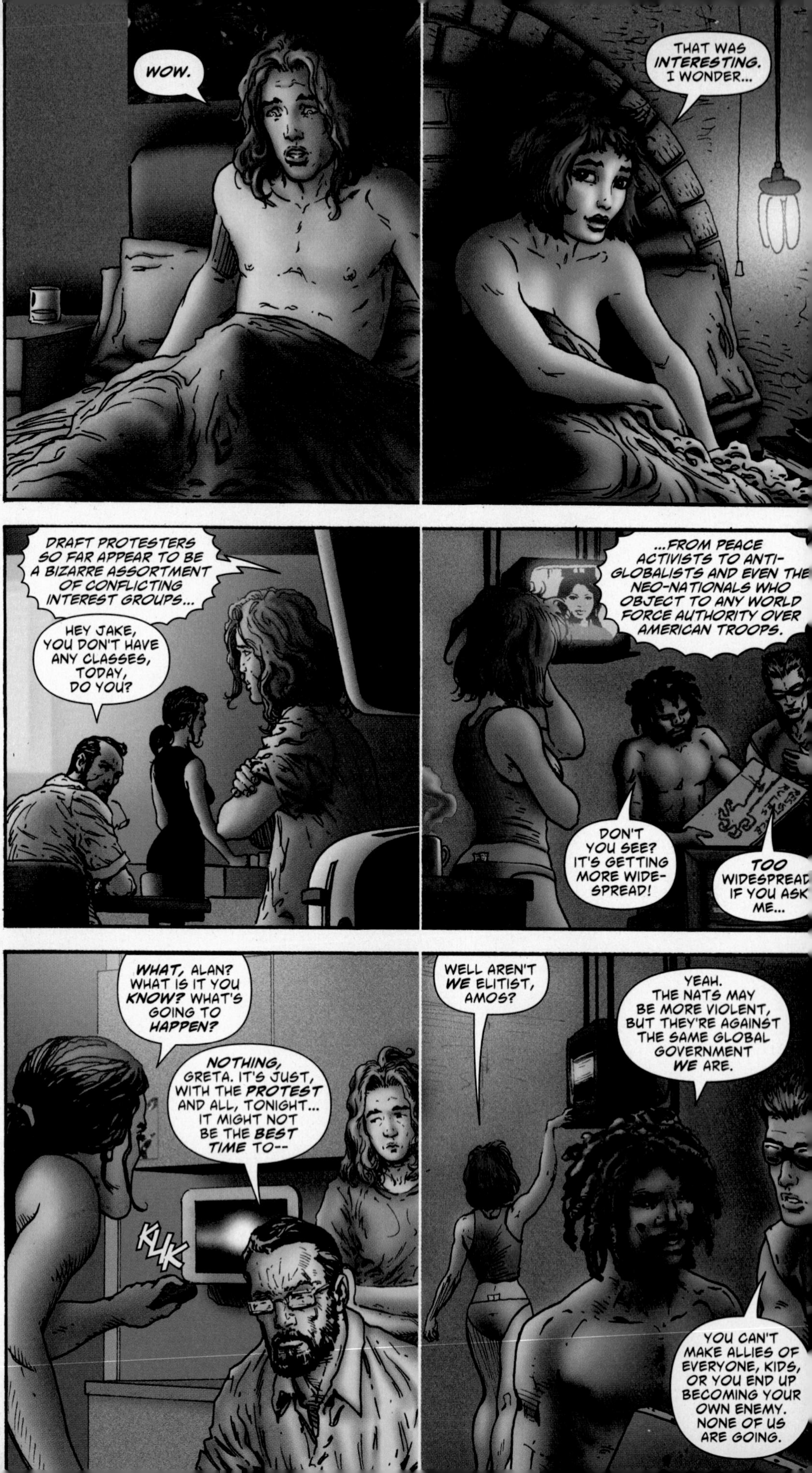
WOW.
THAT WAS INTERESTING. I WONDER...
DRAFT PROTESTERS SO FAR APPEAR TO BE A BIZARRE ASSORTMENT OF CONFLICTING INTEREST GROUPS...
HEY JAKE, YOU DON'T HAVE ANY CLASSES, TODAY, DO YOU?
...FROM PEACE ACTIVISTS TO ANTI-GLOBALISTS AND EVEN THE NEO-NATIONALS WHO OBJECT TO ANY WORLD FORCE AUTHORITY OVER AMERICAN TROOPS.
DON'T YOU SEE? IT'S GETTING MORE WIDE-SPREAD!
TOO WIDESPREAD IF YOU ASK ME...
WHAT, ALAN? WHAT IS IT YOU KNOW? WHAT'S GOING TO HAPPEN?
NOTHING, GRETA. IT'S JUST, WITH THE PROTEST AND ALL, TONIGHT... IT MIGHT NOT BE THE BEST TIME TO--
KLIK
WELL AREN'T WE ELITIST, AMOS?
YEAH. THE NATS MAY BE MORE VIOLENT, BUT THEY'RE AGAINST THE SAME GLOBAL GOVERNMENT WE ARE.
YOU CAN'T MAKE ALLIES OF EVERYONE, KIDS, OR YOU END UP BECOMING YOUR OWN ENEMY. NONE OF US ARE GOING.

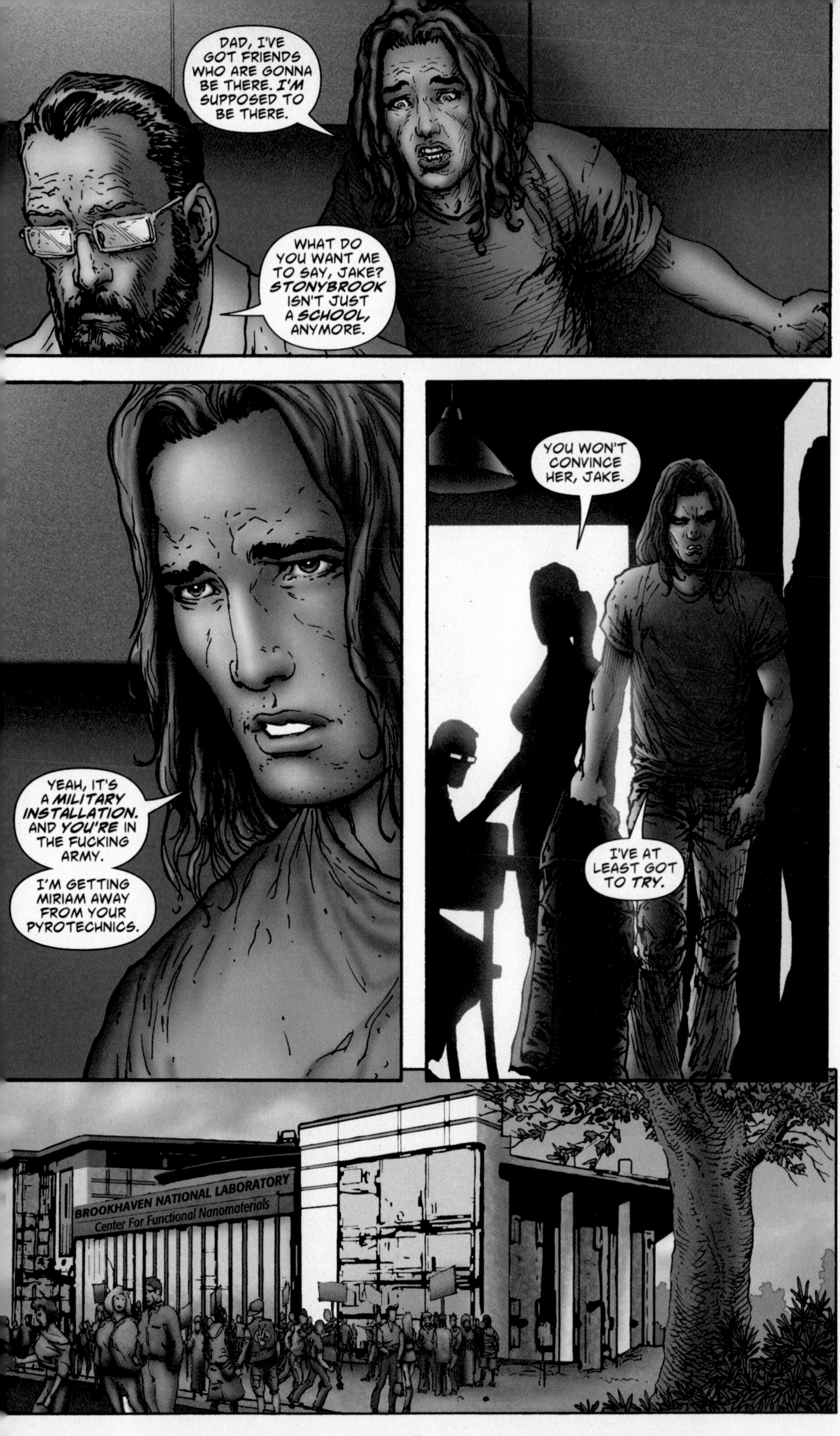
DAD, I'VE GOT FRIENDS WHO ARE GONNA BE THERE. *I'M* SUPPOSED TO BE THERE.
WHAT DO YOU WANT ME TO SAY, JAKE? ***STONYBROOK*** ISN'T JUST A ***SCHOOL***, ANYMORE.
YEAH, IT'S A ***MILITARY INSTALLATION.*** AND ***YOU'RE*** IN THE FUCKING ARMY.
I'M GETTING MIRIAM AWAY FROM YOUR PYROTECHNICS.
YOU WON'T CONVINCE HER, JAKE.
I'VE AT LEAST GOT TO *TRY*.
BROOKHAVEN NATIONAL LABORATORY
Center For Functional Nanomaterials

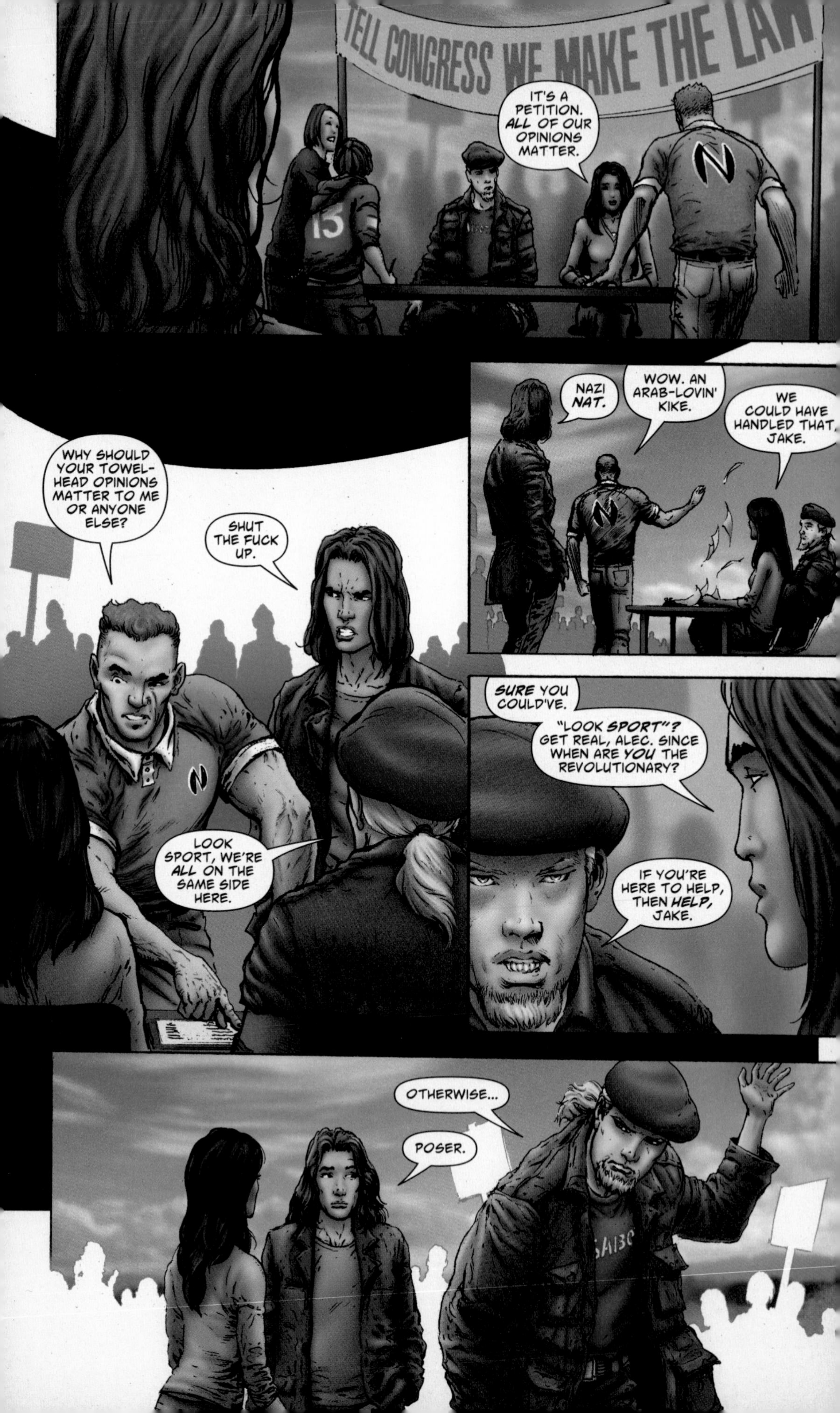
TELL CONGRESS WE MAKE THE LAW
IT'S A PETITION. ALL OF OUR OPINIONS MATTER.
WHY SHOULD YOUR TOWEL-HEAD OPINIONS MATTER TO ME OR ANYONE ELSE?
SHUT THE FUCK UP.
LOOK SPORT, WE'RE ALL ON THE SAME SIDE HERE.
NAZI NAT.
WOW. AN ARAB-LOVIN' KIKE.
WE COULD HAVE HANDLED THAT, JAKE.
SURE YOU COULD'VE.
"LOOK SPORT"? GET REAL, ALEC. SINCE WHEN ARE YOU THE REVOLUTIONARY?
IF YOU'RE HERE TO HELP, THEN HELP, JAKE.
OTHERWISE...
POSER.

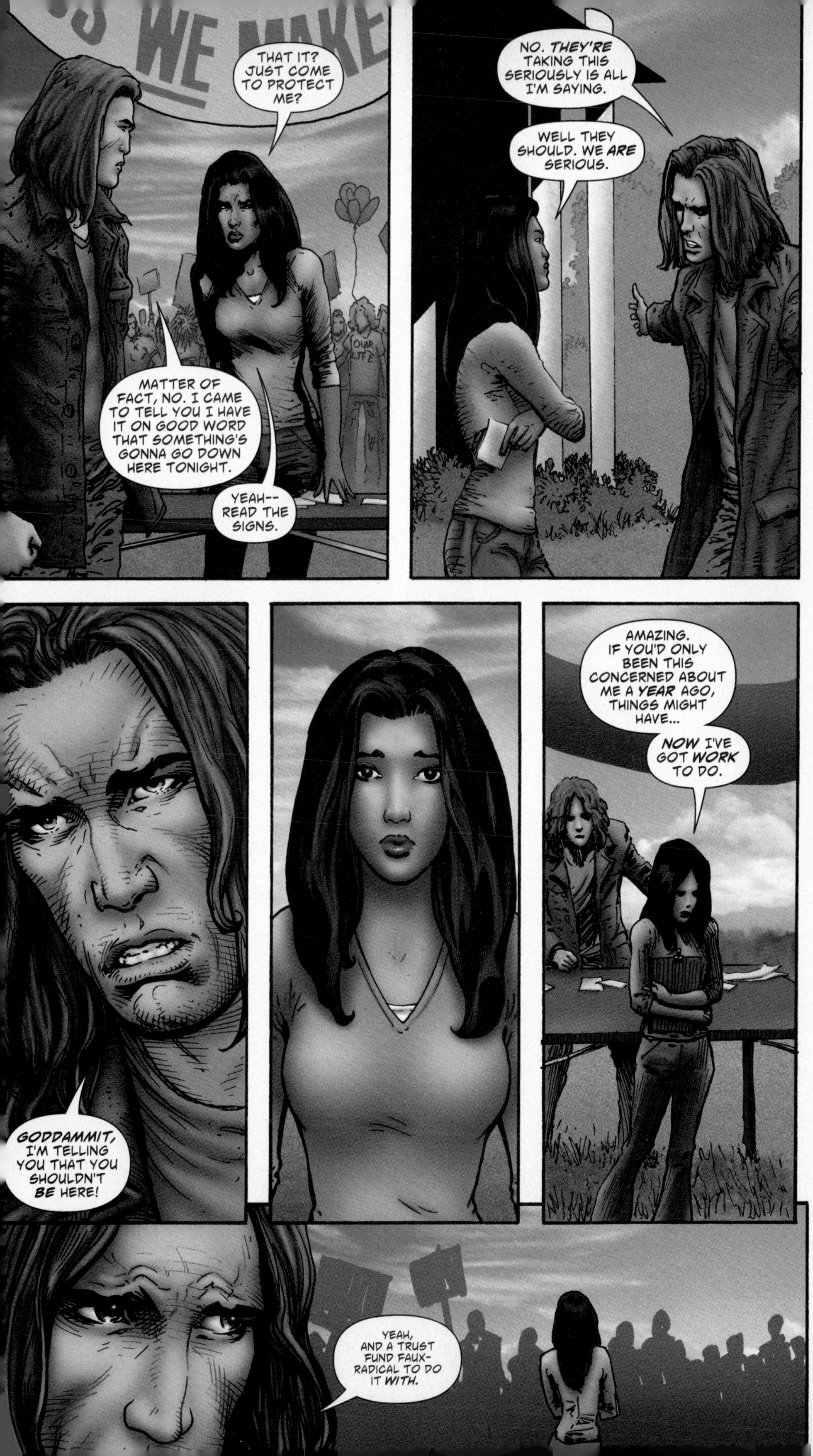
WE MAKE
THAT IT? JUST COME TO PROTECT ME?
MATTER OF FACT, NO. I CAME TO TELL YOU I HAVE IT ON GOOD WORD THAT SOMETHING'S GONNA GO DOWN HERE TONIGHT.
YEAH-- READ THE SIGNS.
NO. THEY'RE TAKING THIS SERIOUSLY IS ALL I'M SAYING.
WELL THEY SHOULD. WE ARE SERIOUS.
GODDAMMIT, I'M TELLING YOU THAT YOU SHOULDN'T BE HERE!
AMAZING. IF YOU'D ONLY BEEN THIS CONCERNED ABOUT ME A YEAR AGO, THINGS MIGHT HAVE...
NOW I'VE GOT WORK TO DO.
YEAH, AND A TRUST FUND FAUX-RADICAL TO DO IT WITH.

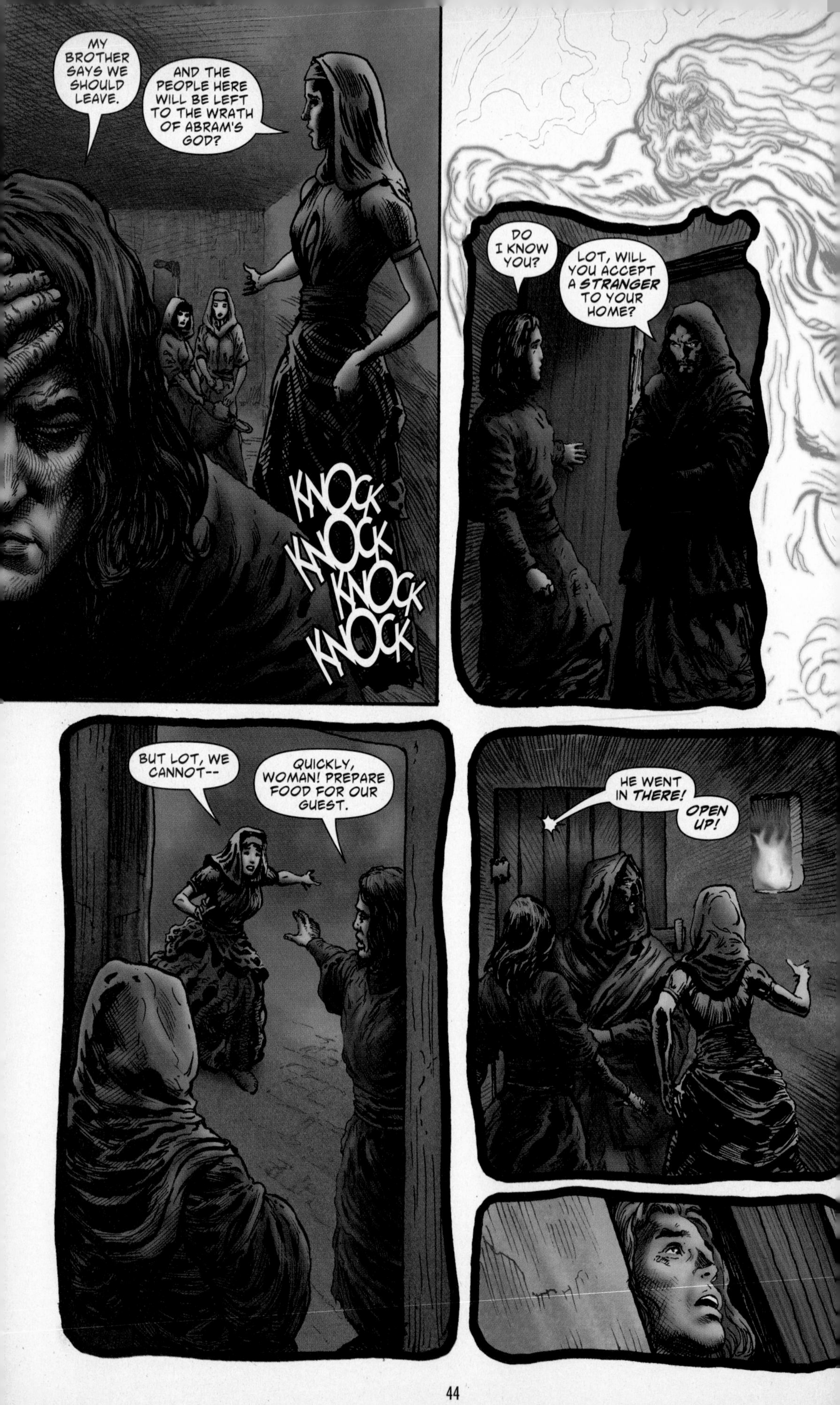
MY BROTHER SAYS WE SHOULD LEAVE.
AND THE PEOPLE HERE WILL BE LEFT TO THE WRATH OF ABRAM'S GOD?
KNOCK KNOCK KNOCK KNOCK
DO I KNOW YOU?
LOT, WILL YOU ACCEPT A STRANGER TO YOUR HOME?
BUT LOT, WE CANNOT--
QUICKLY, WOMAN! PREPARE FOOD FOR OUR GUEST.
HE WENT IN THERE!
OPEN UP!

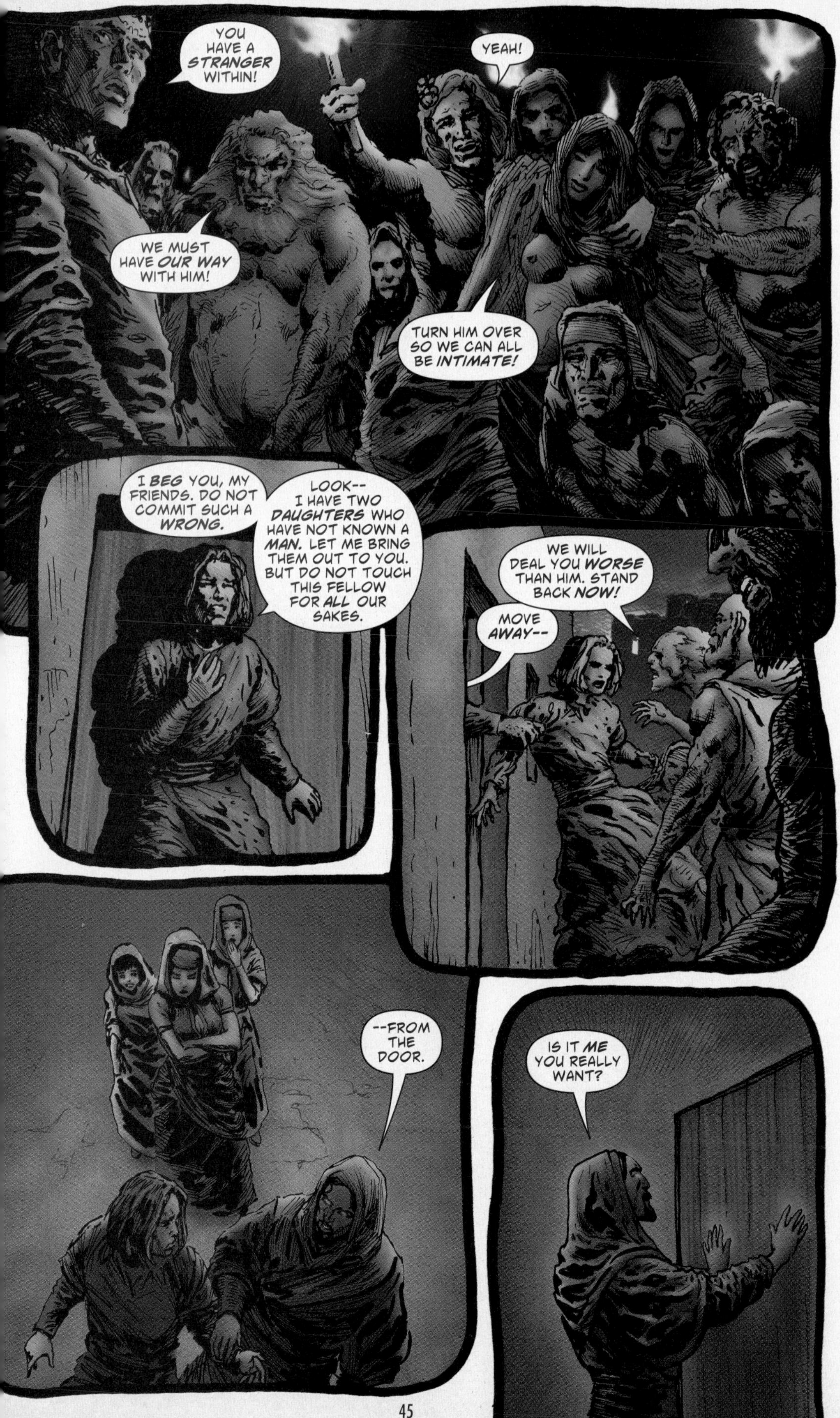
YOU HAVE A STRANGER WITHIN!
YEAH!
WE MUST HAVE OUR WAY WITH HIM!
TURN HIM OVER SO WE CAN ALL BE INTIMATE!
I BEG YOU, MY FRIENDS. DO NOT COMMIT SUCH A WRONG.
LOOK-- I HAVE TWO DAUGHTERS WHO HAVE NOT KNOWN A MAN. LET ME BRING THEM OUT TO YOU. BUT DO NOT TOUCH THIS FELLOW FOR ALL OUR SAKES.
WE WILL DEAL YOU WORSE THAN HIM. STAND BACK NOW!
MOVE AWAY--
--FROM THE DOOR.
IS IT ME YOU REALLY WANT?

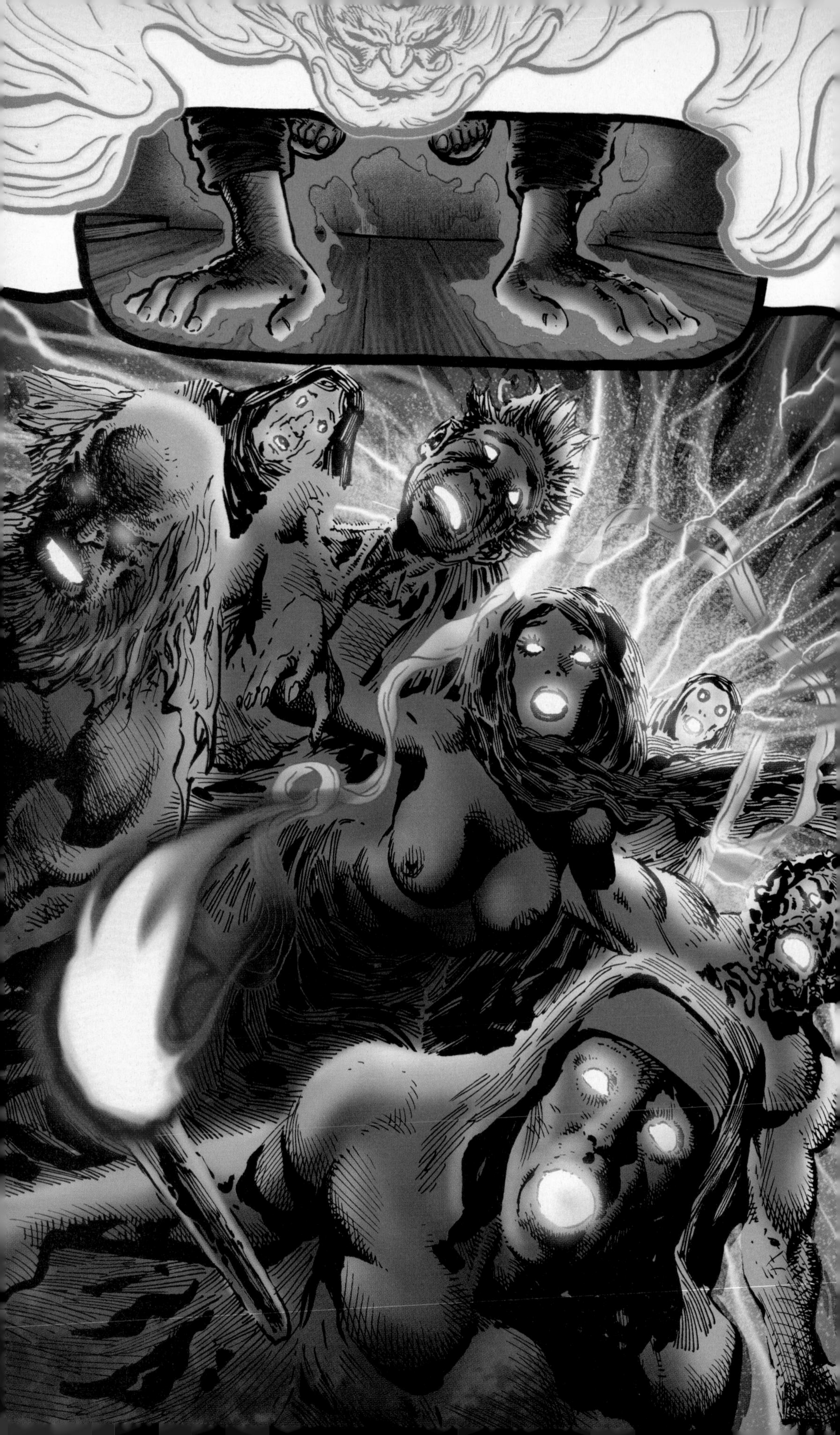

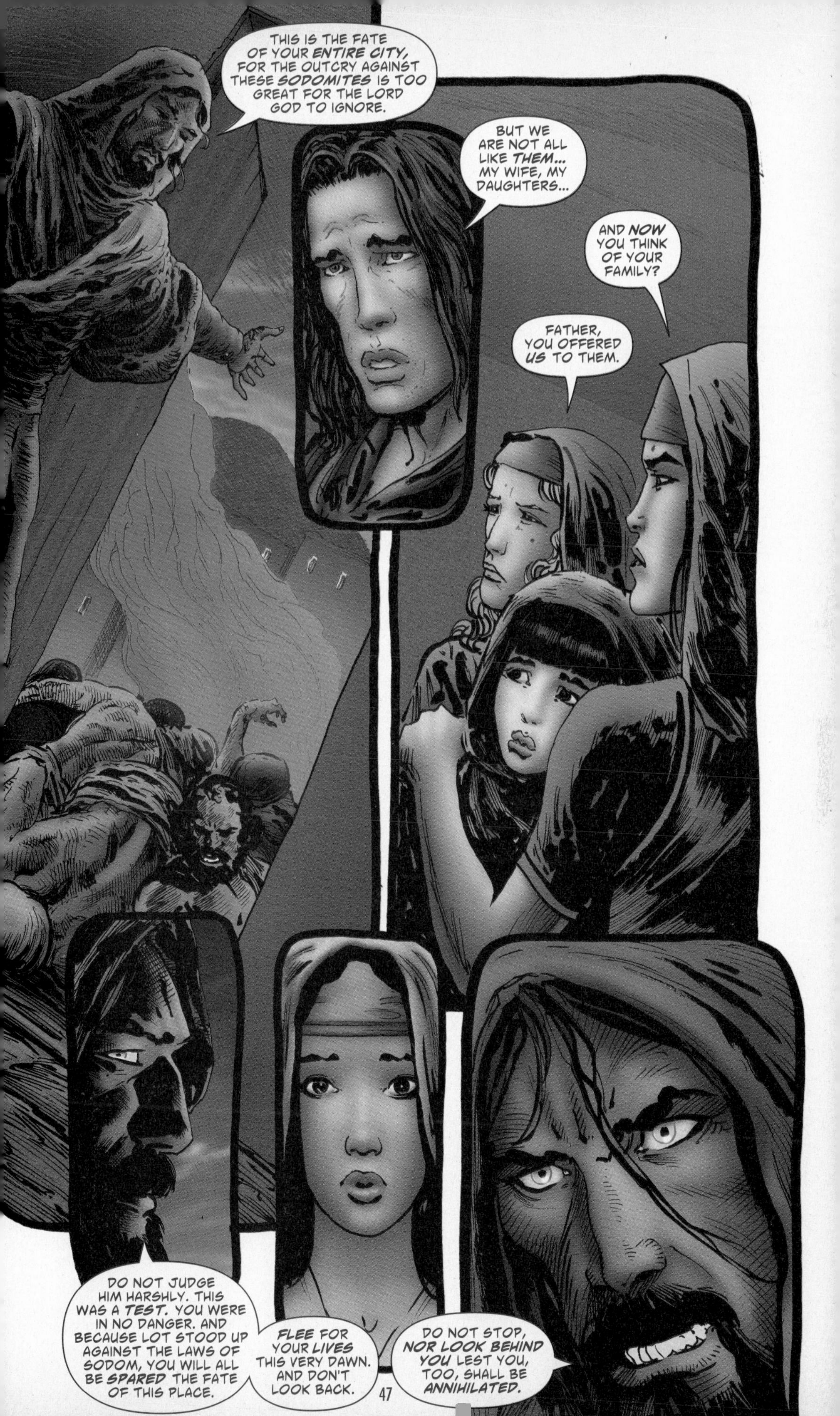

THIS IS THE FATE OF YOUR *ENTIRE CITY*, FOR THE OUTCRY AGAINST THESE *SODOMITES* IS TOO GREAT FOR THE LORD GOD TO IGNORE.
BUT WE ARE NOT ALL LIKE *THEM*... MY WIFE, MY DAUGHTERS...
AND *NOW* YOU THINK OF YOUR FAMILY?
FATHER, YOU OFFERED *US* TO THEM.
DO NOT JUDGE HIM HARSHLY. THIS WAS A *TEST*. YOU WERE IN NO DANGER. AND BECAUSE LOT STOOD UP AGAINST THE LAWS OF SODOM, YOU WILL ALL BE *SPARED* THE FATE OF THIS PLACE.
FLEE FOR YOUR *LIVES* THIS VERY DAWN. AND DON'T LOOK BACK.
DO NOT STOP, *NOR LOOK BEHIND YOU* LEST YOU, TOO, SHALL BE *ANNIHILATED*.

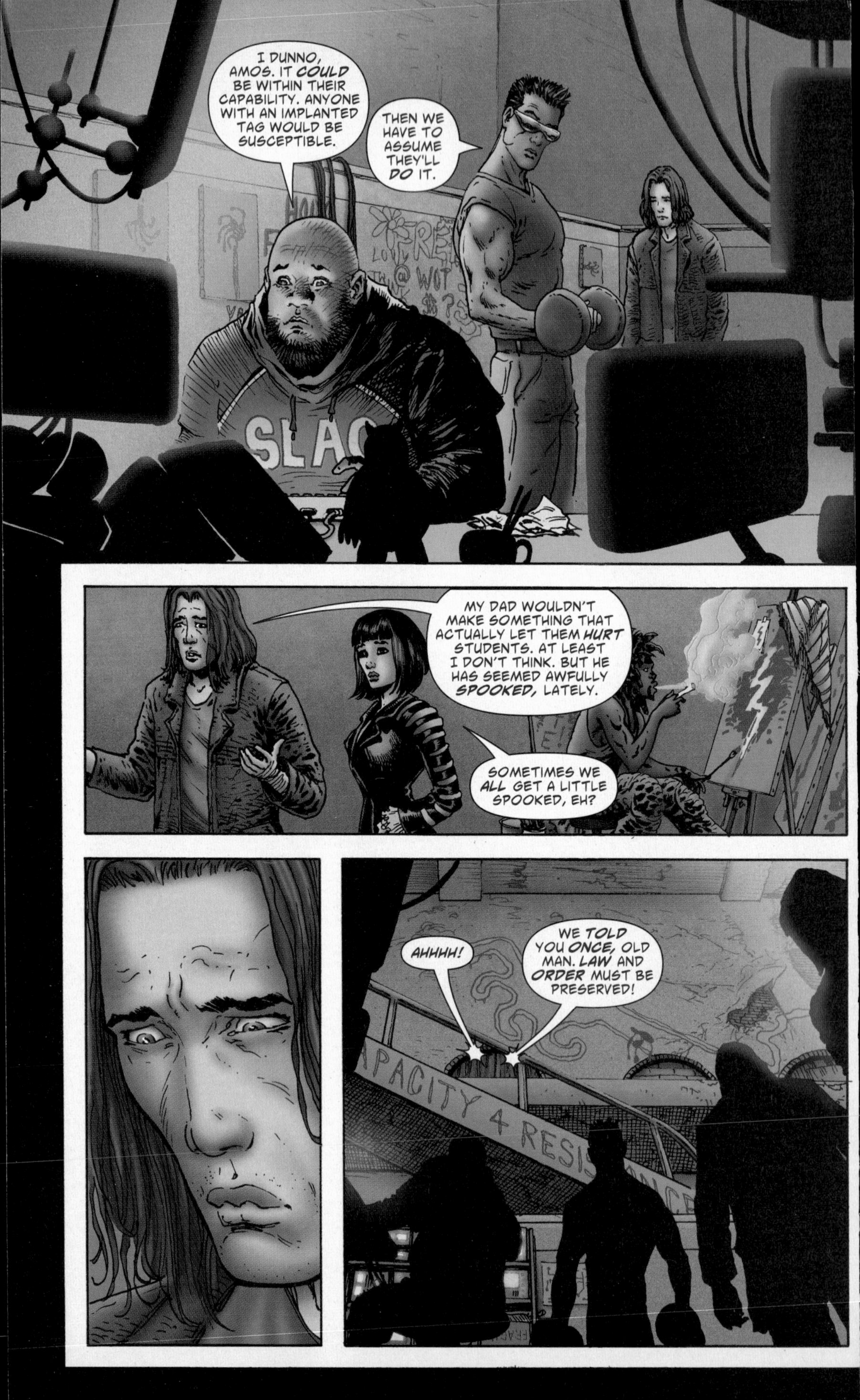
I DUNNO, AMOS. IT COULD BE WITHIN THEIR CAPABILITY. ANYONE WITH AN IMPLANTED TAG WOULD BE SUSCEPTIBLE.
THEN WE HAVE TO ASSUME THEY'LL DO IT.
MY DAD WOULDN'T MAKE SOMETHING THAT ACTUALLY LET THEM HURT STUDENTS. AT LEAST I DON'T THINK. BUT HE HAS SEEMED AWFULLY SPOOKED, LATELY.
SOMETIMES WE ALL GET A LITTLE SPOOKED, EH?
AHHHH!
WE TOLD YOU ONCE, OLD MAN. LAW AND ORDER MUST BE PRESERVED!

UCKING
'S. THEY'RE
NA KILL THE
LD GUY!

WE HAFTA
DO SOME-
THING.

THERE'S
GOT TO BE A
DOZEN OF
THEM.

I GOT
AN IDEA...

SO ARE
ALL NATS
GAY, OR JUST
YOUR LITTLE
CREW?

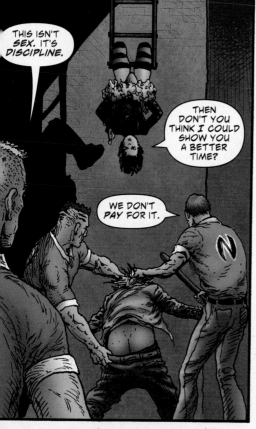

THIS ISN'T
SEX. IT'S
DISCIPLINE.

THEN
DON'T YOU
THINK I COULD
SHOW YOU A
BETTER
TIME?

WE DON'T
PAY FOR IT.

HEY!
OVER
HERE!

WHAT'D YOU PUNKS
THINK YOU WERE
GONNA DO? SNEAK UP
WHILE YOUR WHORE
DISTRACTED US?

YOU'RE
GONNA PAY
WAY WORSE
THAN THIS
OLD FOOL.

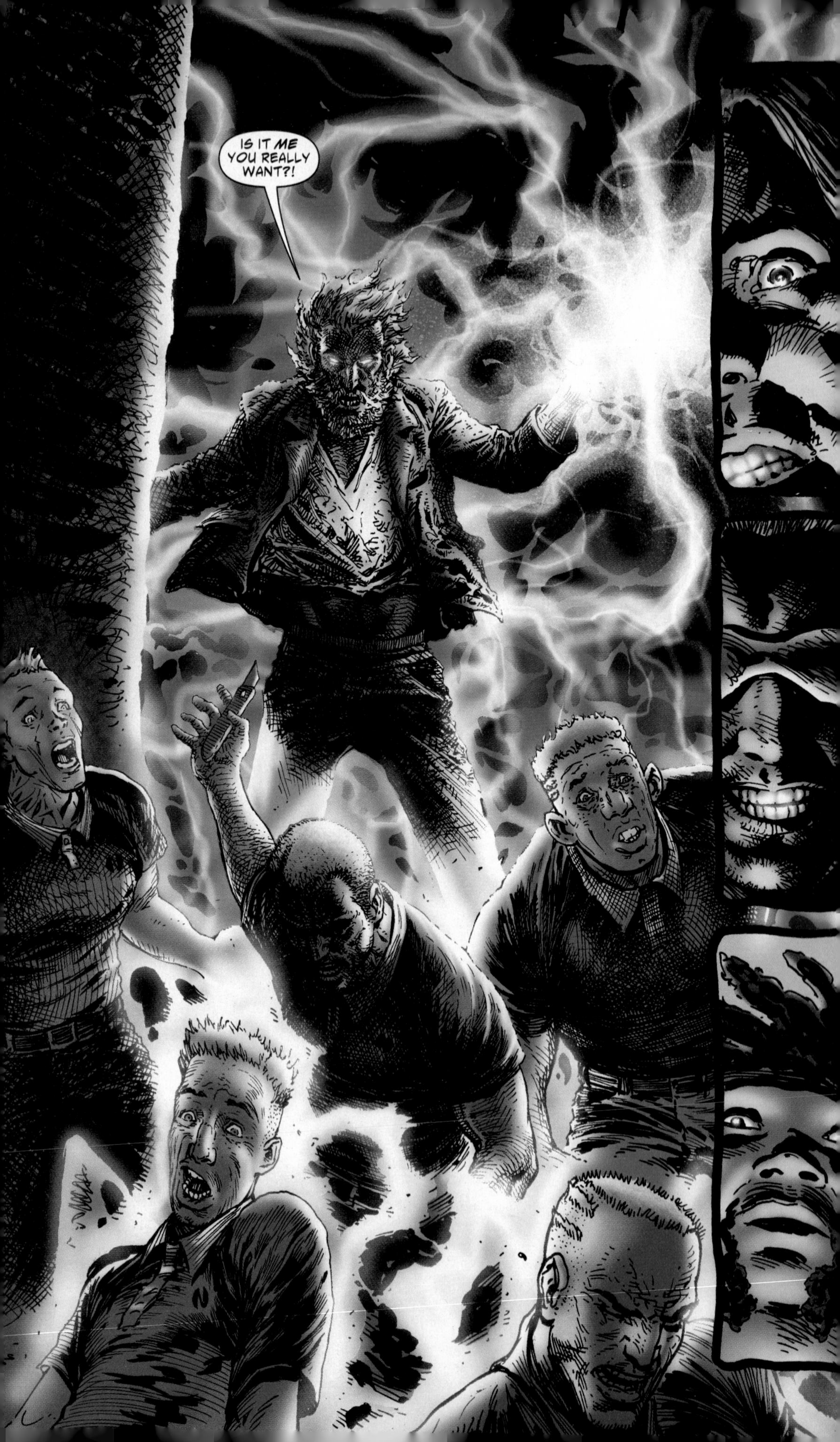
IS IT ME YOU REALLY WANT?!

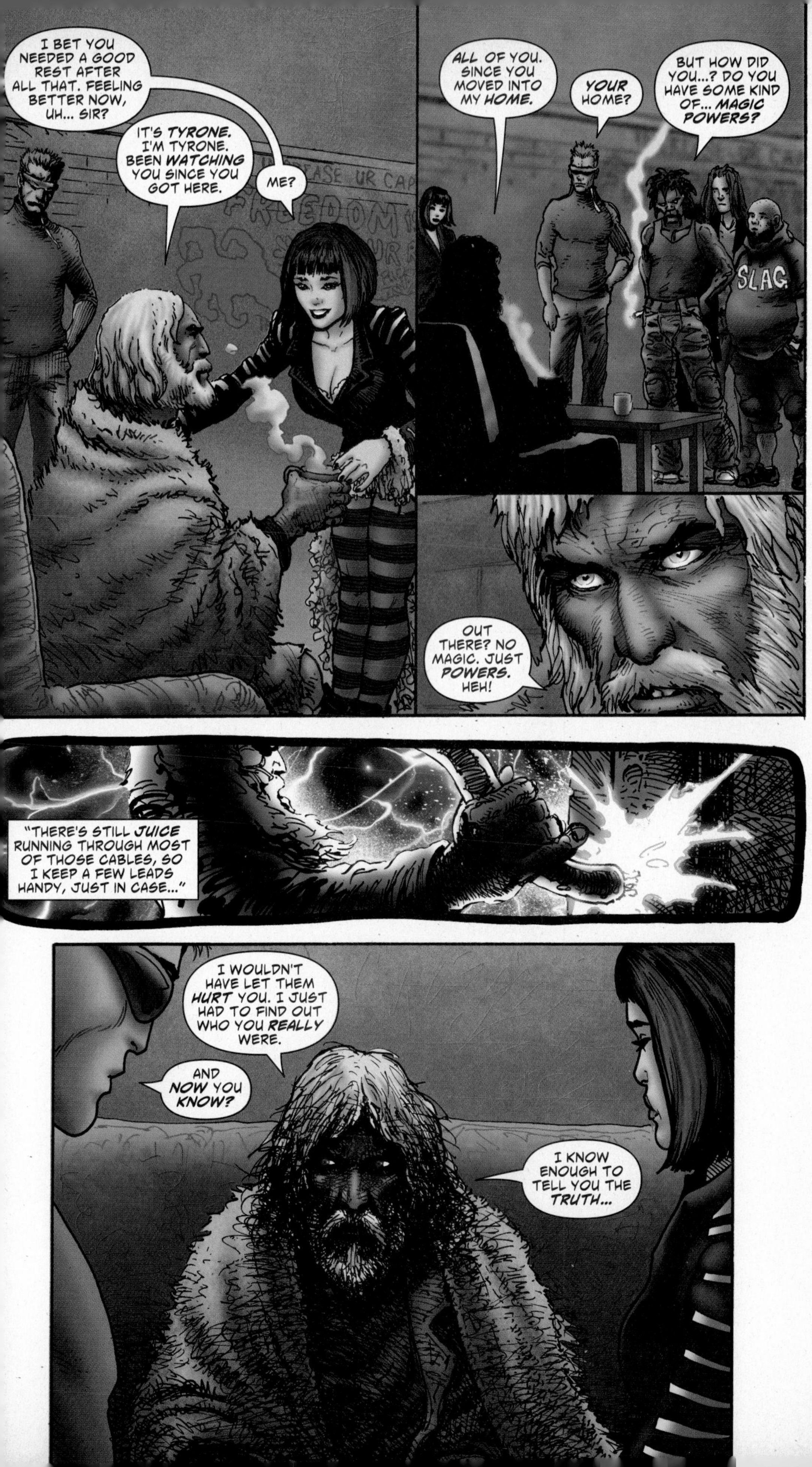
I BET YOU NEEDED A GOOD REST AFTER ALL THAT. FEELING BETTER NOW, UH... SIR?
IT'S TYRONE. I'M TYRONE. BEEN WATCHING YOU SINCE YOU GOT HERE.
ME?
ALL OF YOU. SINCE YOU MOVED INTO MY HOME.
YOUR HOME?
BUT HOW DID YOU...? DO YOU HAVE SOME KIND OF... MAGIC POWERS?
SLAG.
OUT THERE? NO MAGIC. JUST POWERS. HEH!
"THERE'S STILL JUICE RUNNING THROUGH MOST OF THOSE CABLES, SO I KEEP A FEW LEADS HANDY, JUST IN CASE..."
I WOULDN'T HAVE LET THEM HURT YOU. I JUST HAD TO FIND OUT WHO YOU REALLY WERE.
AND NOW YOU KNOW?
I KNOW ENOUGH TO TELL YOU THE TRUTH...

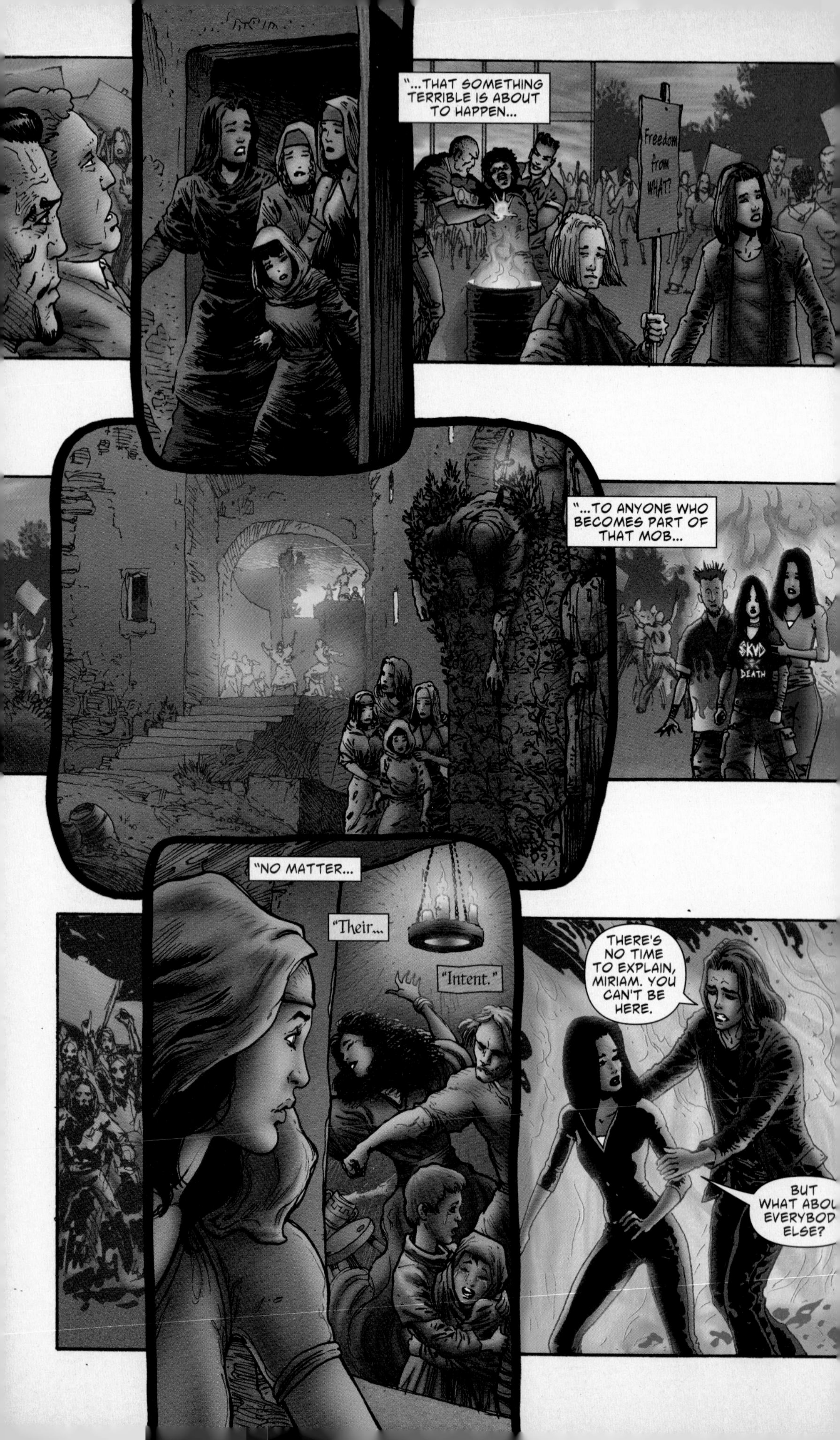
"...THAT SOMETHING TERRIBLE IS ABOUT TO HAPPEN...
Freedom from WHAT?
"...TO ANYONE WHO BECOMES PART OF THAT MOB...
SKVD
DEATH
"NO MATTER...
"Their...
"Intent."
THERE'S NO TIME TO EXPLAIN, MIRIAM. YOU CAN'T BE HERE.
BUT WHAT ABOU EVERYBOD ELSE?

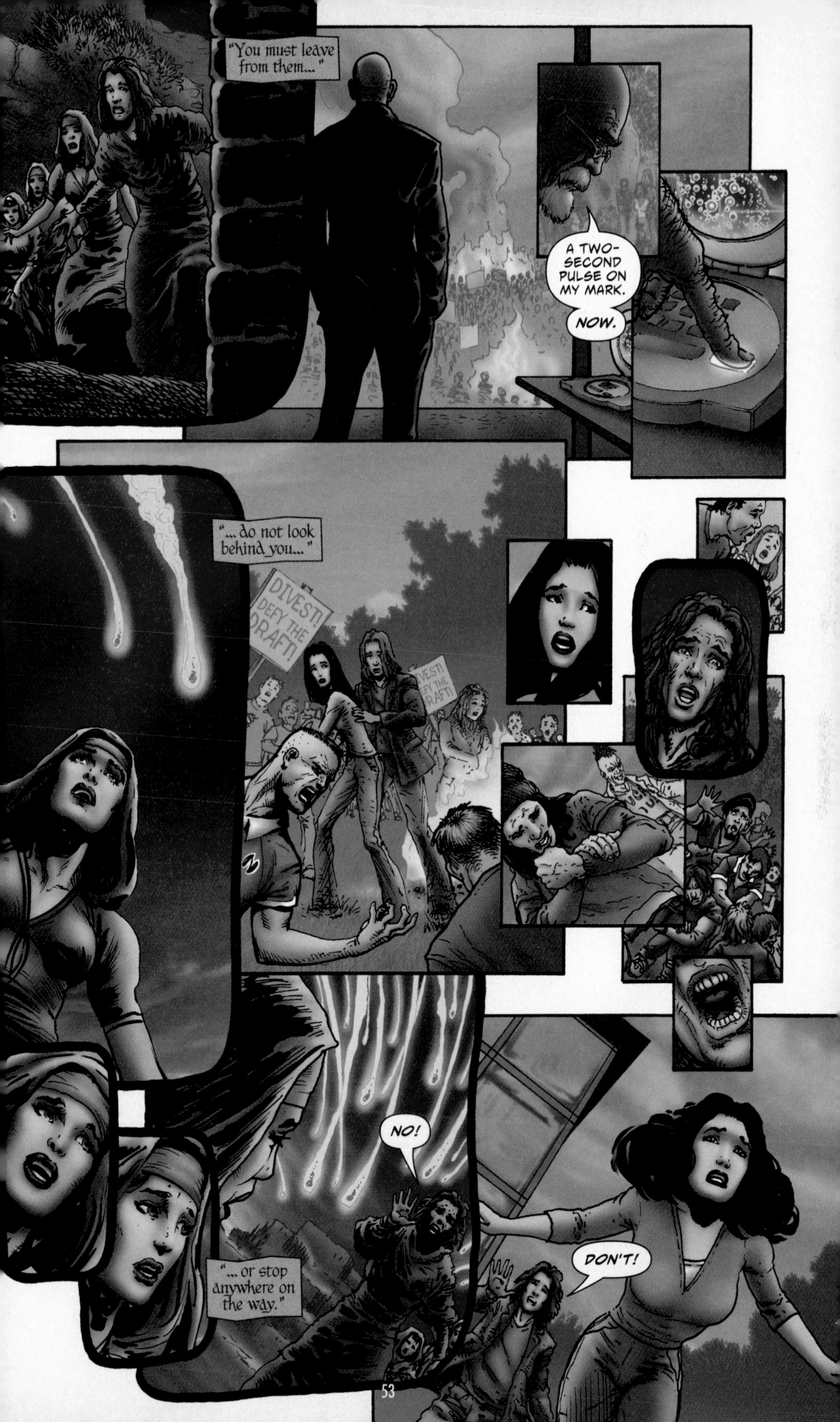

"You must leave from them..."
A TWO-SECOND PULSE ON MY MARK.
NOW.
"...do not look behind you..."
DIVEST! DEFY THE DRAFT!
DIVEST! DEFY THE DRAFT!
NO!
"...or stop anywhere on the way."
DON'T!

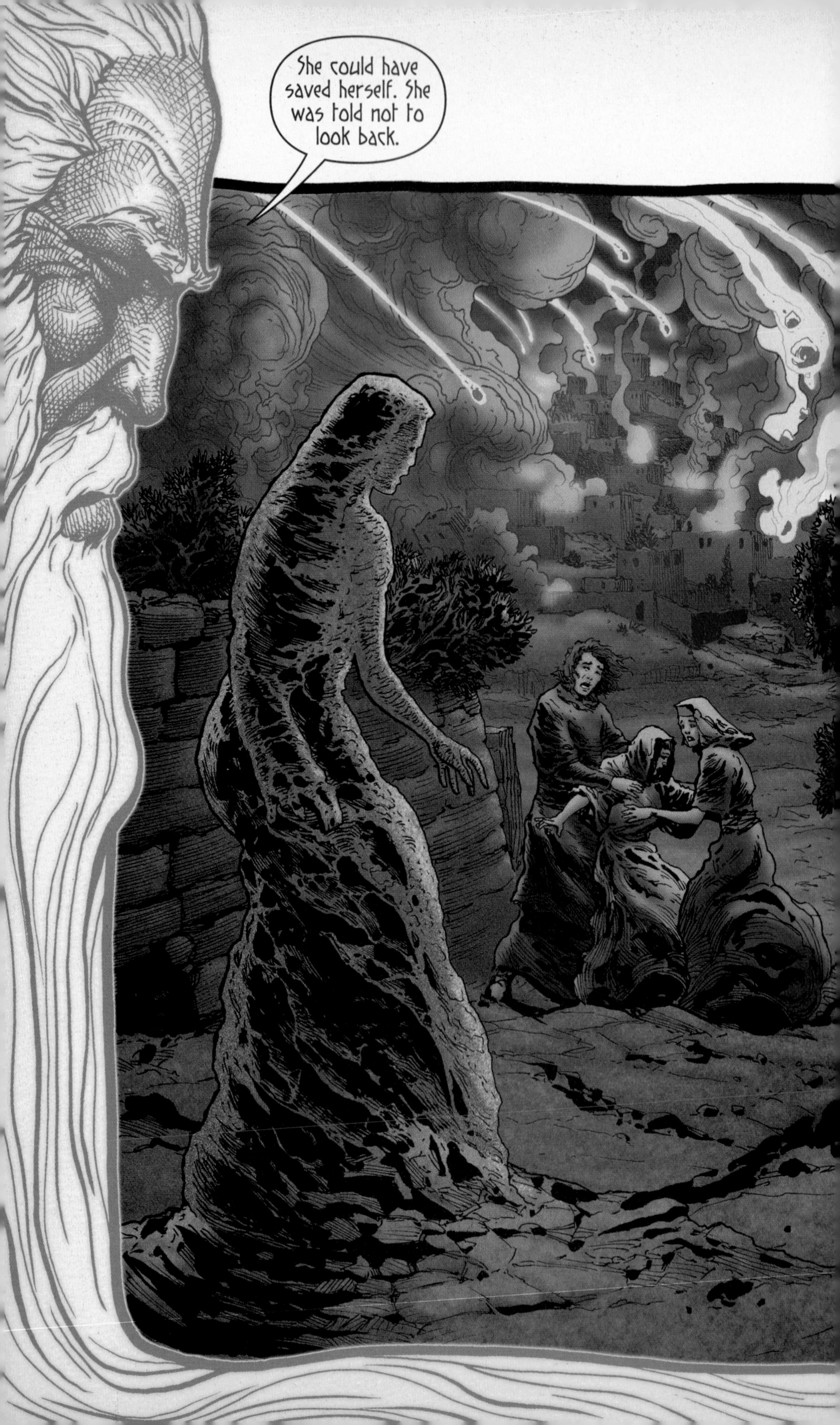
She could have saved herself. She was told not to look back.

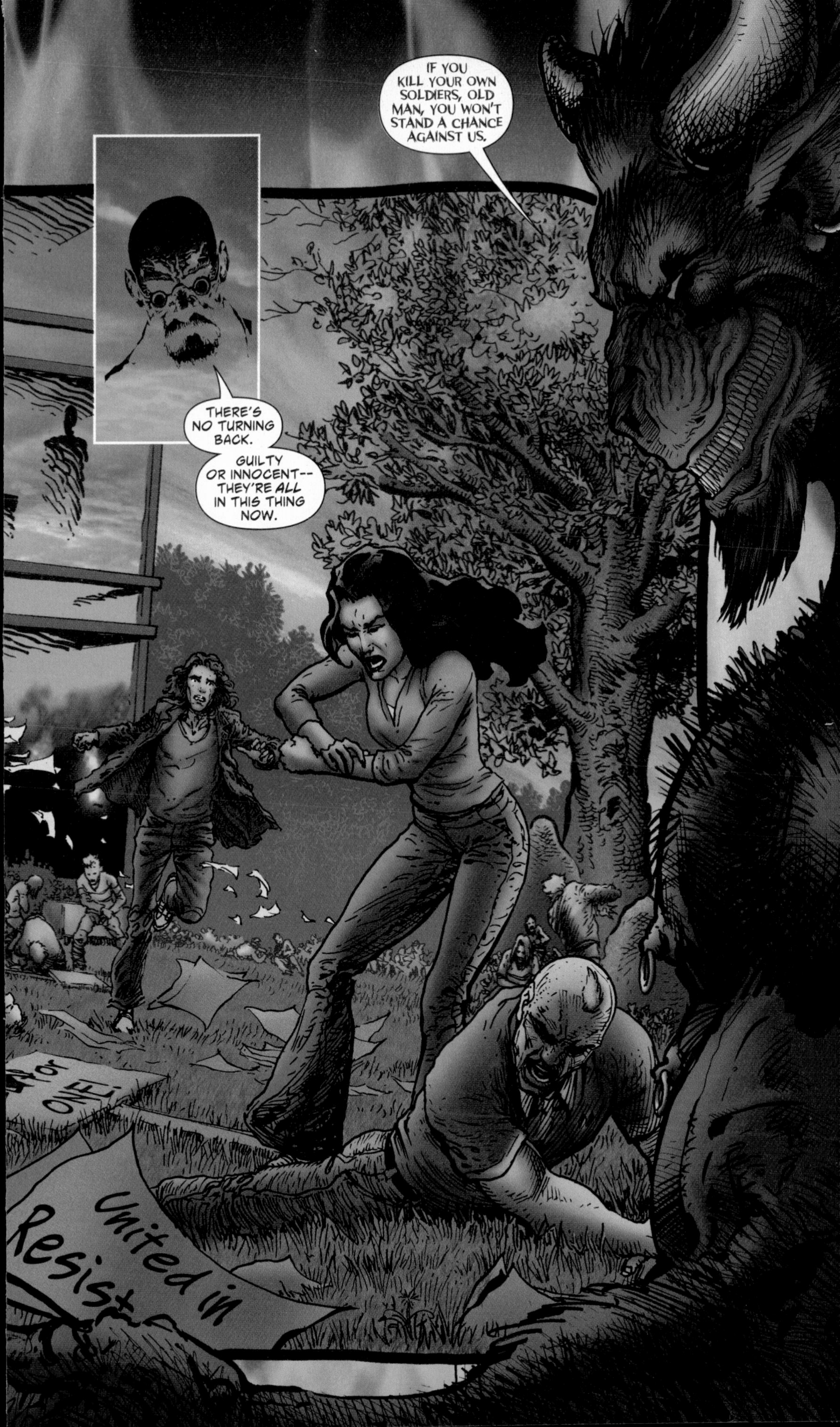
IF YOU KILL YOUR OWN SOLDIERS, OLD MAN, YOU WON'T STAND A CHANCE AGAINST US.
THERE'S NO TURNING BACK.
GUILTY OR INNOCENT-- THEY'RE *ALL* IN THIS THING NOW.
ONE!
United in
Resist

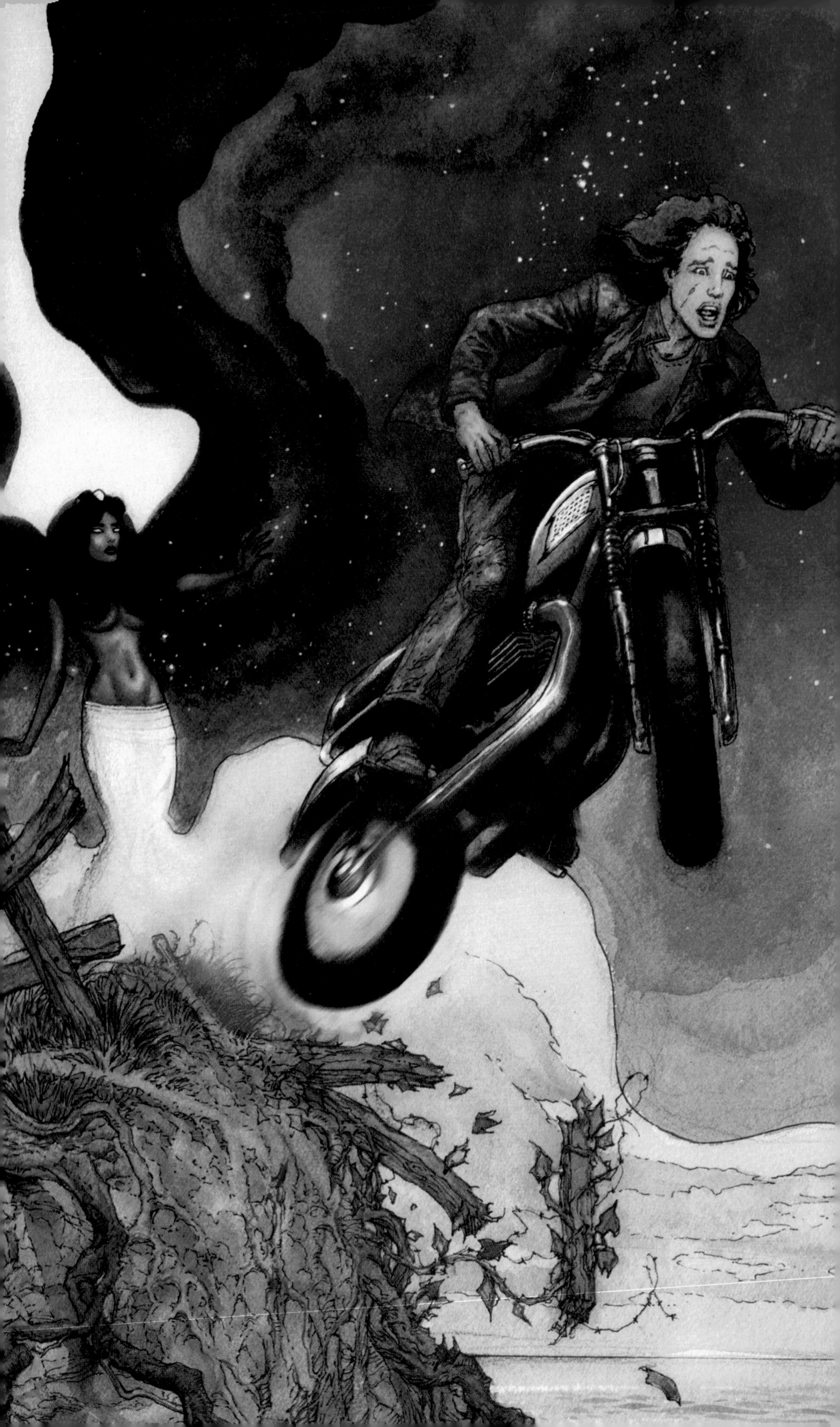

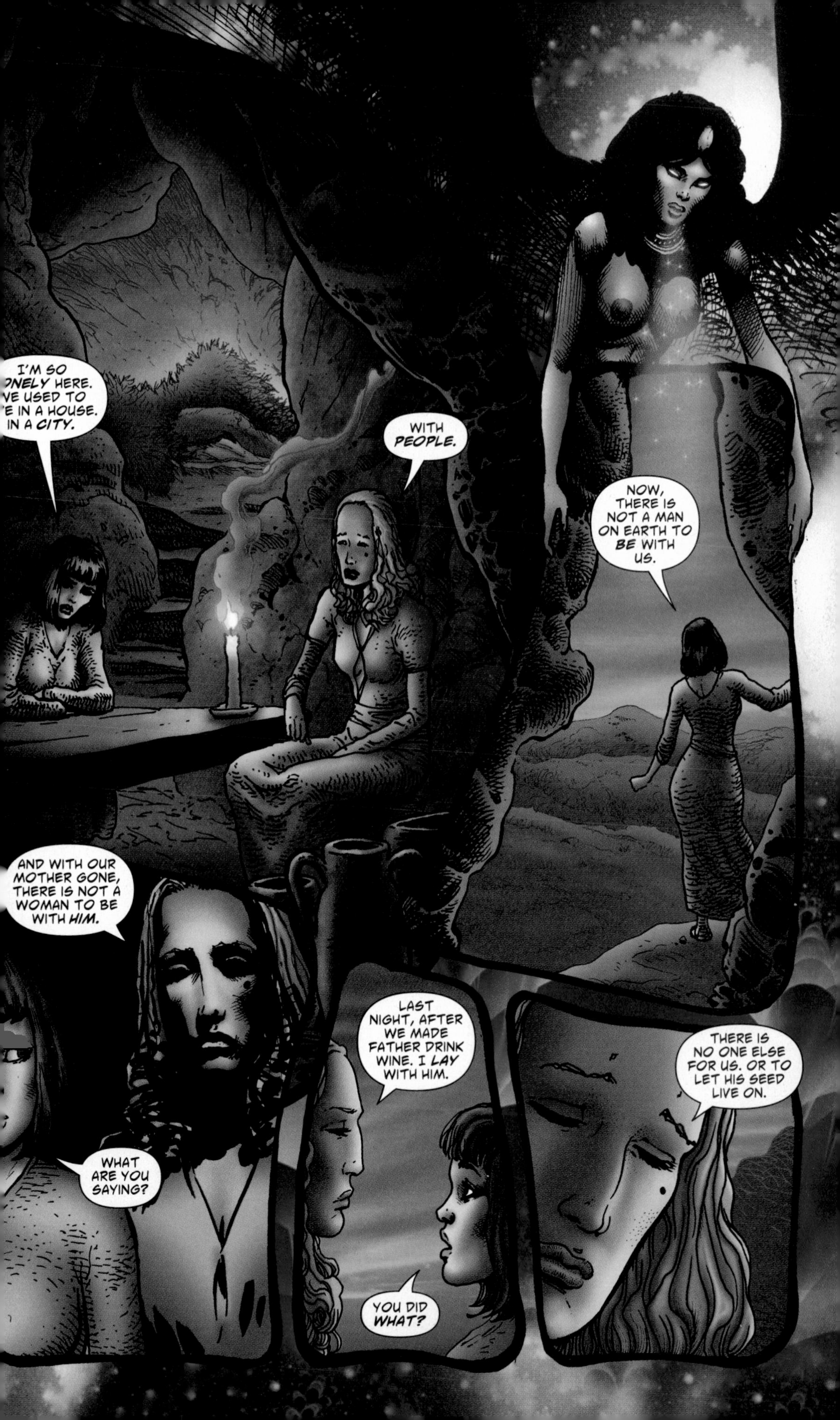
I'M SO ONELY HERE. VE USED TO E IN A HOUSE. IN A CITY.
WITH PEOPLE.
NOW, THERE IS NOT A MAN ON EARTH TO BE WITH US.
AND WITH OUR MOTHER GONE, THERE IS NOT A WOMAN TO BE WITH HIM.
WHAT ARE YOU SAYING?
LAST NIGHT, AFTER WE MADE FATHER DRINK WINE, I LAY WITH HIM.
YOU DID WHAT?
THERE IS NO ONE ELSE FOR US. OR TO LET HIS SEED LIVE ON.

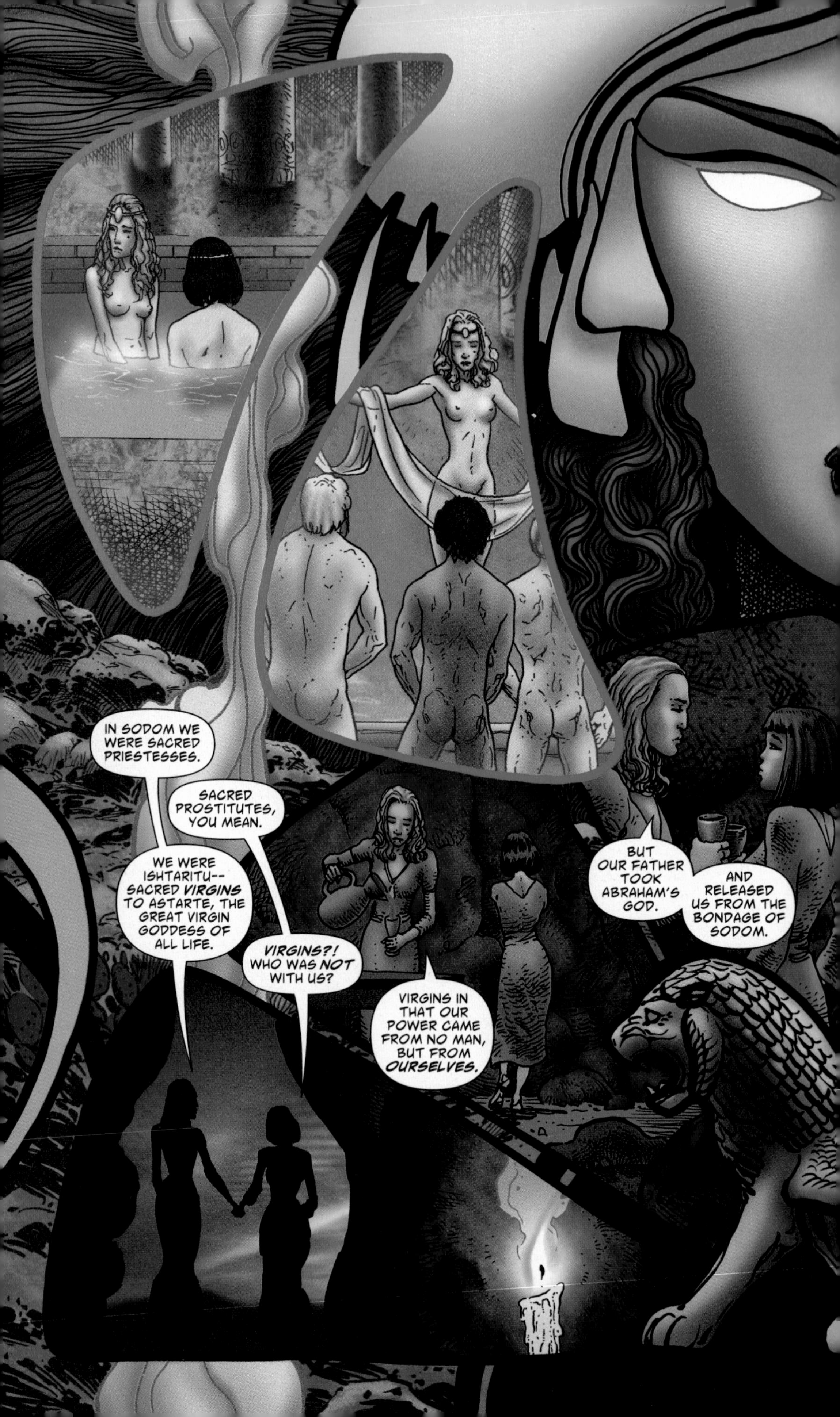
IN SODOM WE WERE SACRED PRIESTESSES.
SACRED PROSTITUTES, YOU MEAN.
WE WERE ISHTARITU-- SACRED *VIRGINS* TO ASTARTE, THE GREAT VIRGIN GODDESS OF ALL LIFE.
VIRGINS?! WHO WAS *NOT* WITH US?
VIRGINS IN THAT OUR POWER CAME FROM NO MAN, BUT FROM *OURSELVES.*
BUT OUR FATHER TOOK ABRAHAM'S GOD.
AND RELEASED US FROM THE BONDAGE OF SODOM.

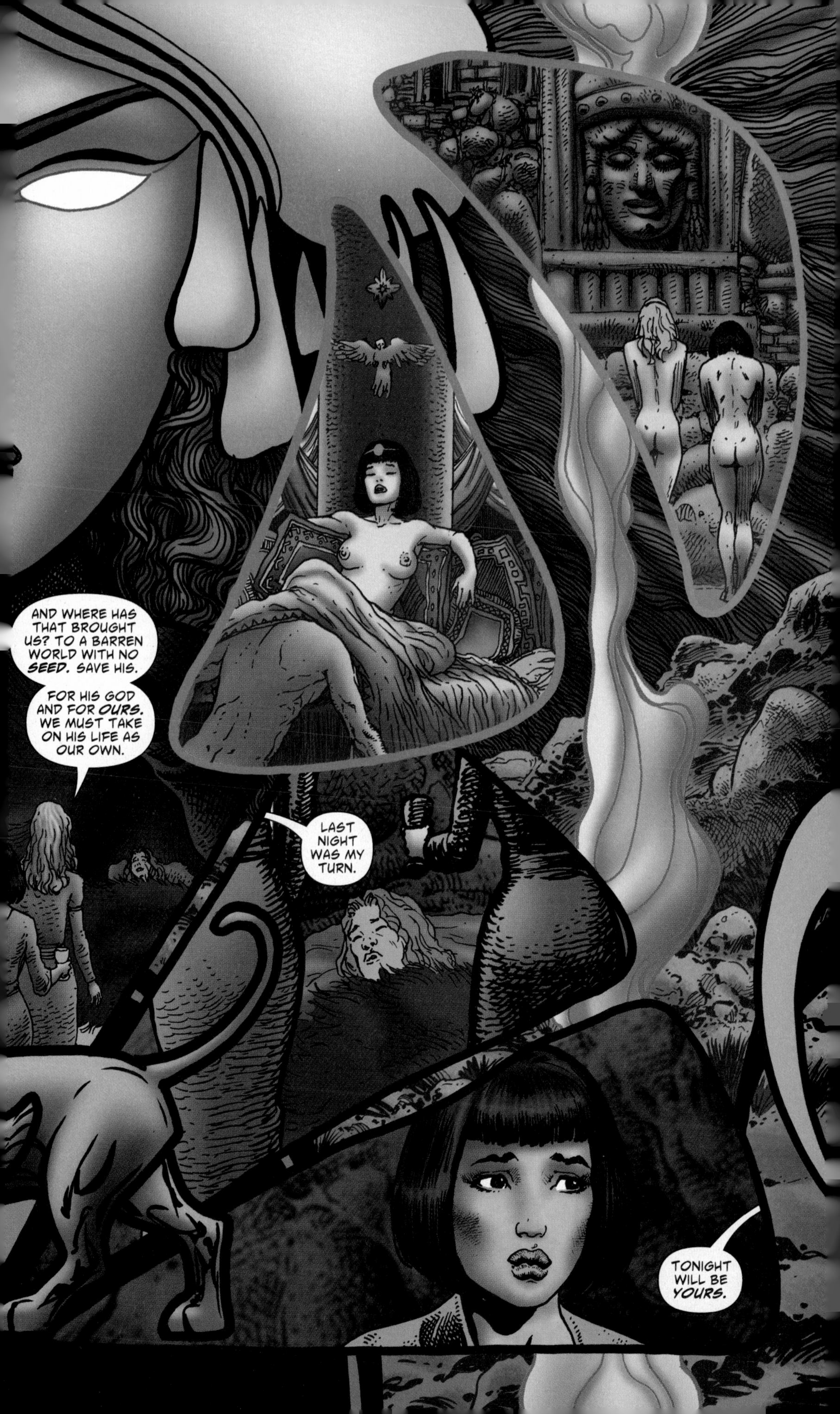
AND WHERE HAS THAT BROUGHT US? TO A BARREN WORLD WITH NO SEED. SAVE HIS.
FOR HIS GOD AND FOR OURS. WE MUST TAKE ON HIS LIFE AS OUR OWN.
LAST NIGHT WAS MY TURN.
TONIGHT WILL BE YOURS.

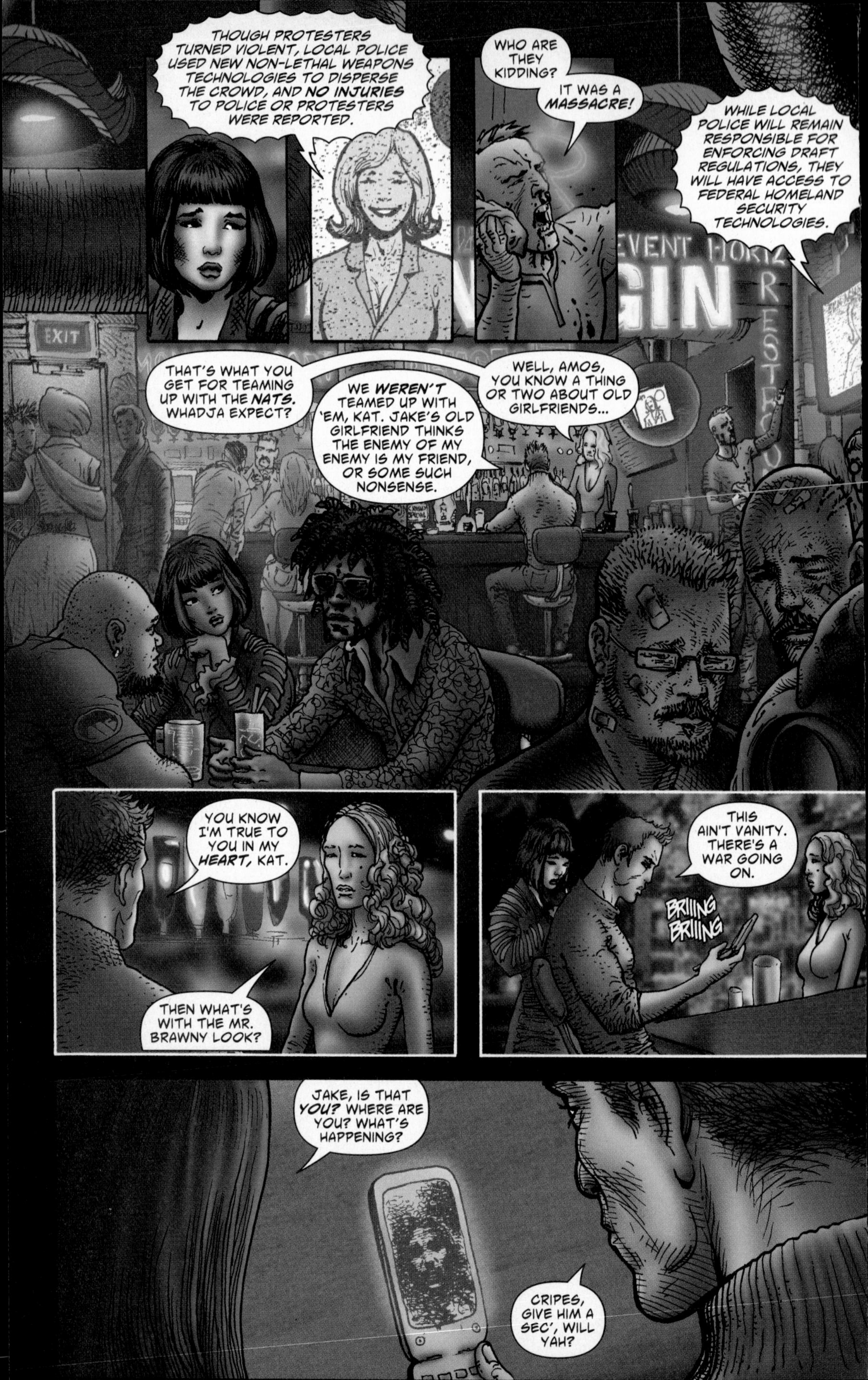
THOUGH PROTESTERS TURNED VIOLENT, LOCAL POLICE USED NEW NON-LETHAL WEAPONS TECHNOLOGIES TO DISPERSE THE CROWD, AND NO INJURIES TO POLICE OR PROTESTERS WERE REPORTED.
WHO ARE THEY KIDDING?
IT WAS A MASSACRE!
WHILE LOCAL POLICE WILL REMAIN RESPONSIBLE FOR ENFORCING DRAFT REGULATIONS, THEY WILL HAVE ACCESS TO FEDERAL HOMELAND SECURITY TECHNOLOGIES.
EVENT HORIZ
GIN
EXIT
THAT'S WHAT YOU GET FOR TEAMING UP WITH THE NATS. WHADJA EXPECT?
WE WEREN'T TEAMED UP WITH 'EM, KAT. JAKE'S OLD GIRLFRIEND THINKS THE ENEMY OF MY ENEMY IS MY FRIEND, OR SOME SUCH NONSENSE.
WELL, AMOS, YOU KNOW A THING OR TWO ABOUT OLD GIRLFRIENDS...
YOU KNOW I'M TRUE TO YOU IN MY HEART, KAT.
THEN WHAT'S WITH THE MR. BRAWNY LOOK?
THIS AIN'T VANITY. THERE'S A WAR GOING ON.
BRIIING BRIIING
JAKE, IS THAT YOU? WHERE ARE YOU? WHAT'S HAPPENING?
CRIPES, GIVE HIM A SEC', WILL YAH?

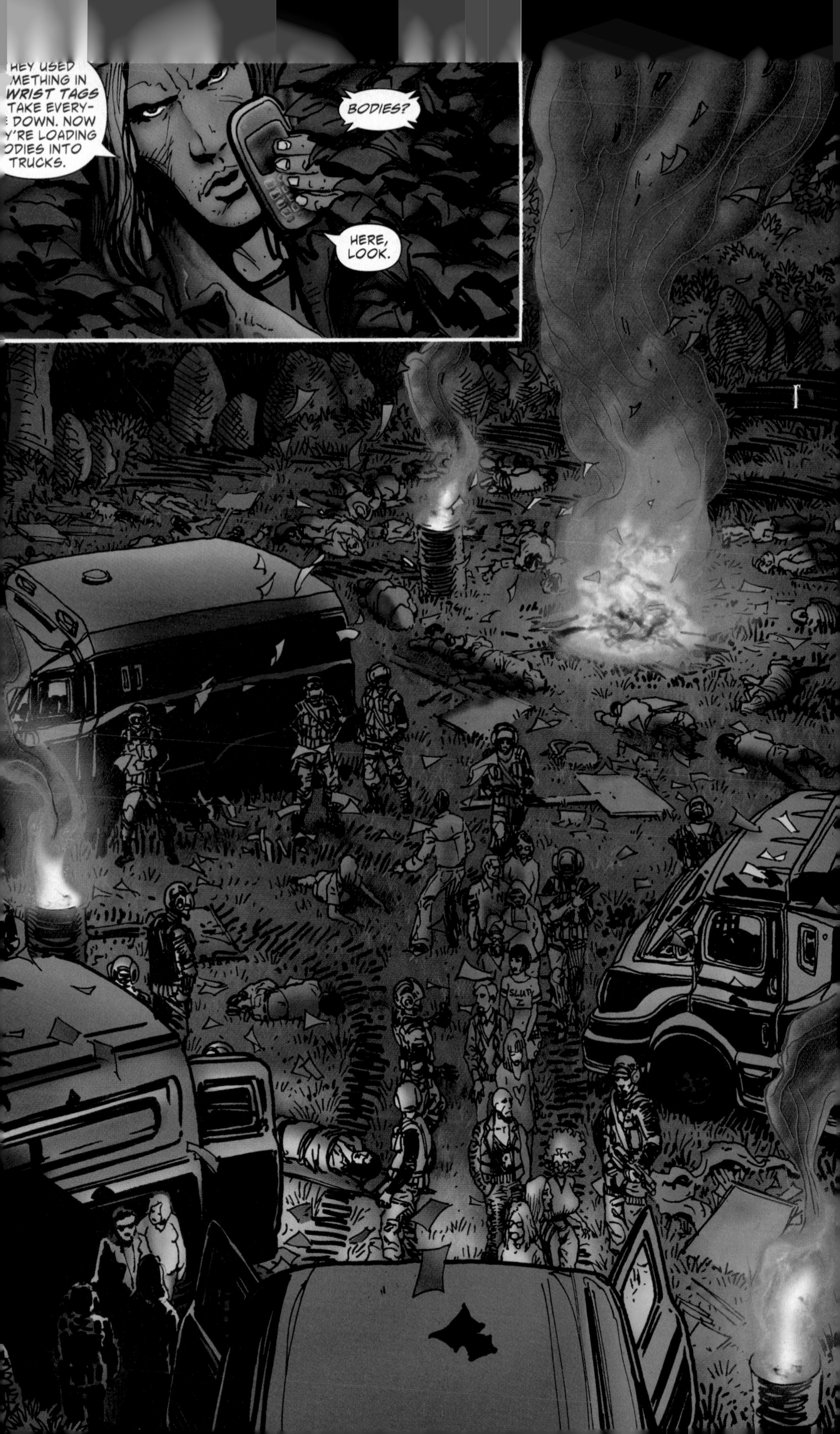
HEY USED
METHING IN
WRIST TAGS
TAKE EVERY-
E DOWN. NOW
Y'RE LOADING
ODIES INTO
TRUCKS.
BODIES?
HERE, LOOK.
SLUT
Z

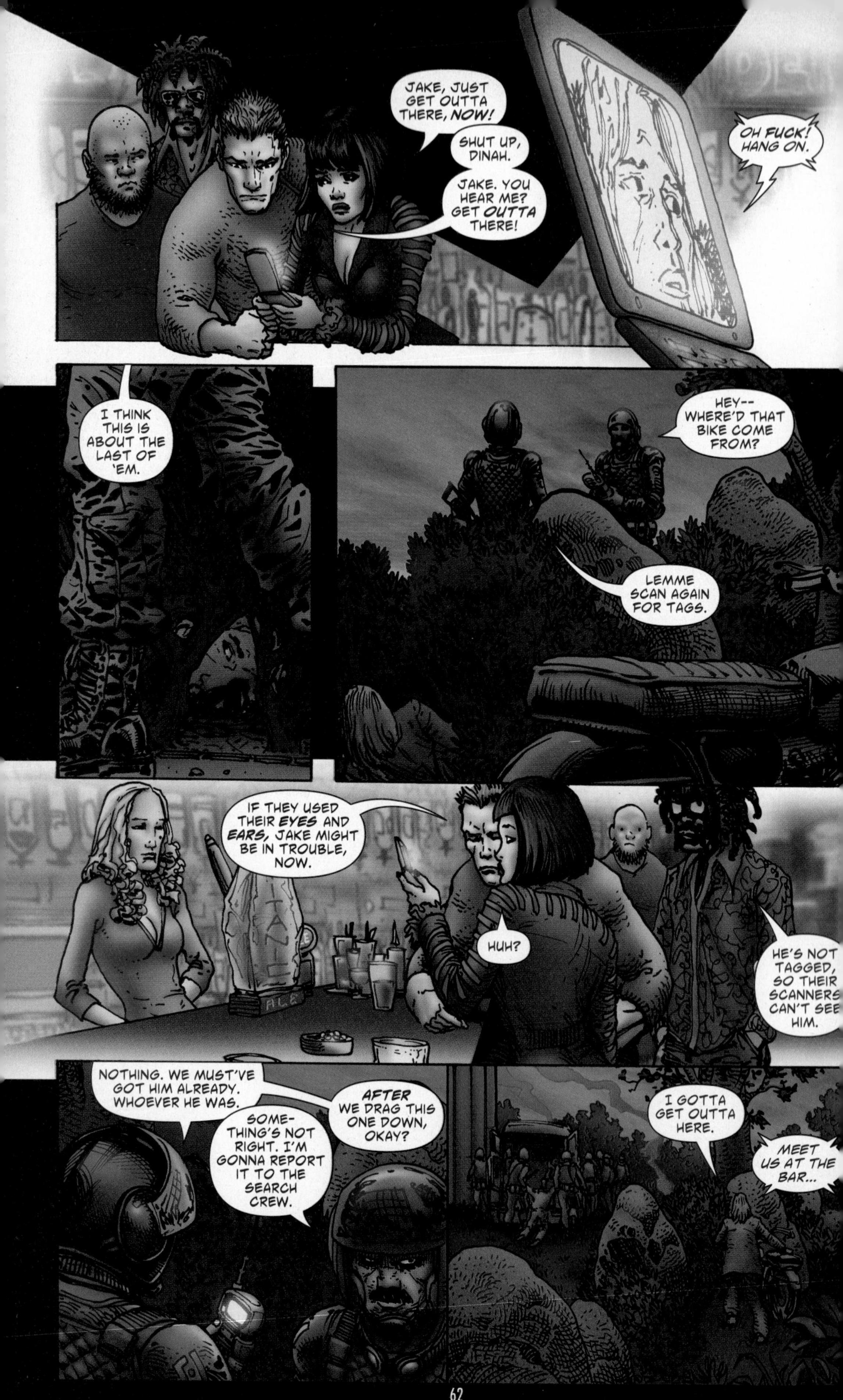
JAKE, JUST GET OUTTA THERE, NOW!
SHUT UP, DINAH.
JAKE. YOU HEAR ME? GET OUTTA THERE!
OH FUCK! HANG ON.
I THINK THIS IS ABOUT THE LAST OF 'EM.
HEY-- WHERE'D THAT BIKE COME FROM?
LEMME SCAN AGAIN FOR TAGS.
IF THEY USED THEIR EYES AND EARS, JAKE MIGHT BE IN TROUBLE, NOW.
HUH?
HE'S NOT TAGGED, SO THEIR SCANNERS CAN'T SEE HIM.
NOTHING. WE MUST'VE GOT HIM ALREADY. WHOEVER HE WAS.
SOME-THING'S NOT RIGHT. I'M GONNA REPORT IT TO THE SEARCH CREW.
AFTER WE DRAG THIS ONE DOWN, OKAY?
I GOTTA GET OUTTA HERE.
MEET US AT THE BAR...

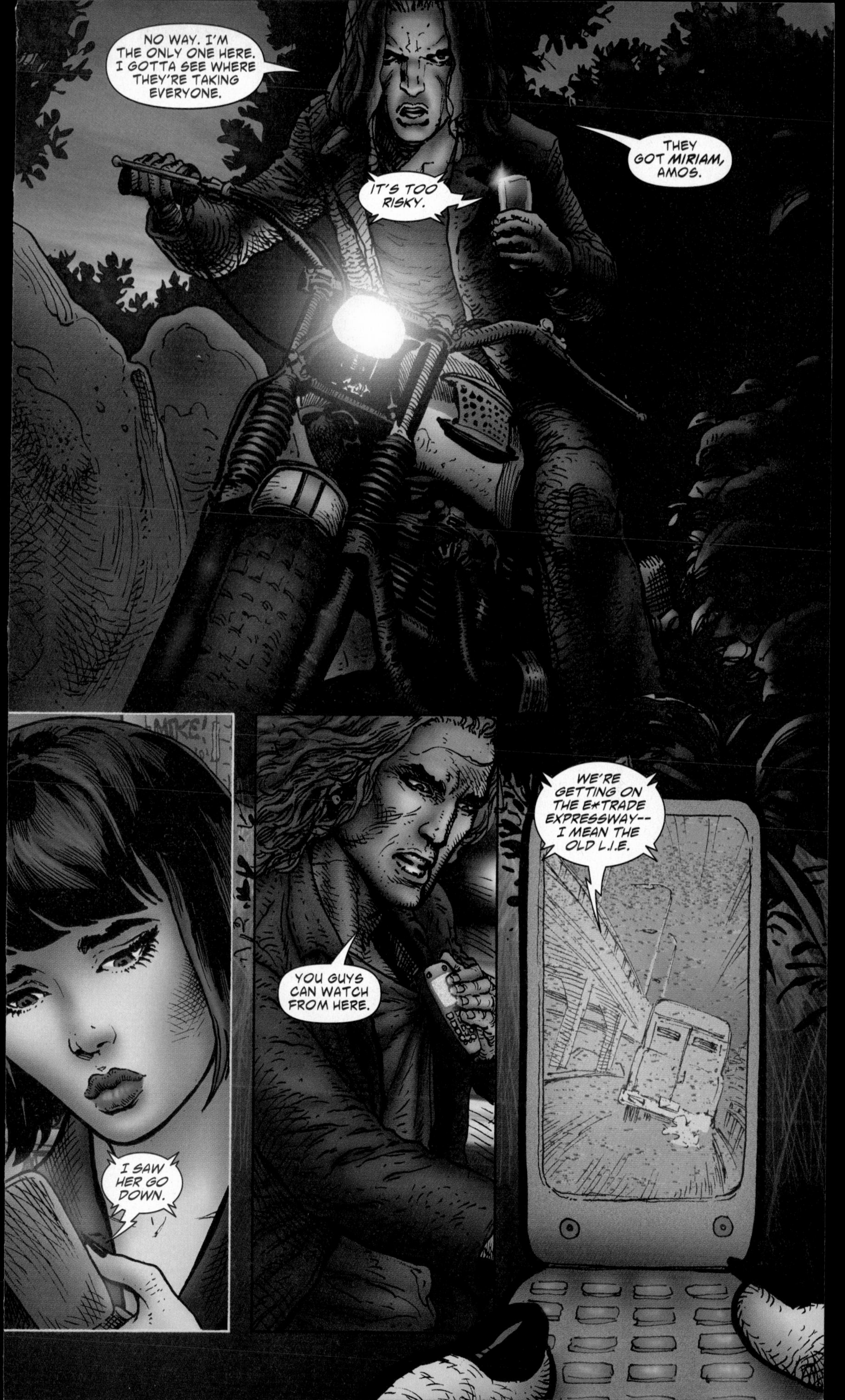

NO WAY. I'M THE ONLY ONE HERE. I GOTTA SEE WHERE THEY'RE TAKING EVERYONE.
IT'S TOO RISKY.
THEY GOT MIRIAM, AMOS.
I SAW HER GO DOWN.
YOU GUYS CAN WATCH FROM HERE.
WE'RE GETTING ON THE E*TRADE EXPRESSWAY-- I MEAN THE OLD L.I.E.

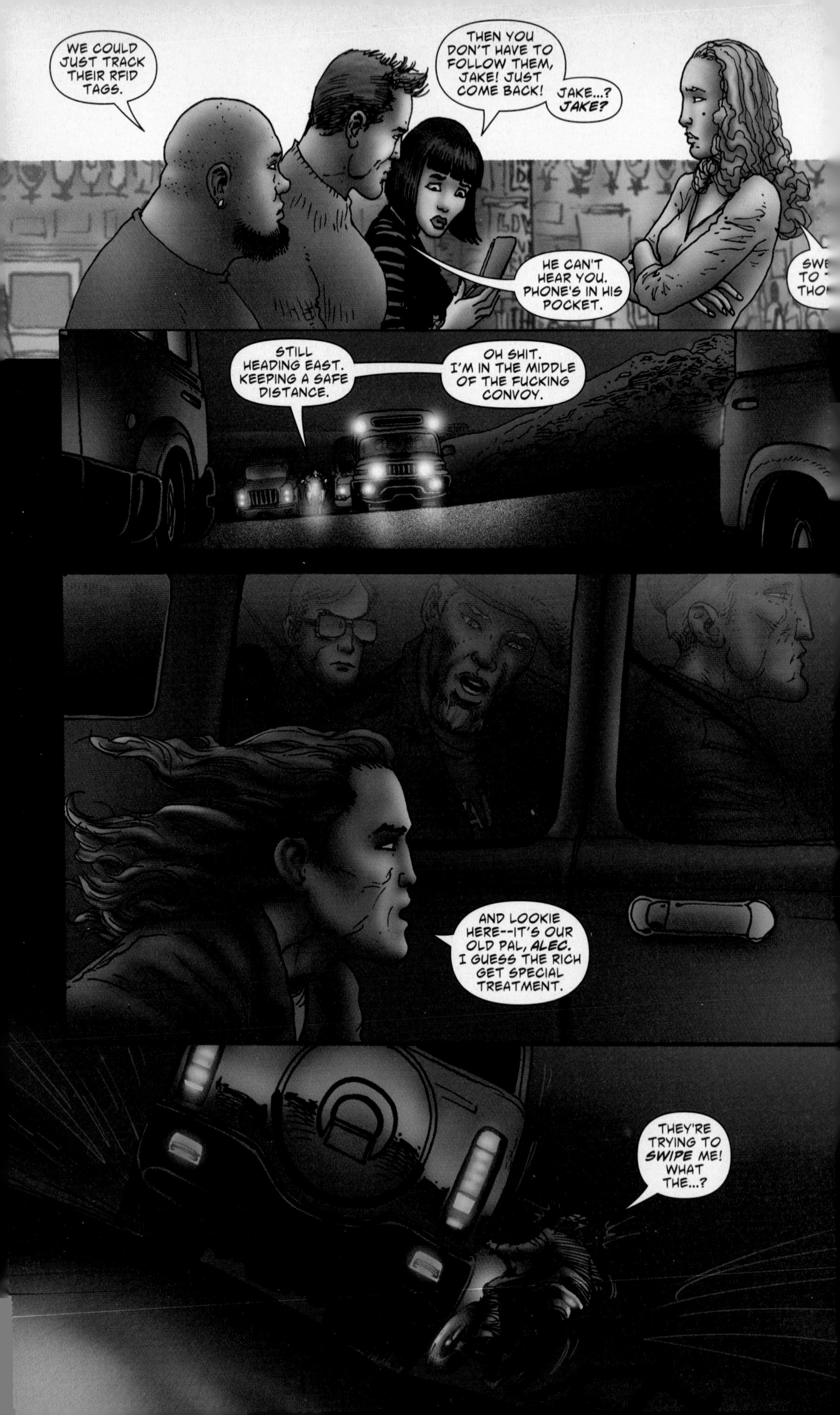
WE COULD JUST TRACK THEIR RFID TAGS.
THEN YOU DON'T HAVE TO FOLLOW THEM, JAKE! JUST COME BACK!
JAKE...? *JAKE?*
HE CAN'T HEAR YOU. PHONE'S IN HIS POCKET.
STILL HEADING EAST. KEEPING A SAFE DISTANCE.
OH SHIT. I'M IN THE MIDDLE OF THE FUCKING CONVOY.
AND LOOKIE HERE--IT'S OUR OLD PAL, *ALEC.* I GUESS THE RICH GET SPECIAL TREATMENT.
THEY'RE TRYING TO *SWIPE* ME! WHAT THE...?

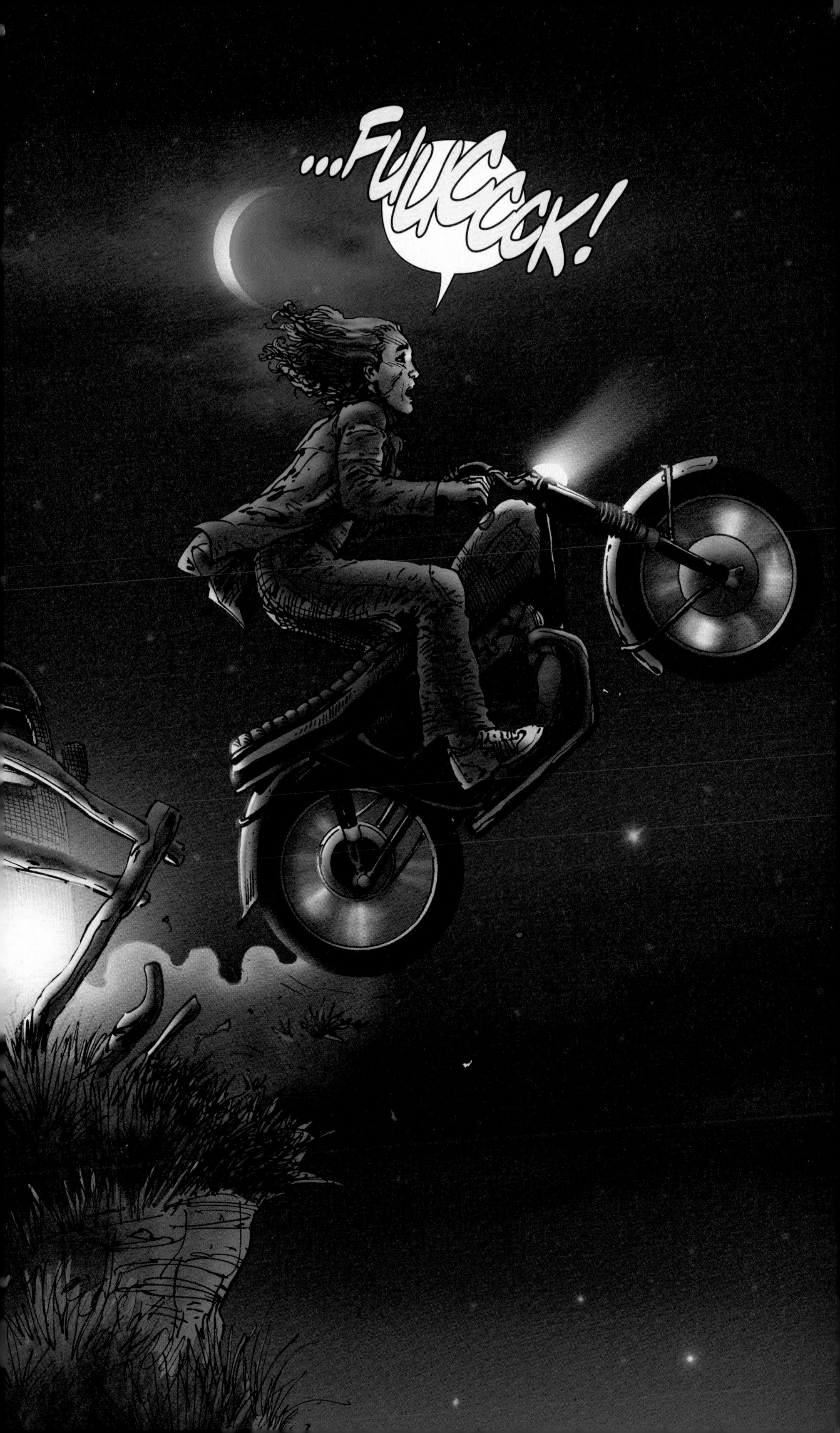
...FUUCCCCK!

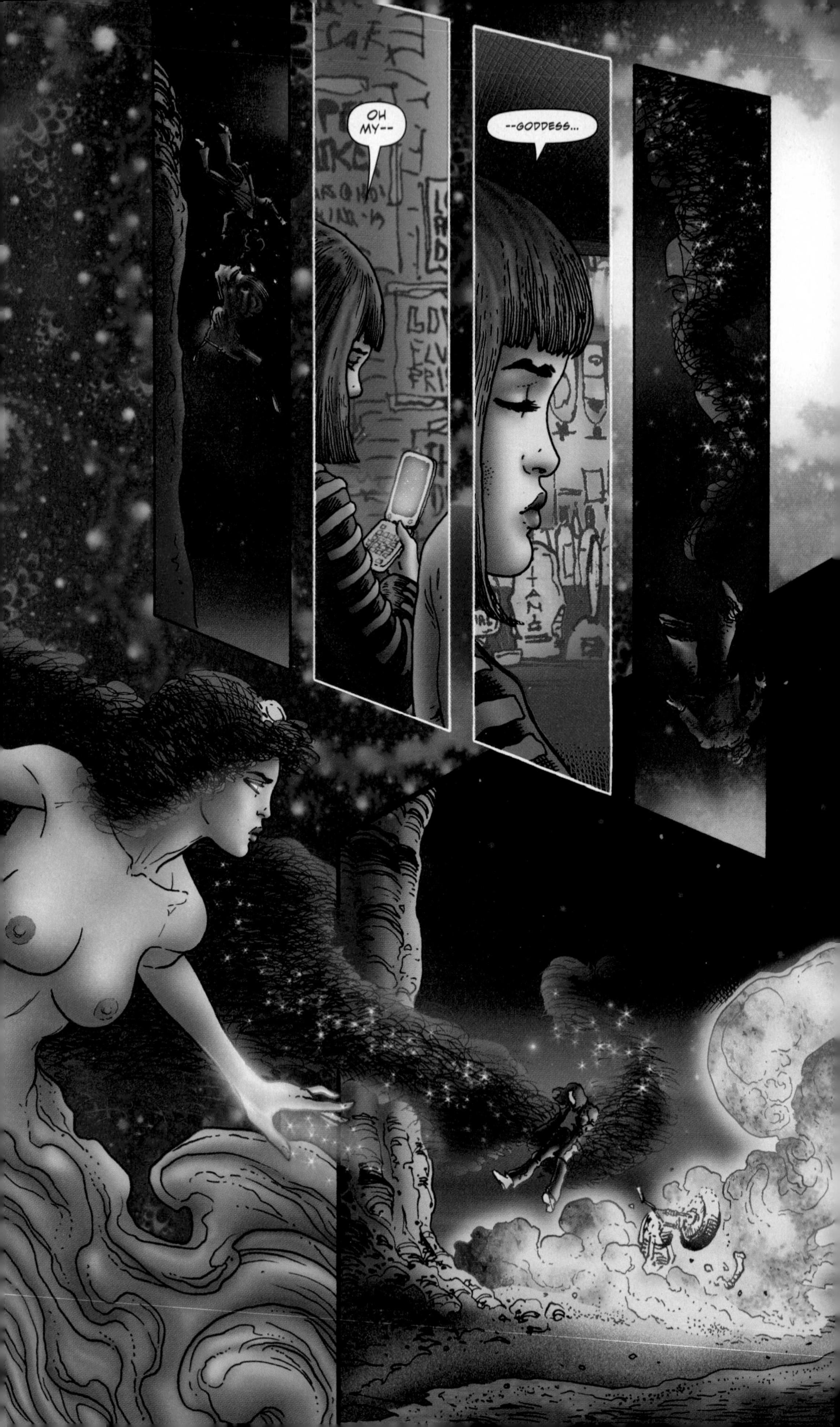
OH MY--
--GODDESS...

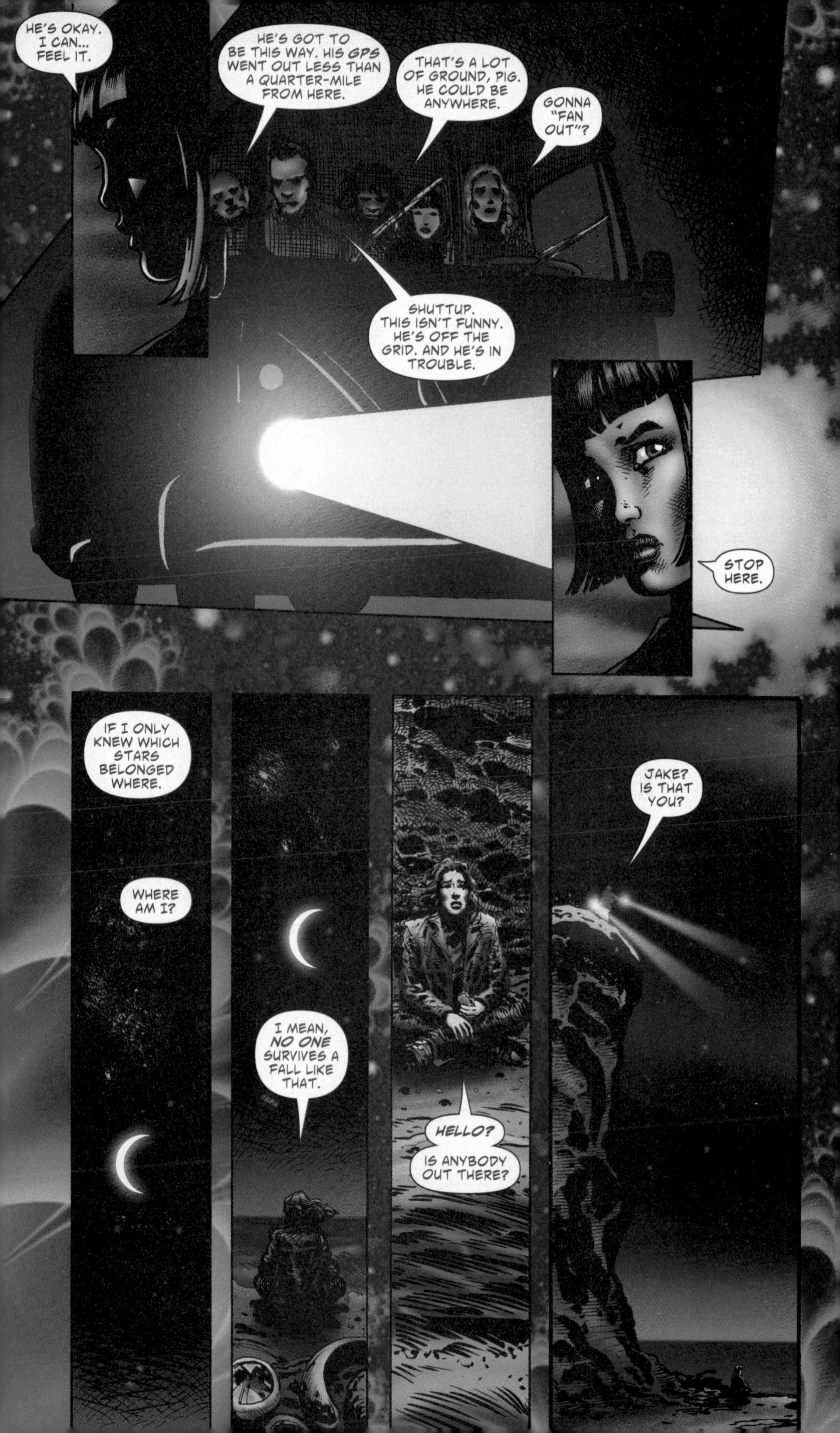
HE'S OKAY. I CAN... FEEL IT.
HE'S GOT TO BE THIS WAY. HIS GPS WENT OUT LESS THAN A QUARTER-MILE FROM HERE.
THAT'S A LOT OF GROUND, PIG. HE COULD BE ANYWHERE.
GONNA "FAN OUT"?
SHUTTUP. THIS ISN'T FUNNY. HE'S OFF THE GRID. AND HE'S IN TROUBLE.
STOP HERE.
IF I ONLY KNEW WHICH STARS BELONGED WHERE.
WHERE AM I?
I MEAN, NO ONE SURVIVES A FALL LIKE THAT.
HELLO?
IS ANYBODY OUT THERE?
JAKE? IS THAT YOU?

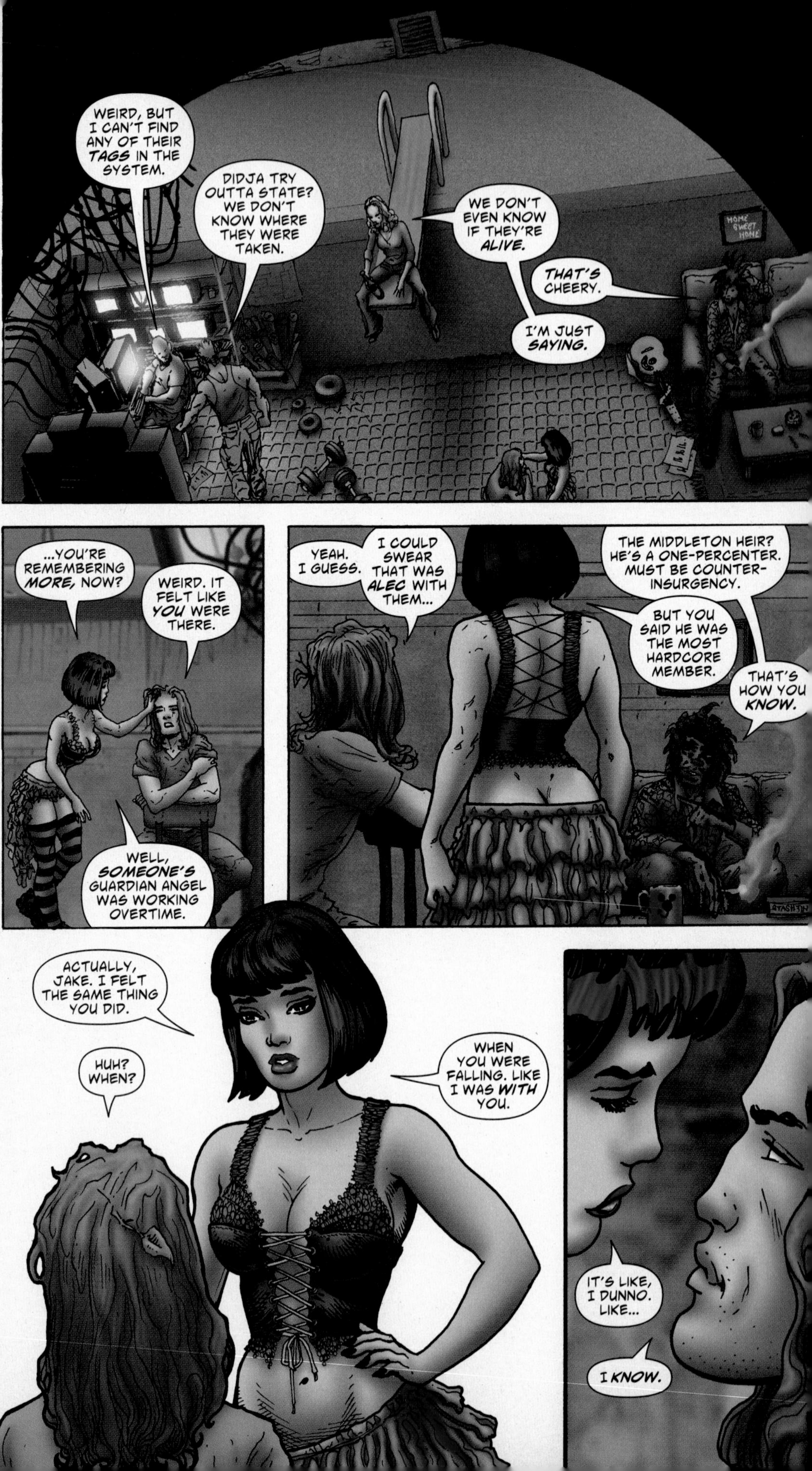

WEIRD, BUT I CAN'T FIND ANY OF THEIR TAGS IN THE SYSTEM.
DIDJA TRY OUTTA STATE? WE DON'T KNOW WHERE THEY WERE TAKEN.
WE DON'T EVEN KNOW IF THEY'RE ALIVE.
THAT'S CHEERY.
I'M JUST SAYING.
HOME SWEET HOME
...YOU'RE REMEMBERING MORE, NOW?
WEIRD. IT FELT LIKE YOU WERE THERE.
WELL, SOMEONE'S GUARDIAN ANGEL WAS WORKING OVERTIME.
YEAH. I GUESS.
I COULD SWEAR THAT WAS ALEC WITH THEM...
THE MIDDLETON HEIR? HE'S A ONE-PERCENTER. MUST BE COUNTER-INSURGENCY.
BUT YOU SAID HE WAS THE MOST HARDCORE MEMBER.
THAT'S HOW YOU KNOW.
STASH
ACTUALLY, JAKE. I FELT THE SAME THING YOU DID.
HUH? WHEN?
WHEN YOU WERE FALLING. LIKE I WAS WITH YOU.
IT'S LIKE, I DUNNO. LIKE...
I KNOW.

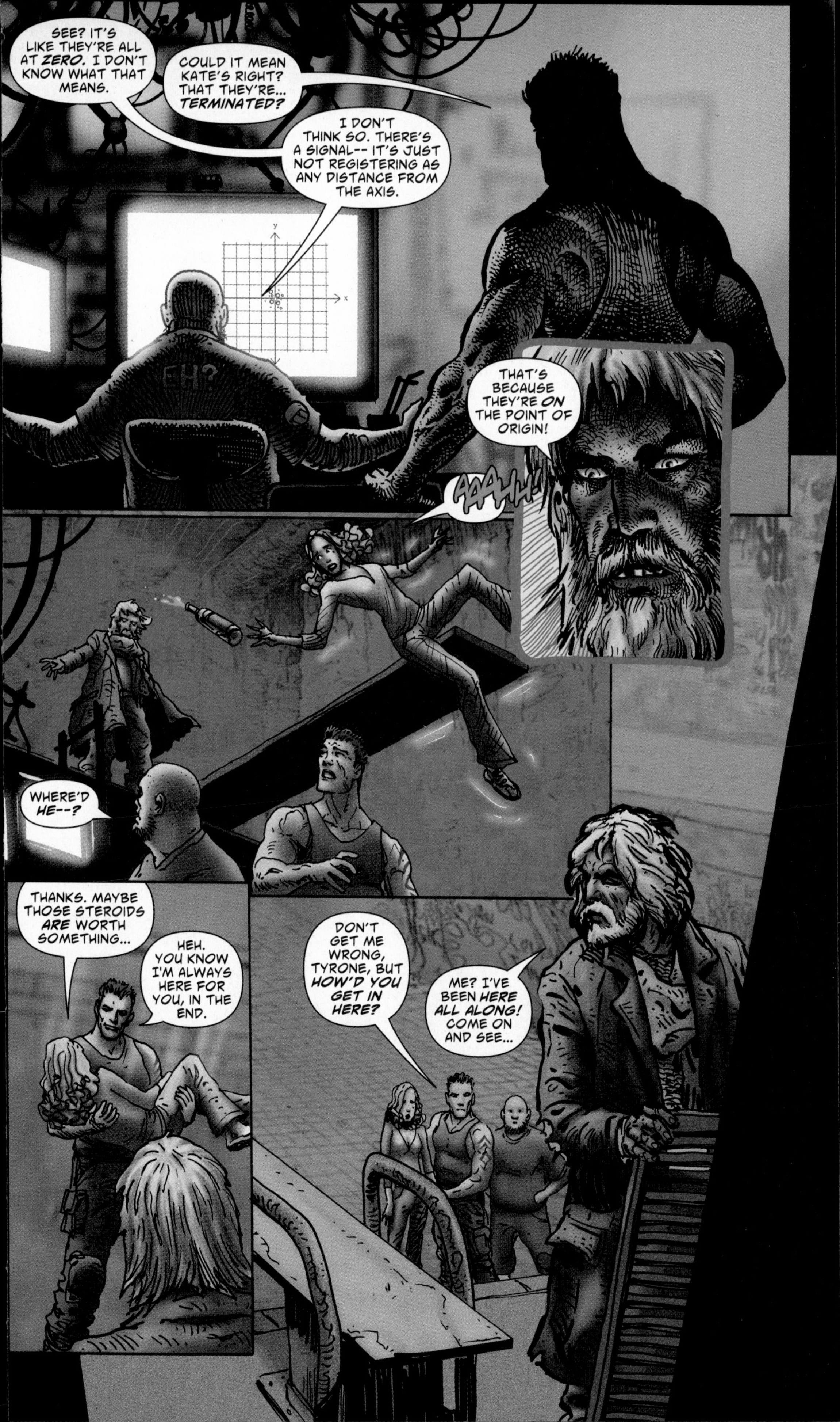

SEE? IT'S LIKE THEY'RE ALL AT *ZERO*. I DON'T KNOW WHAT THAT MEANS.
COULD IT MEAN KATE'S RIGHT? THAT THEY'RE... *TERMINATED?*
I DON'T THINK SO. THERE'S A SIGNAL-- IT'S JUST NOT REGISTERING AS ANY DISTANCE FROM THE AXIS.
EH?
THAT'S BECAUSE THEY'RE *ON* THE POINT OF ORIGIN!
AAAHH!
WHERE'D *HE--?*
THANKS. MAYBE THOSE STEROIDS *ARE* WORTH SOMETHING...
HEH. YOU KNOW I'M ALWAYS HERE FOR YOU, IN THE END.
DON'T GET ME WRONG, TYRONE, BUT *HOW'D YOU GET IN HERE?*
ME? I'VE BEEN *HERE ALL ALONG!* COME ON AND SEE...

WELCOME BACK TO THE *STORY!* I'VE BEEN WAITING FOR YOU A LONG, LONG TIME...

I DON'T KNOW ABOUT THIS GUY.

YOU THINK HE WAS PUT HERE? TO WATCH US?

I WOULD... EXCEPT FOR THE FACT IT LOOKS LIKE *HE* WAS HERE BEFORE *WE* WERE.

YOUR FRIENDS ARE ON THE ALTAR ITSELF. ON THE CROSS.

IS THAT WHAT YOU MEAN BY "POINT OF ORIGIN"? WHERE THE AXES CROSS?

YOU *UNDERSTAND* HIM?

CHECK OUT THESE STATUES.

THEY'RE ALL OF *US.* KINDA SPOOKY.

HE MUST HAVE BEEN WATCHING US FOR A WHILE.

YOU EVER FEEL LIKE YOU *KNOW* WHAT'S GOING TO HAPPEN?

AND THAT LIFE IS JUS' GOING THROU THE *MOTION* PRETENDING Y DON'T KNOW IT'S GOING T TURN OUT?

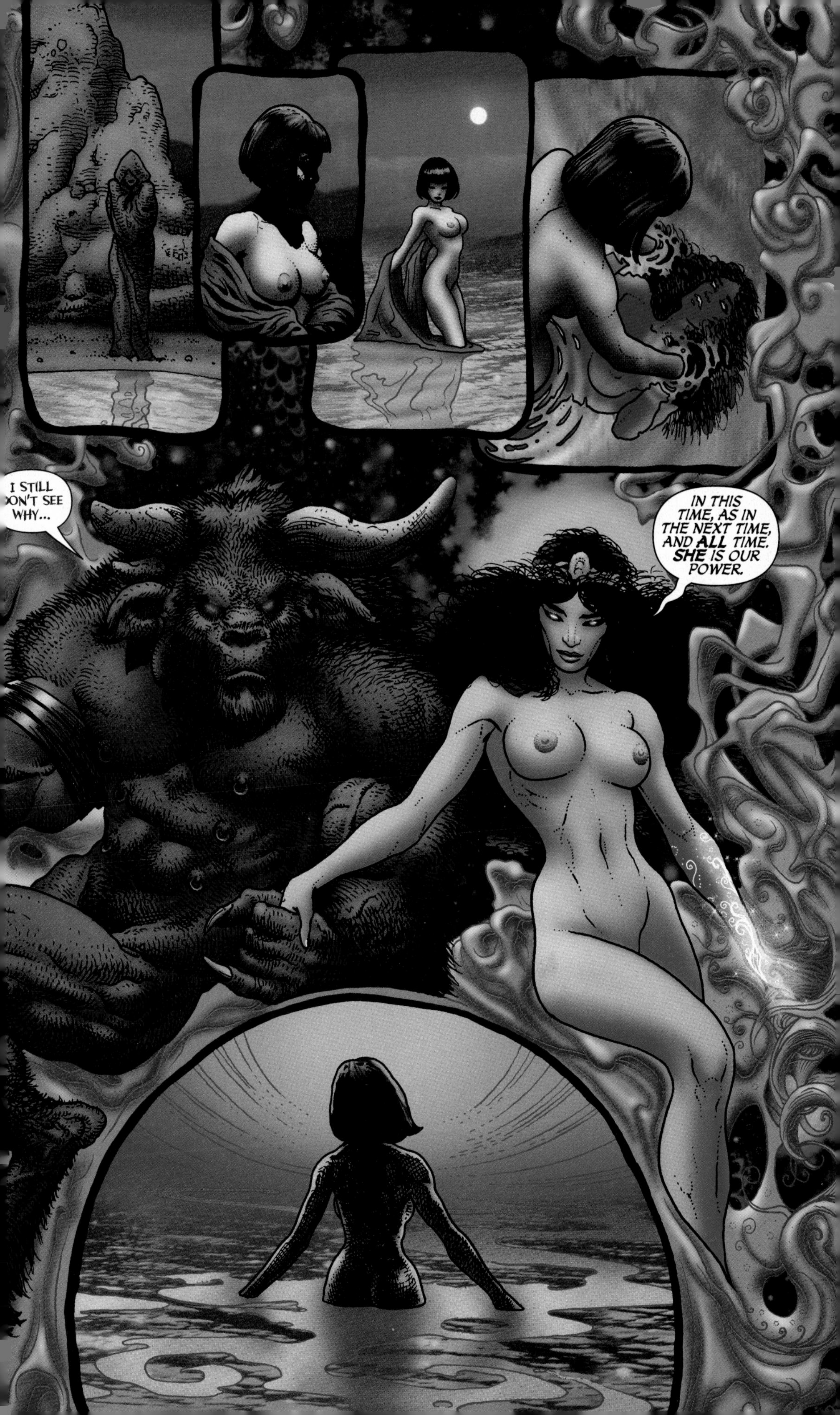
I STILL DON'T SEE WHY...
IN THIS TIME, AS IN THE NEXT TIME, AND ALL TIME. SHE IS OUR POWER.

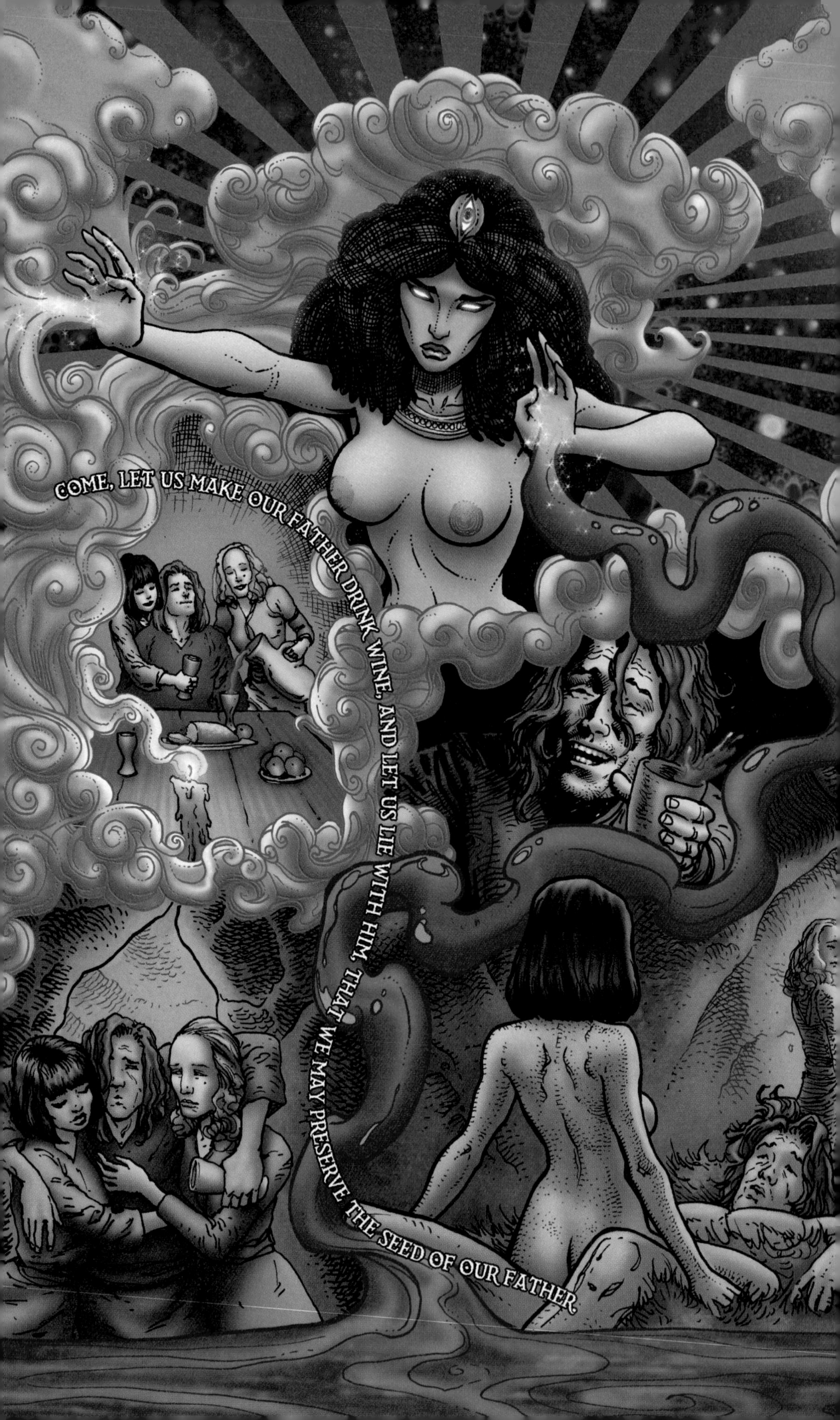
COME, LET US MAKE OUR FATHER DRINK WINE, AND LET US LIE WITH HIM, THAT WE MAY PRESERVE THE SEED OF OUR FATHER

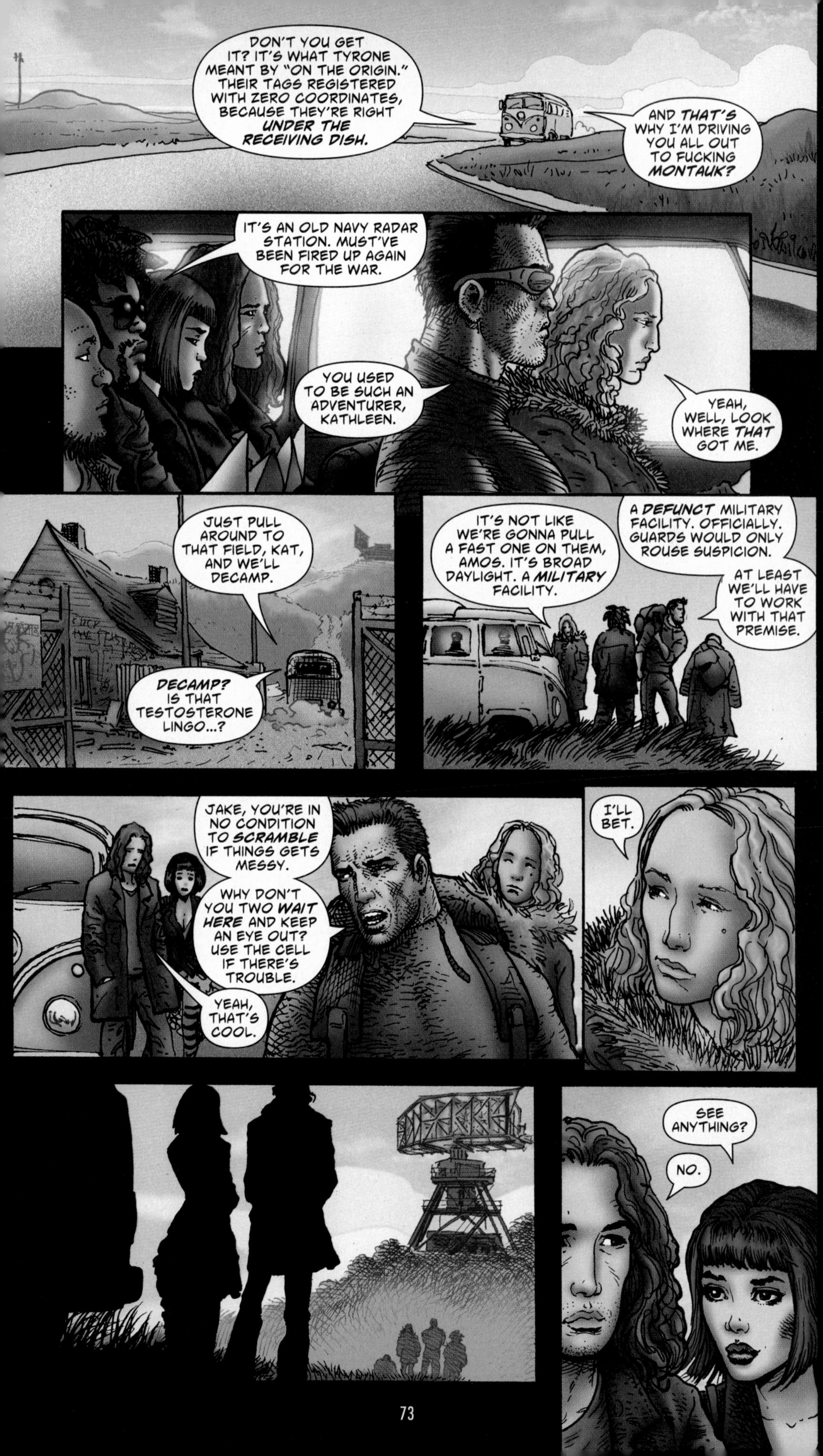
DON'T YOU GET IT? IT'S WHAT TYRONE MEANT BY "ON THE ORIGIN." THEIR TAGS REGISTERED WITH ZERO COORDINATES, BECAUSE THEY'RE RIGHT UNDER THE RECEIVING DISH.
AND THAT'S WHY I'M DRIVING YOU ALL OUT TO FUCKING MONTAUK?
IT'S AN OLD NAVY RADAR STATION. MUST'VE BEEN FIRED UP AGAIN FOR THE WAR.
YOU USED TO BE SUCH AN ADVENTURER, KATHLEEN.
YEAH, WELL, LOOK WHERE THAT GOT ME.
JUST PULL AROUND TO THAT FIELD, KAT, AND WE'LL DECAMP.
DECAMP? IS THAT TESTOSTERONE LINGO...?
IT'S NOT LIKE WE'RE GONNA PULL A FAST ONE ON THEM, AMOS. IT'S BROAD DAYLIGHT. A MILITARY FACILITY.
A DEFUNCT MILITARY FACILITY. OFFICIALLY. GUARDS WOULD ONLY ROUSE SUSPICION.
AT LEAST WE'LL HAVE TO WORK WITH THAT PREMISE.
JAKE, YOU'RE IN NO CONDITION TO SCRAMBLE IF THINGS GETS MESSY.
WHY DON'T YOU TWO WAIT HERE AND KEEP AN EYE OUT? USE THE CELL IF THERE'S TROUBLE.
YEAH, THAT'S COOL.
I'LL BET.
SEE ANYTHING?
NO.

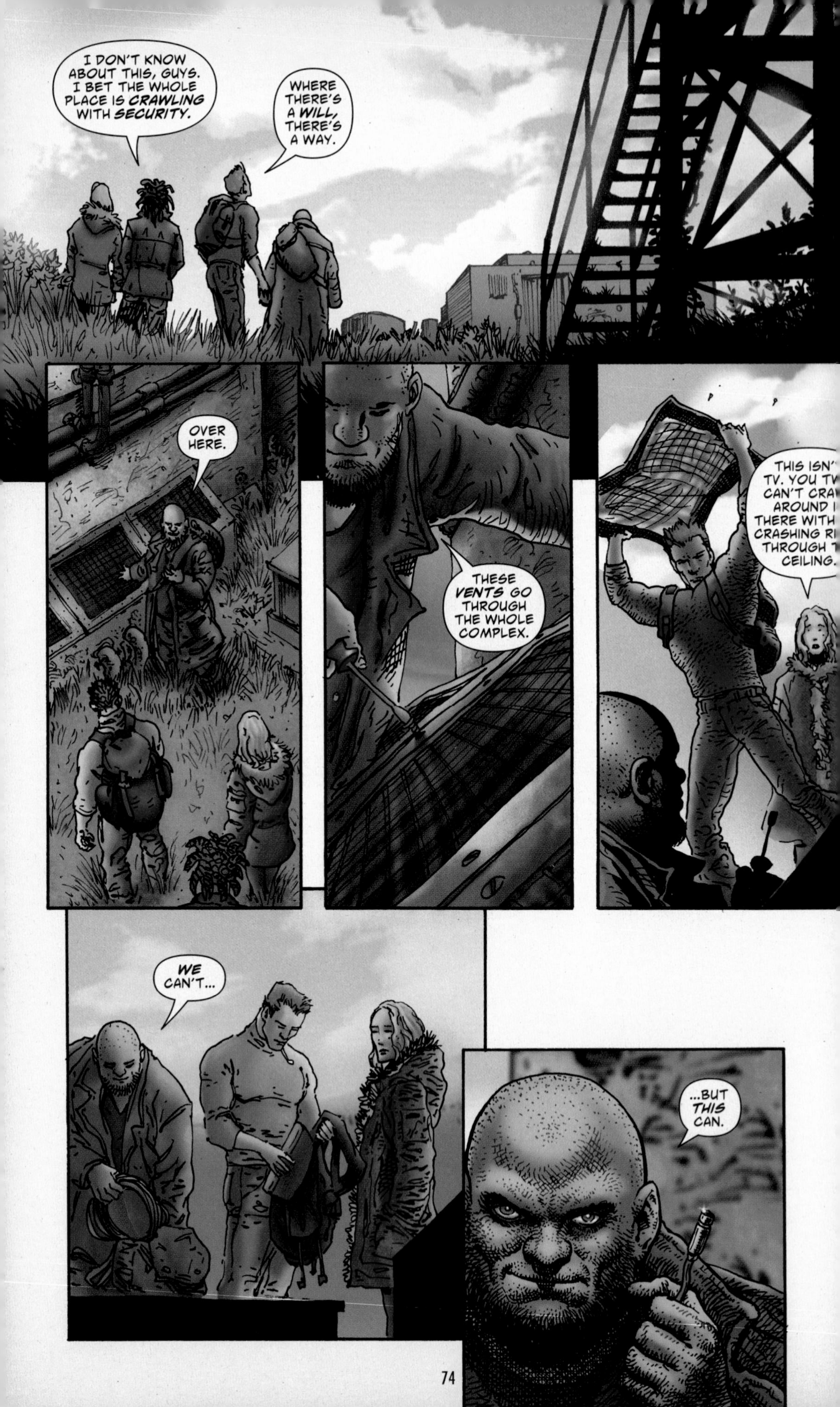
I DON'T KNOW ABOUT THIS, GUYS. I BET THE WHOLE PLACE IS CRAWLING WITH SECURITY.
WHERE THERE'S A WILL, THERE'S A WAY.
OVER HERE.
THESE VENTS GO THROUGH THE WHOLE COMPLEX.
THIS ISN'T TV. YOU TW CAN'T CRA AROUND I THERE WITH CRASHING RI THROUGH T CEILING.
WE CAN'T...
...BUT THIS CAN.

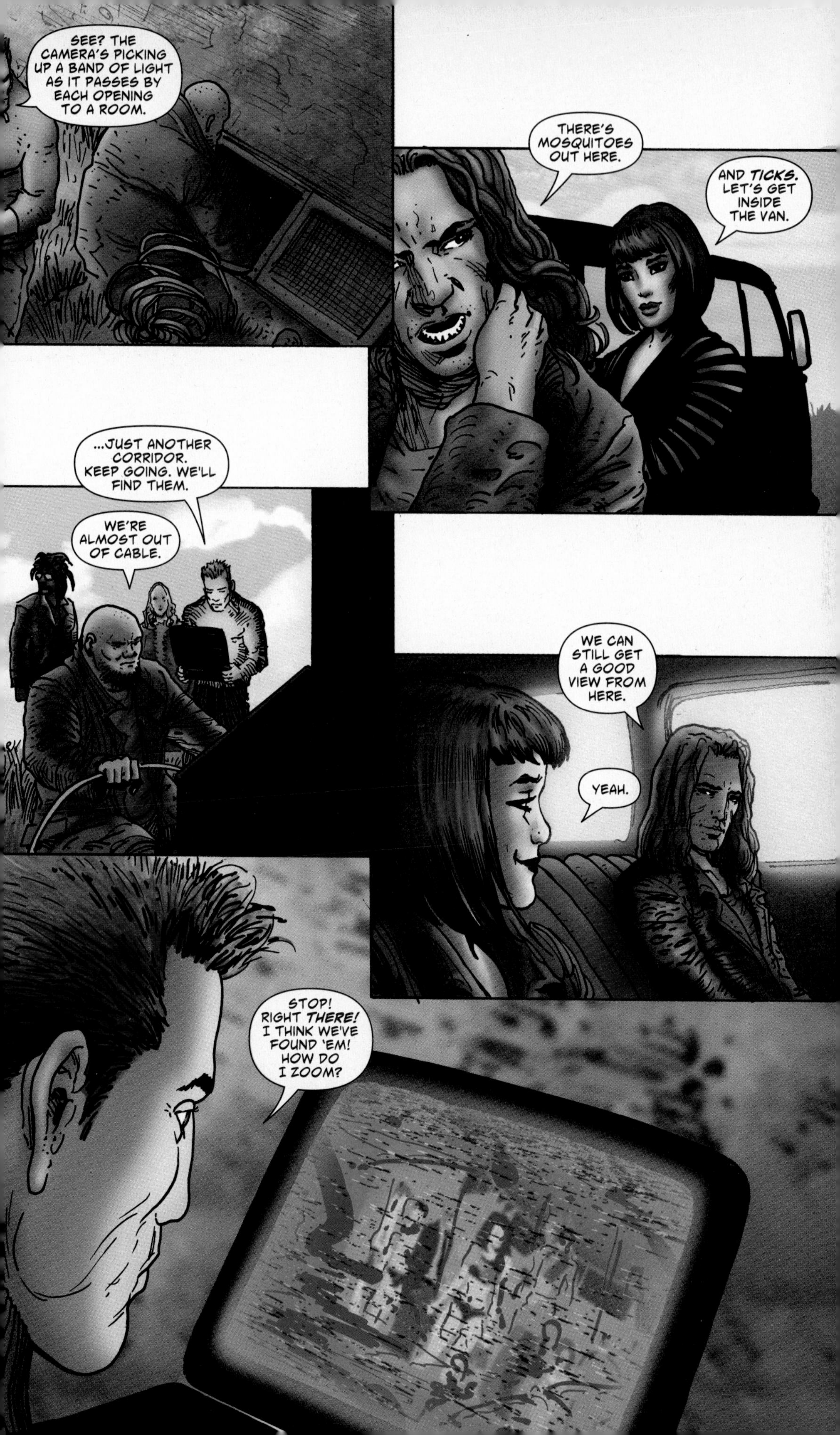
SEE? THE CAMERA'S PICKING UP A BAND OF LIGHT AS IT PASSES BY EACH OPENING TO A ROOM.
THERE'S MOSQUITOES OUT HERE.
AND TICKS. LET'S GET INSIDE THE VAN.
...JUST ANOTHER CORRIDOR. KEEP GOING. WE'LL FIND THEM.
WE'RE ALMOST OUT OF CABLE.
WE CAN STILL GET A GOOD VIEW FROM HERE.
YEAH.
STOP! RIGHT THERE! I THINK WE'VE FOUND 'EM! HOW DO I ZOOM?

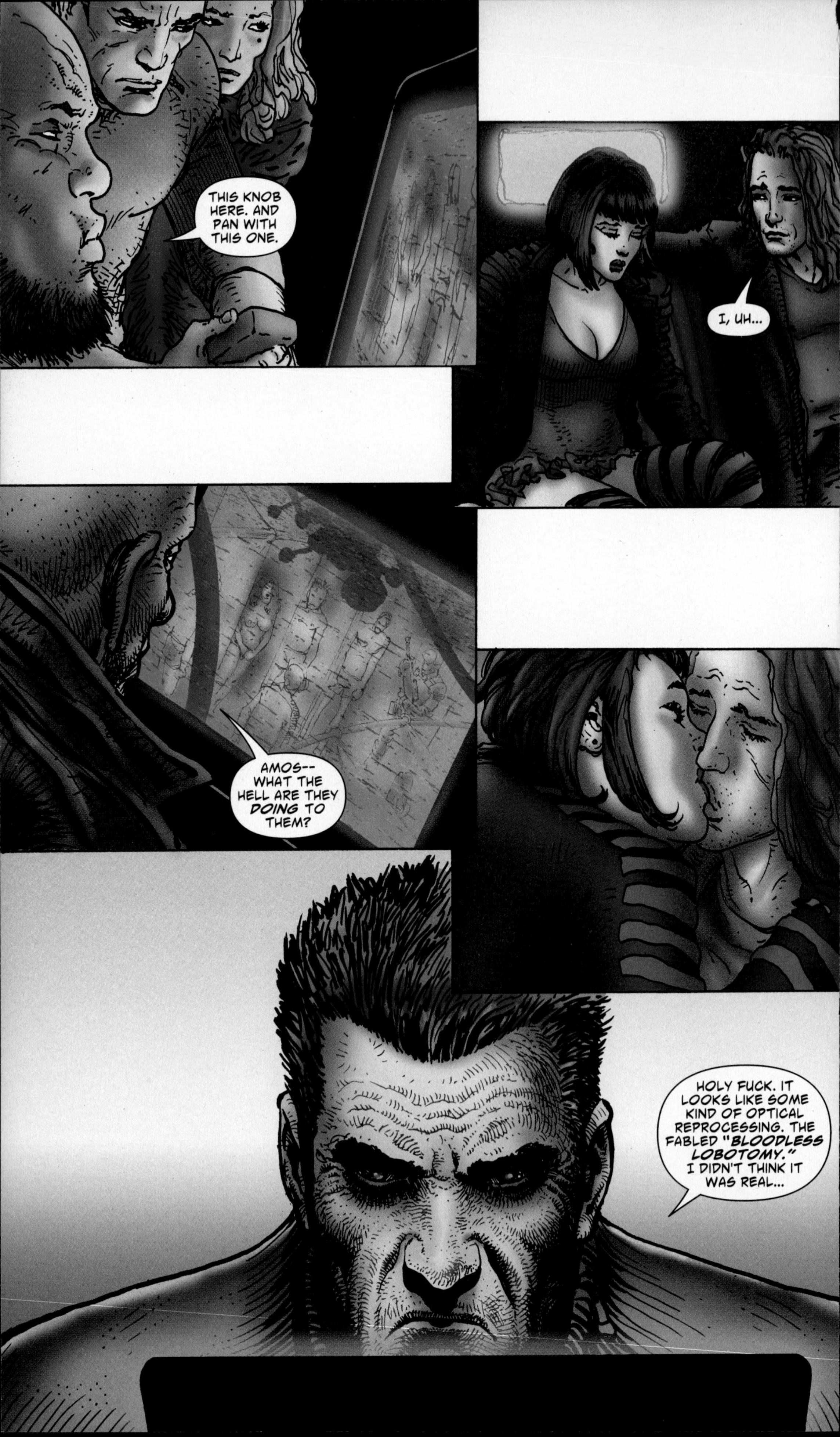
THIS KNOB HERE. AND PAN WITH THIS ONE.
I, UH...
AMOS-- WHAT THE HELL ARE THEY *DOING* TO THEM?
HOLY FUCK. IT LOOKS LIKE SOME KIND OF OPTICAL REPROCESSING. THE FABLED "*BLOODLESS LOBOTOMY.*" I DIDN'T THINK IT WAS REAL...

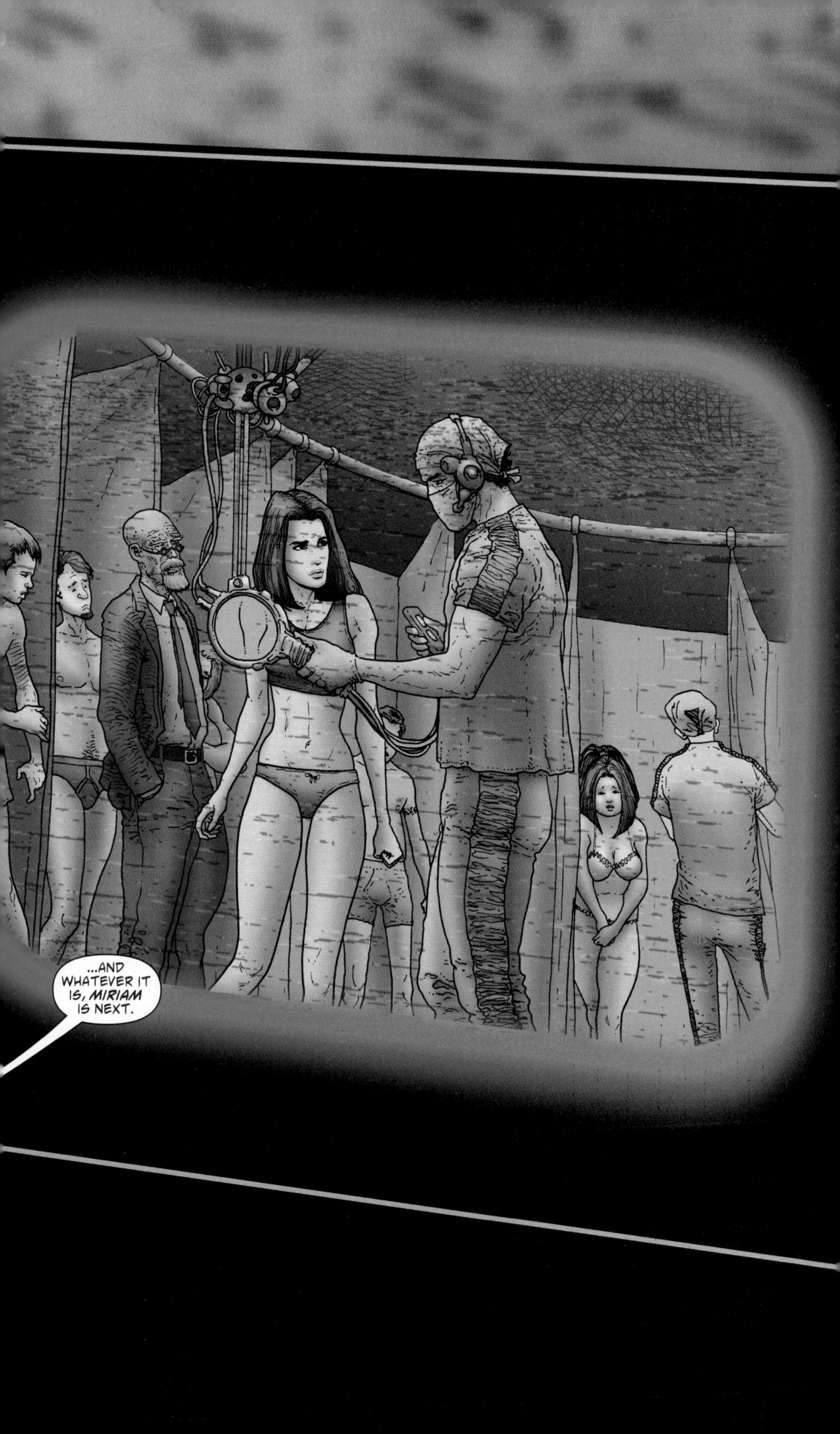
...AND WHATEVER IT IS, MIRIAM IS NEXT.

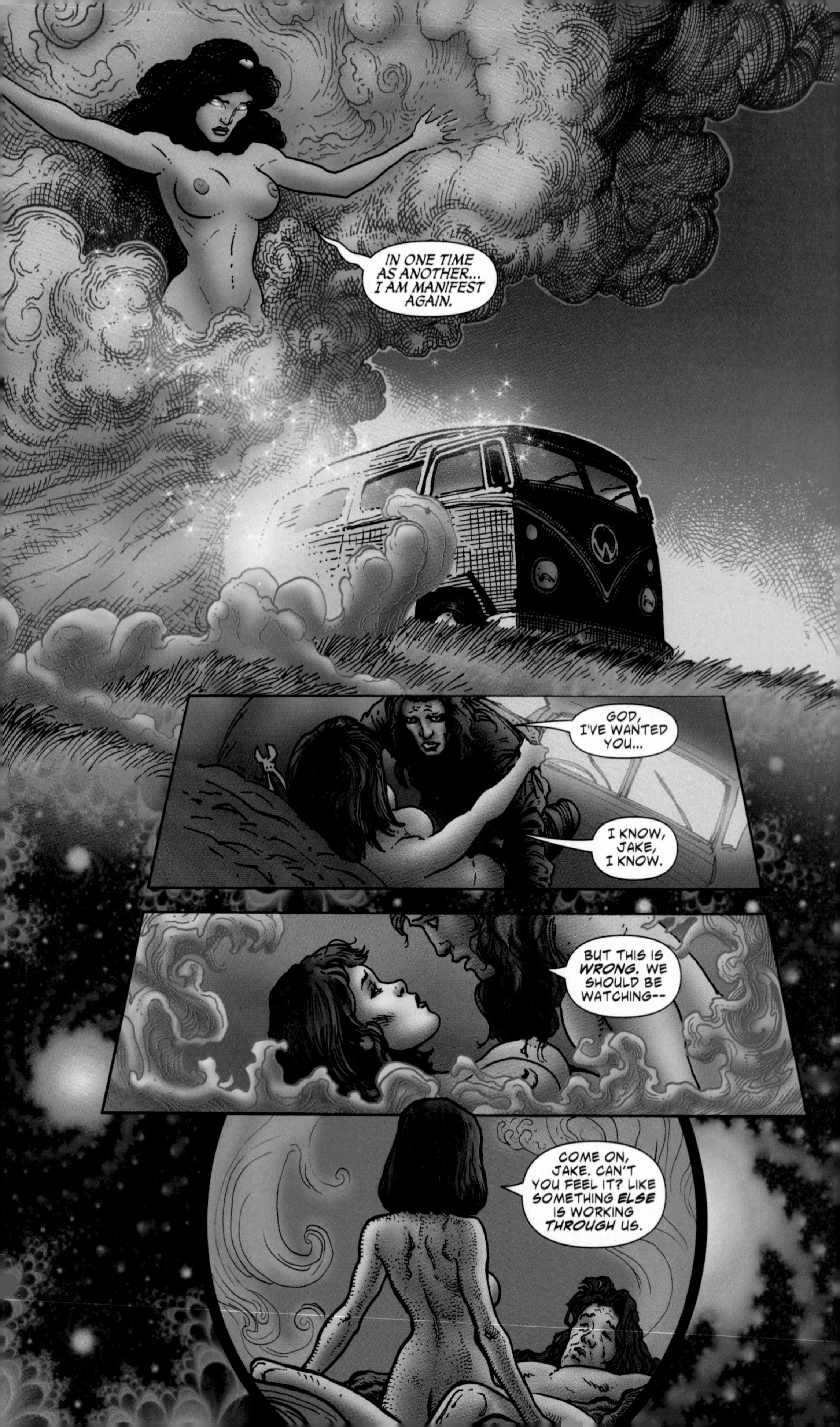
IN ONE TIME AS ANOTHER... I AM MANIFEST AGAIN.
GOD, I'VE WANTED YOU...
I KNOW, JAKE, I KNOW.
BUT THIS IS WRONG. WE SHOULD BE WATCHING--
COME ON, JAKE. CAN'T YOU FEEL IT? LIKE SOMETHING ELSE IS WORKING THROUGH US.

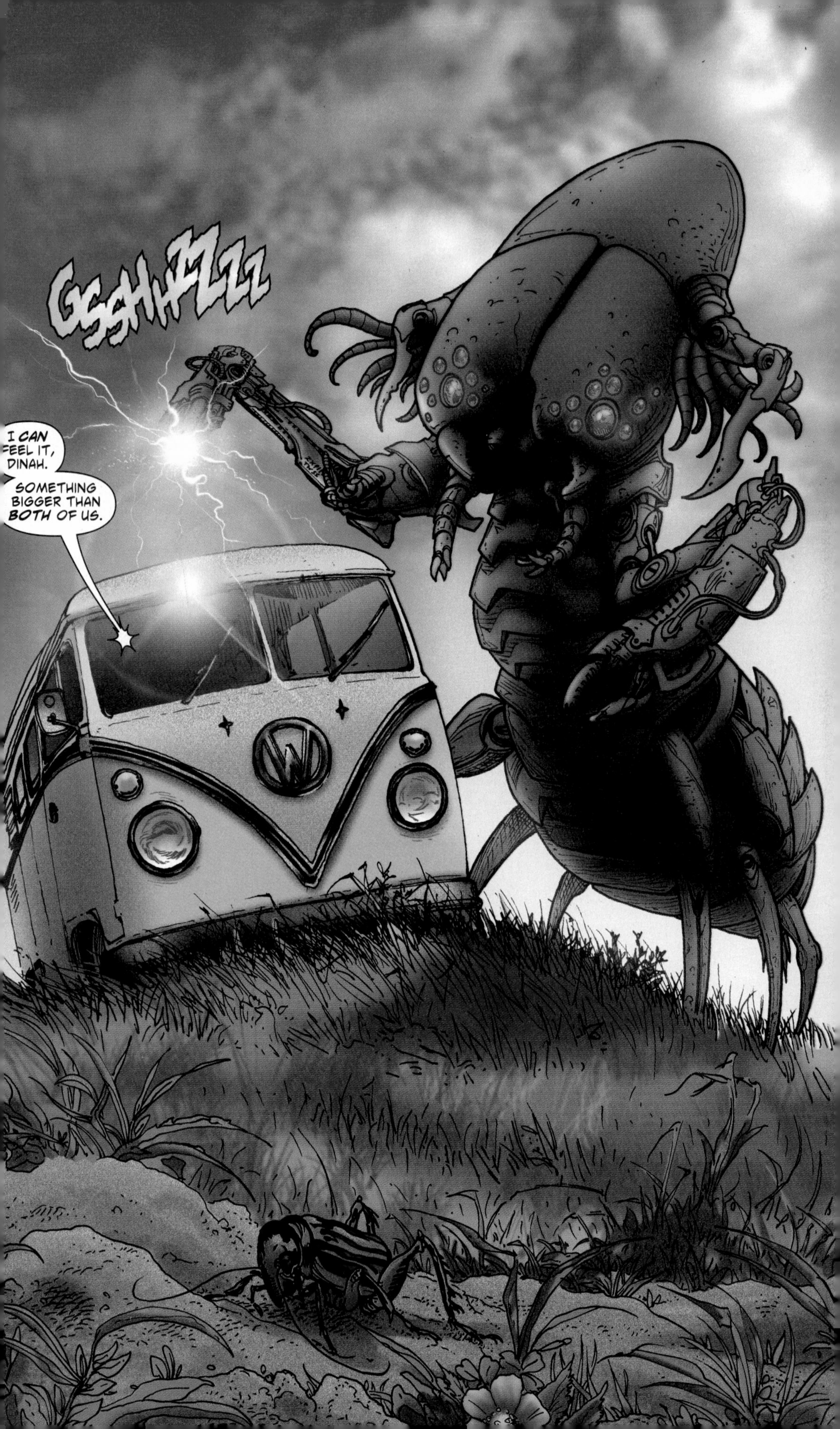
GSSHHZZzz
I CAN FEEL IT, DINAH.
SOMETHING BIGGER THAN BOTH OF US.

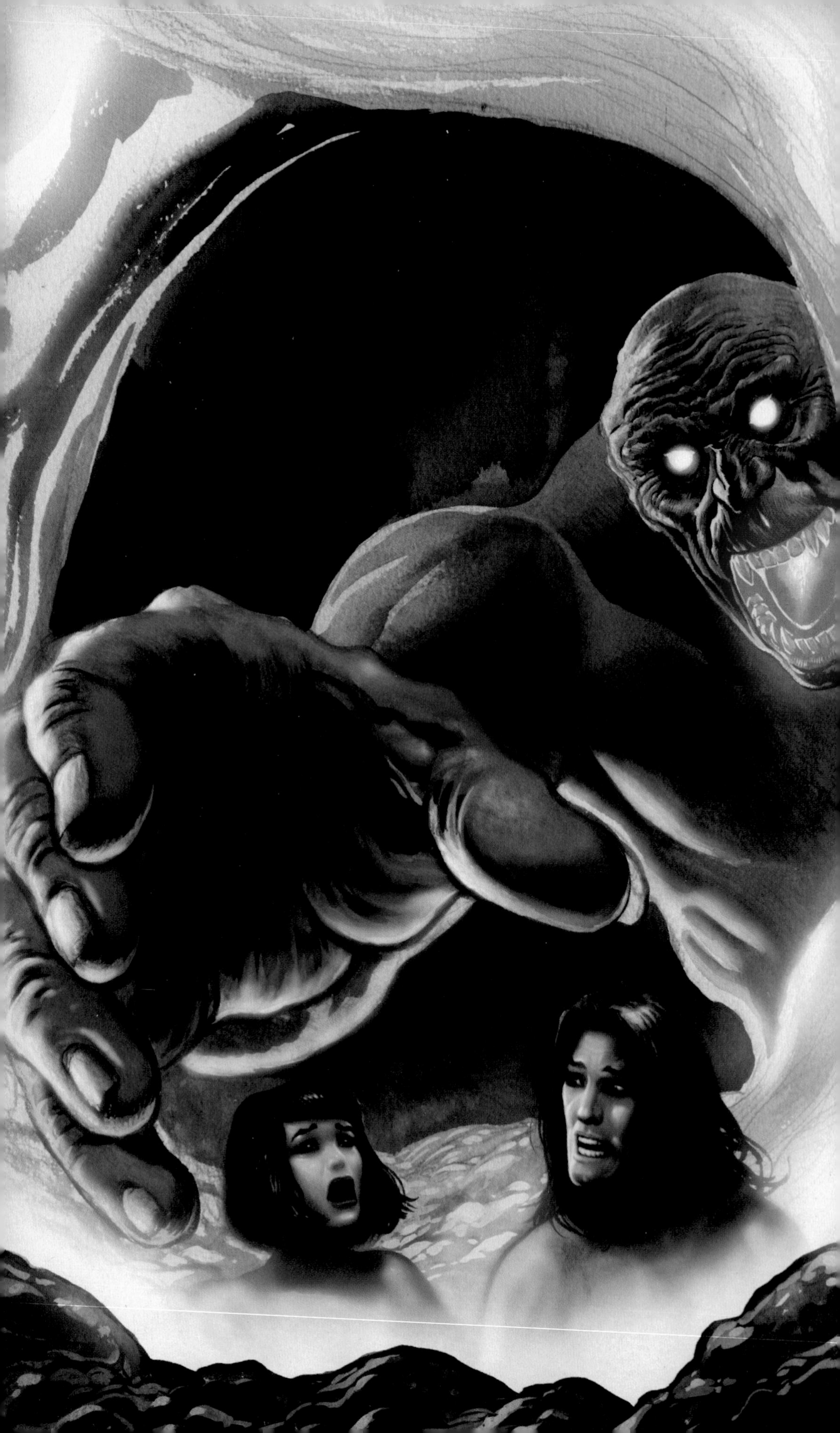

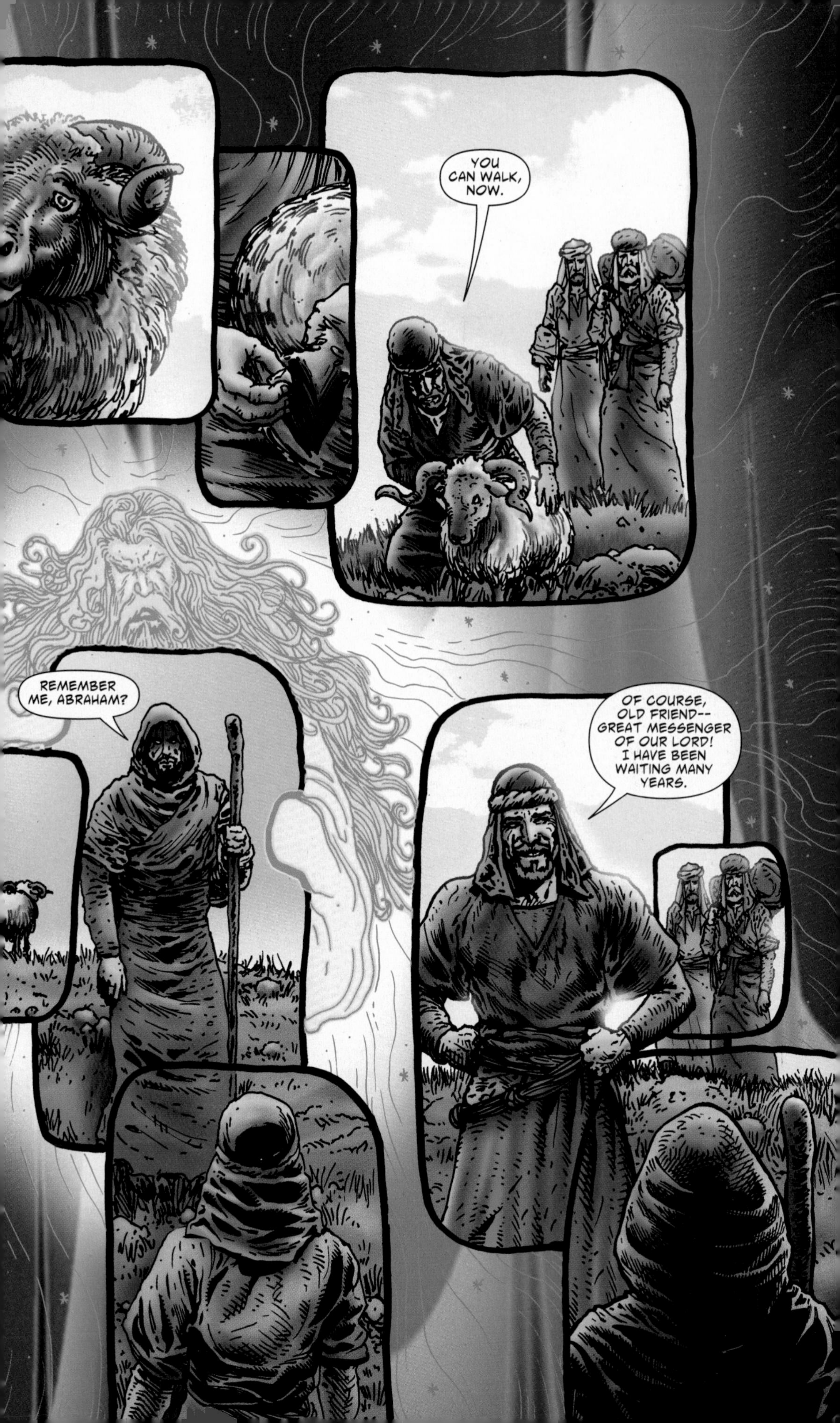
YOU CAN WALK, NOW.
REMEMBER ME, ABRAHAM?
OF COURSE, OLD FRIEND-- GREAT MESSENGER OF OUR LORD! I HAVE BEEN WAITING MANY YEARS.

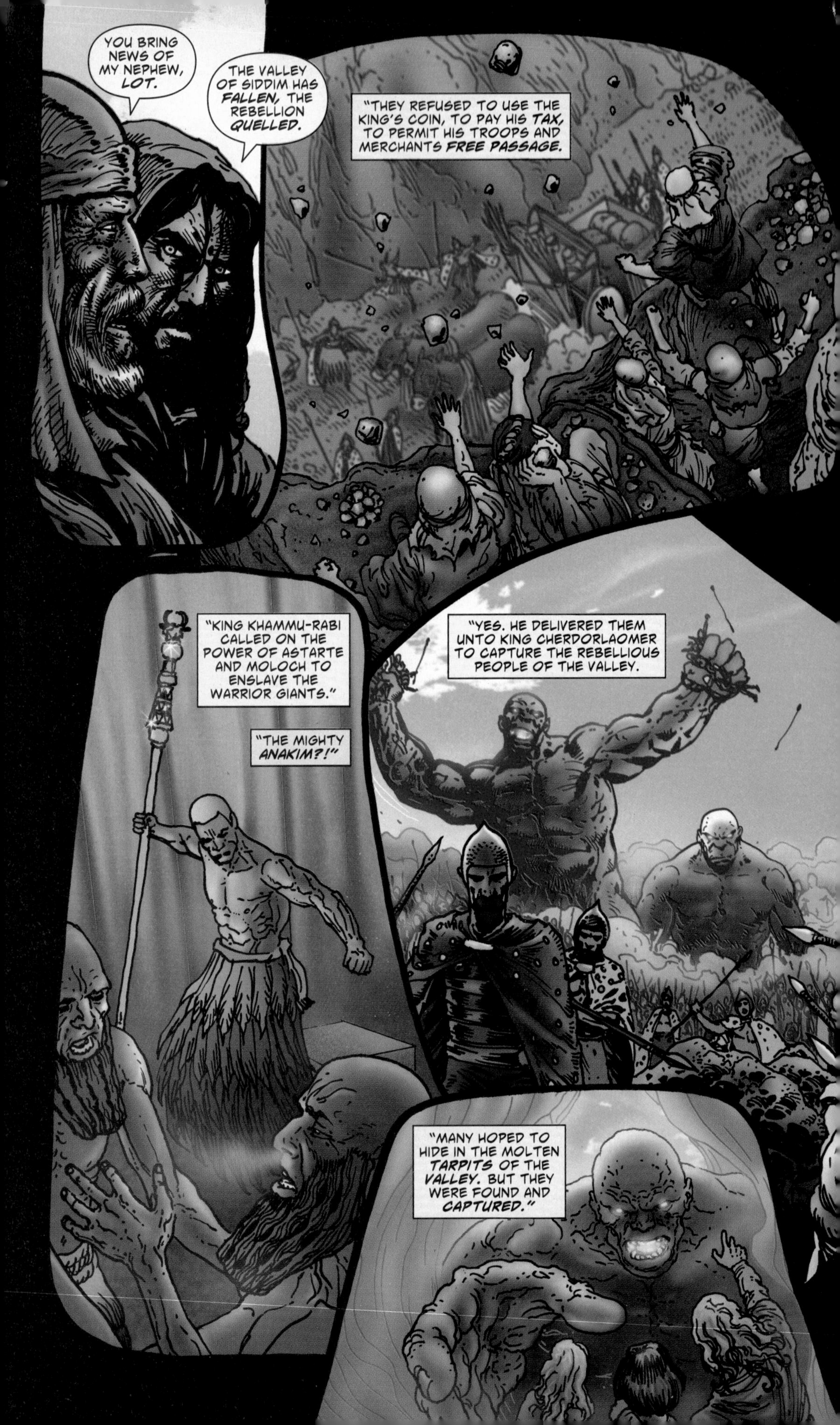

YOU BRING NEWS OF MY NEPHEW, LOT.
THE VALLEY OF SIDDIM HAS FALLEN, THE REBELLION QUELLED.
"THEY REFUSED TO USE THE KING'S COIN, TO PAY HIS TAX, TO PERMIT HIS TROOPS AND MERCHANTS FREE PASSAGE.
"KING KHAMMU-RABI CALLED ON THE POWER OF ASTARTE AND MOLOCH TO ENSLAVE THE WARRIOR GIANTS."
"THE MIGHTY ANAKIM?!"
"YES. HE DELIVERED THEM UNTO KING CHERDORLAOMER TO CAPTURE THE REBELLIOUS PEOPLE OF THE VALLEY.
"MANY HOPED TO HIDE IN THE MOLTEN TARPITS OF THE VALLEY. BUT THEY WERE FOUND AND CAPTURED."

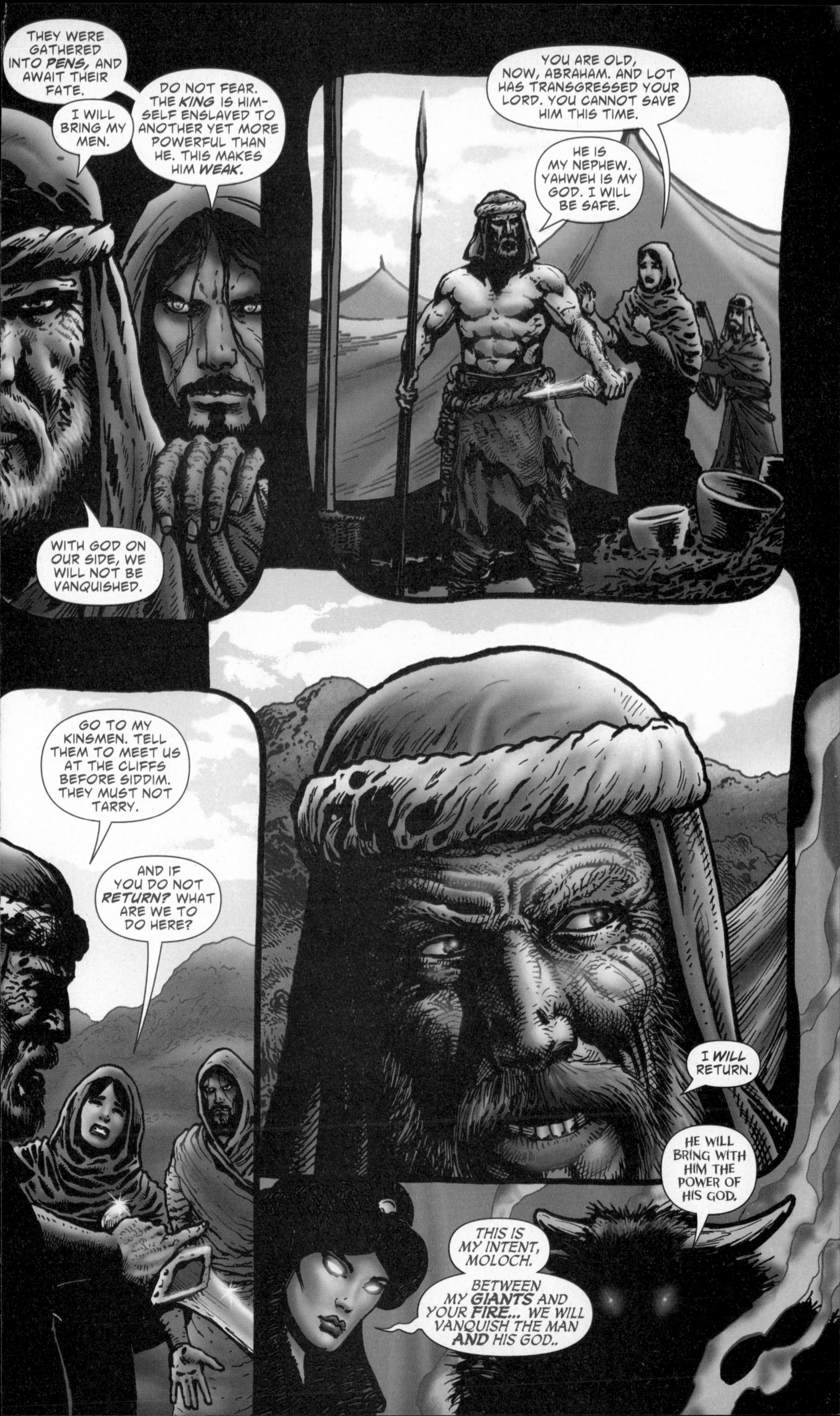
THEY WERE GATHERED INTO PENS, AND AWAIT THEIR FATE.
I WILL BRING MY MEN.
DO NOT FEAR. THE KING IS HIMSELF ENSLAVED TO ANOTHER YET MORE POWERFUL THAN HE. THIS MAKES HIM WEAK.
WITH GOD ON OUR SIDE, WE WILL NOT BE VANQUISHED.
YOU ARE OLD, NOW, ABRAHAM. AND LOT HAS TRANSGRESSED YOUR LORD. YOU CANNOT SAVE HIM THIS TIME.
HE IS MY NEPHEW. YAHWEH IS MY GOD. I WILL BE SAFE.
GO TO MY KINSMEN. TELL THEM TO MEET US AT THE CLIFFS BEFORE SIDDIM. THEY MUST NOT TARRY.
AND IF YOU DO NOT RETURN? WHAT ARE WE TO DO HERE?
I WILL RETURN.
HE WILL BRING WITH HIM THE POWER OF HIS GOD.
THIS IS MY INTENT, MOLOCH.
BETWEEN MY GIANTS AND YOUR FIRE... WE WILL VANQUISH THE MAN AND HIS GOD..

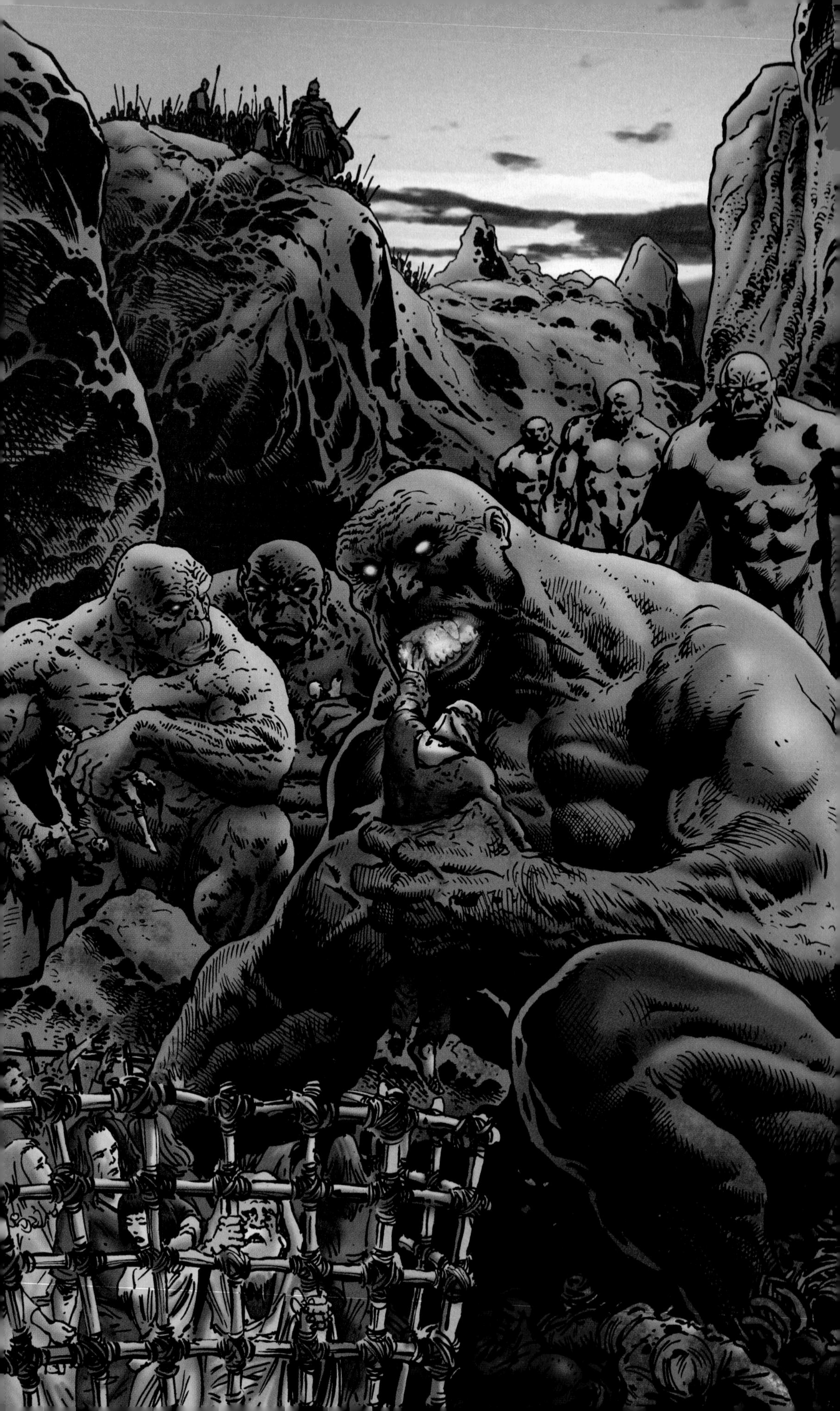

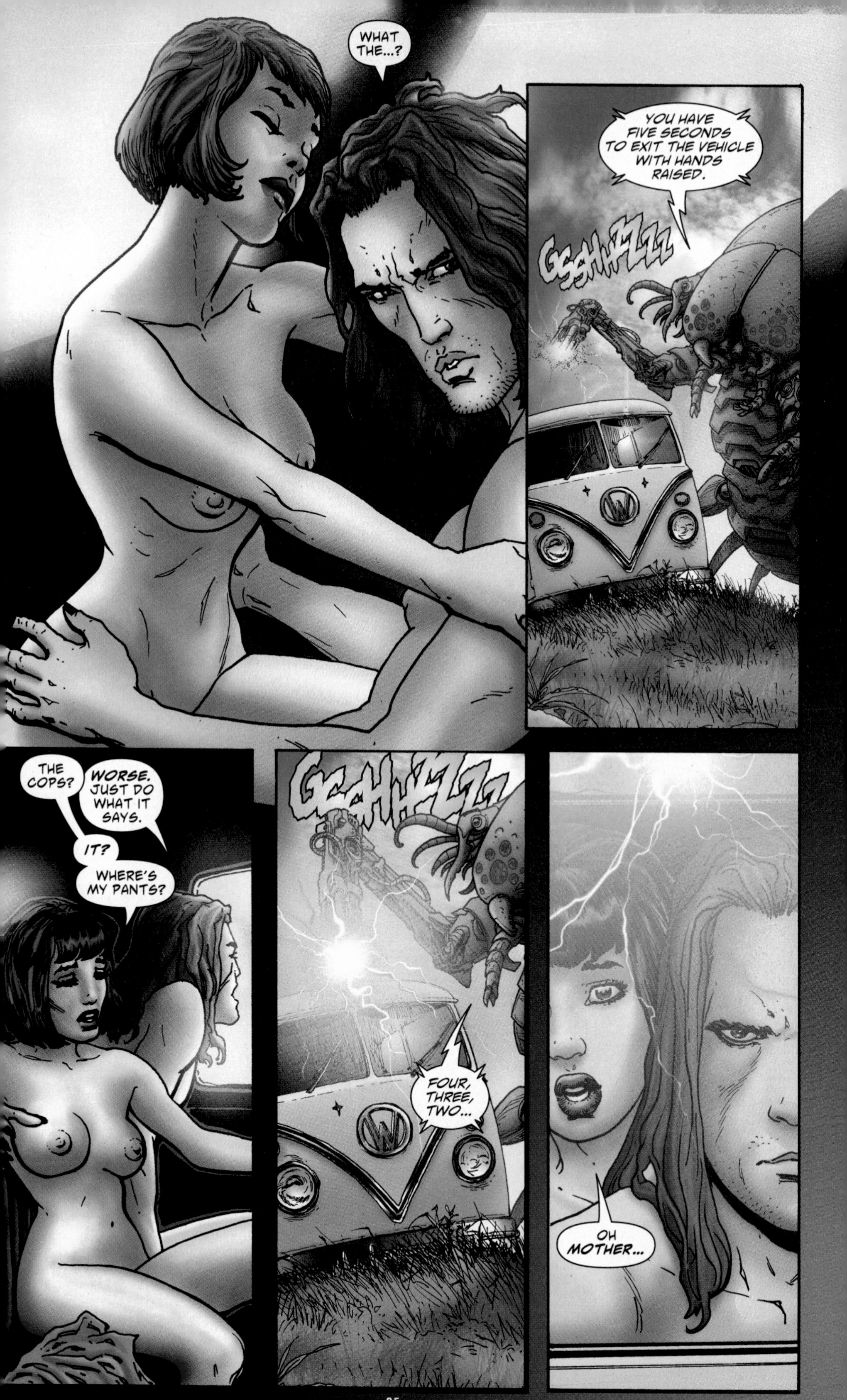
WHAT THE...?
YOU HAVE FIVE SECONDS TO EXIT THE VEHICLE WITH HANDS RAISED.
GSSHHZZZZ
THE COPS?
WORSE. JUST DO WHAT IT SAYS.
IT?
WHERE'S MY PANTS?
GSHHZZZ
FOUR, THREE, TWO...
OH MOTHER...

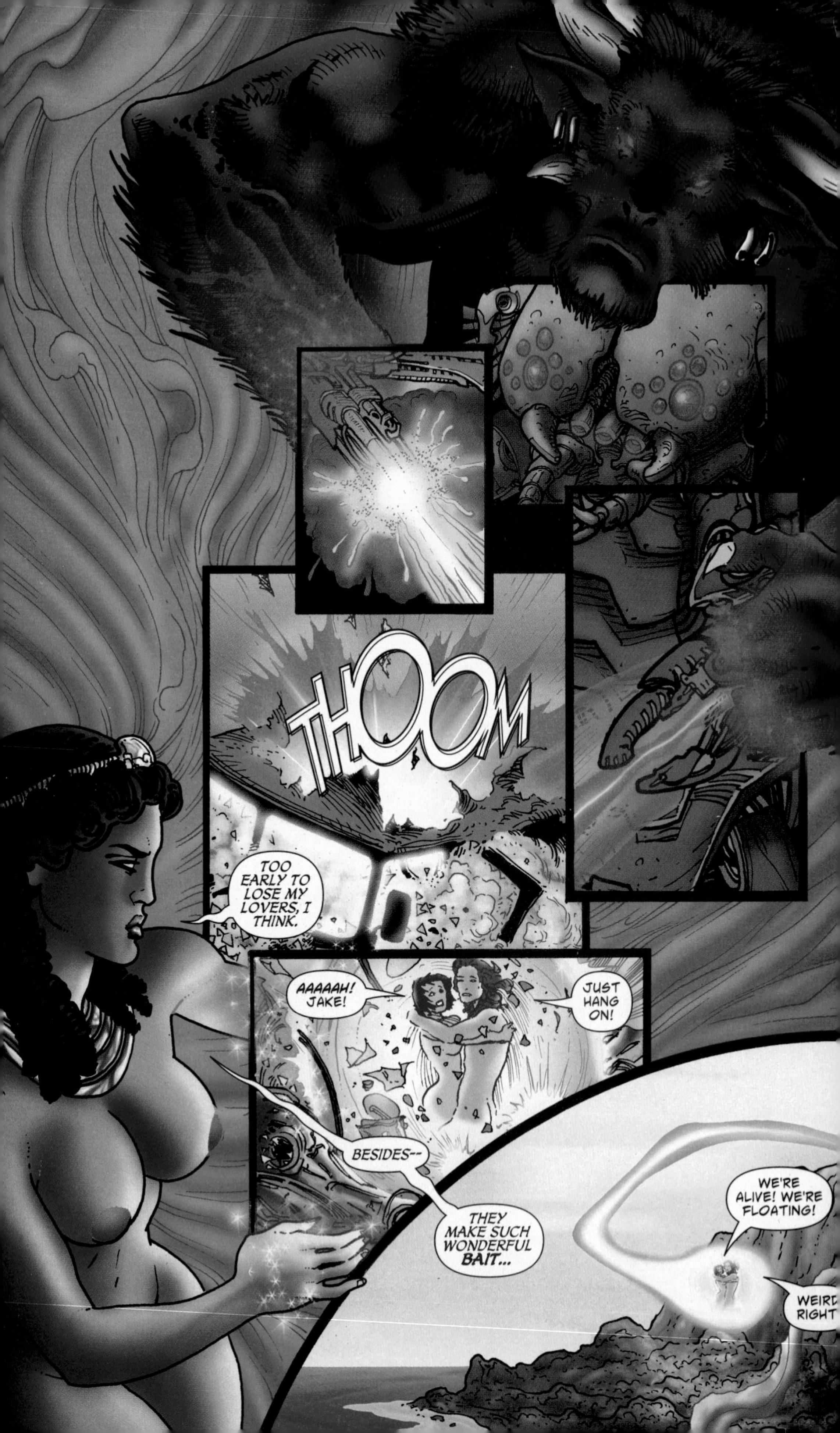
THOOM
TOO EARLY TO LOSE MY LOVERS, I THINK.
AAAAAH! JAKE!
JUST HANG ON!
BESIDES--
THEY MAKE SUCH WONDERFUL BAIT...
WE'RE ALIVE! WE'RE FLOATING!
WEIRD RIGHT

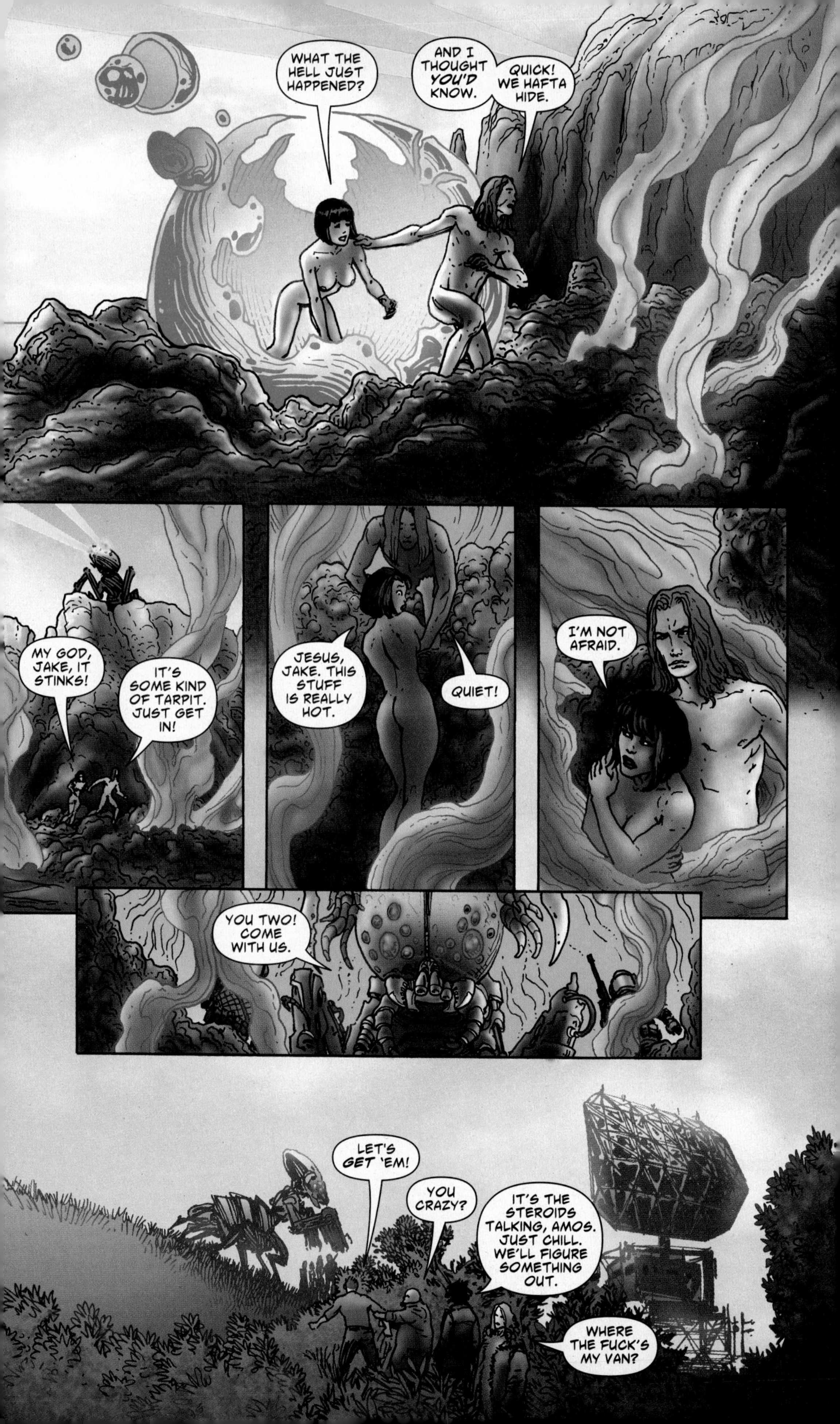

WHAT THE HELL JUST HAPPENED?
AND I THOUGHT *YOU'D* KNOW.
QUICK! WE HAFTA HIDE.
MY GOD, JAKE, IT STINKS!
IT'S SOME KIND OF TARPIT. JUST GET IN!
JESUS, JAKE. THIS STUFF IS REALLY HOT.
QUIET!
I'M NOT AFRAID.
YOU TWO! COME WITH US.
LET'S *GET* 'EM!
YOU CRAZY?
IT'S THE STEROIDS TALKING, AMOS. JUST CHILL. WE'LL FIGURE SOMETHING OUT.
WHERE THE FUCK'S MY VAN?

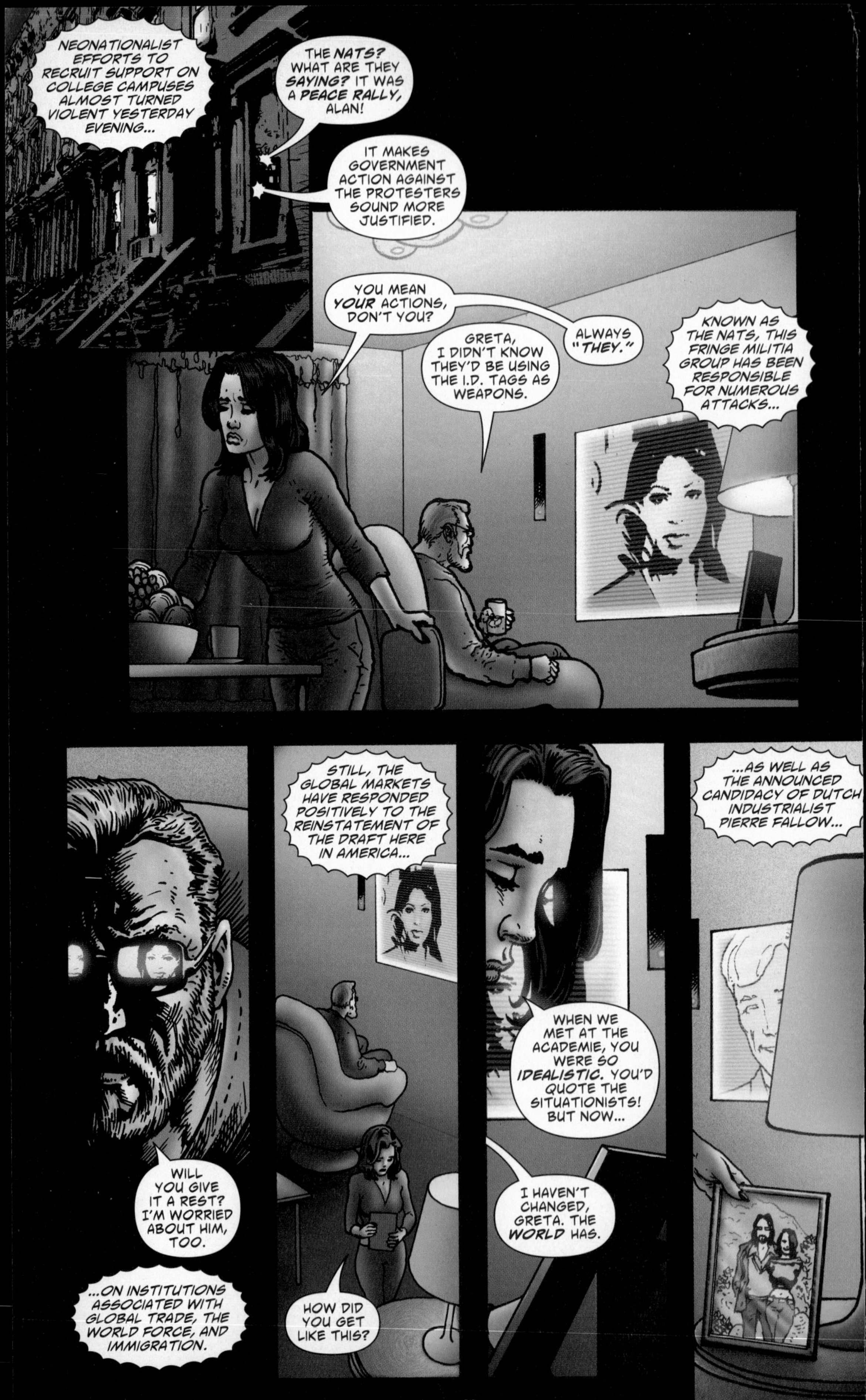
NEONATIONALIST EFFORTS TO RECRUIT SUPPORT ON COLLEGE CAMPUSES ALMOST TURNED VIOLENT YESTERDAY EVENING...
THE NATS? WHAT ARE THEY SAYING? IT WAS A PEACE RALLY, ALAN!
IT MAKES GOVERNMENT ACTION AGAINST THE PROTESTERS SOUND MORE JUSTIFIED.
YOU MEAN YOUR ACTIONS, DON'T YOU?
GRETA, I DIDN'T KNOW THEY'D BE USING THE I.D. TAGS AS WEAPONS.
ALWAYS "THEY."
KNOWN AS THE NATS, THIS FRINGE MILITIA GROUP HAS BEEN RESPONSIBLE FOR NUMEROUS ATTACKS...
WILL YOU GIVE IT A REST? I'M WORRIED ABOUT HIM, TOO.
...ON INSTITUTIONS ASSOCIATED WITH GLOBAL TRADE, THE WORLD FORCE, AND IMMIGRATION.
STILL, THE GLOBAL MARKETS HAVE RESPONDED POSITIVELY TO THE REINSTATEMENT OF THE DRAFT HERE IN AMERICA...
HOW DID YOU GET LIKE THIS?
WHEN WE MET AT THE ACADEMIE, YOU WERE SO IDEALISTIC. YOU'D QUOTE THE SITUATIONISTS! BUT NOW...
I HAVEN'T CHANGED, GRETA. THE WORLD HAS.
...AS WELL AS THE ANNOUNCED CANDIDACY OF DUTCH INDUSTRIALIST PIERRE FALLOW...

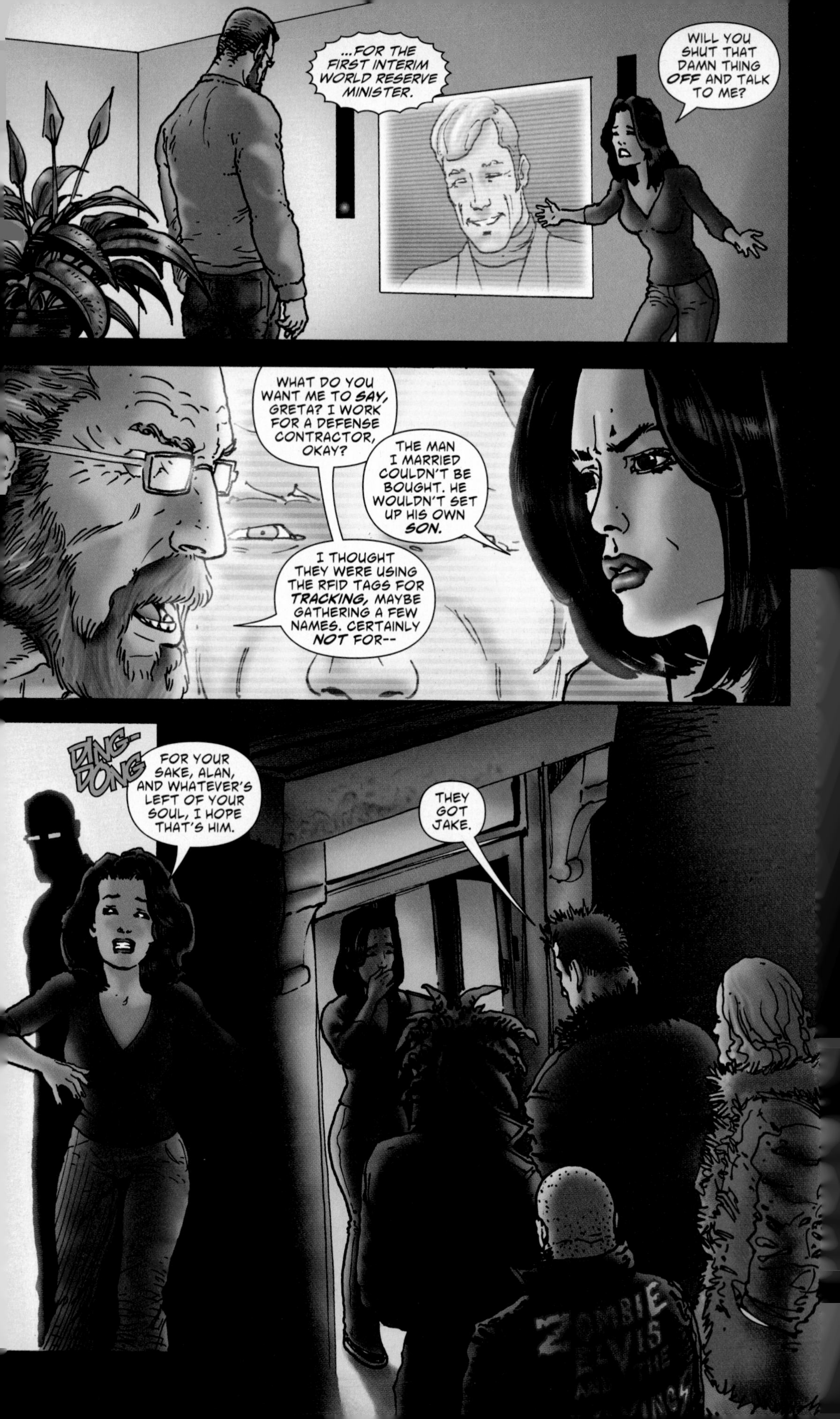
...FOR THE FIRST INTERIM WORLD RESERVE MINISTER.
WILL YOU SHUT THAT DAMN THING OFF AND TALK TO ME?
WHAT DO YOU WANT ME TO SAY, GRETA? I WORK FOR A DEFENSE CONTRACTOR, OKAY?
THE MAN I MARRIED COULDN'T BE BOUGHT. HE WOULDN'T SET UP HIS OWN SON.
I THOUGHT THEY WERE USING THE RFID TAGS FOR TRACKING, MAYBE GATHERING A FEW NAMES. CERTAINLY NOT FOR--
DING-DONG
FOR YOUR SAKE, ALAN, AND WHATEVER'S LEFT OF YOUR SOUL, I HOPE THAT'S HIM.
THEY GOT JAKE.

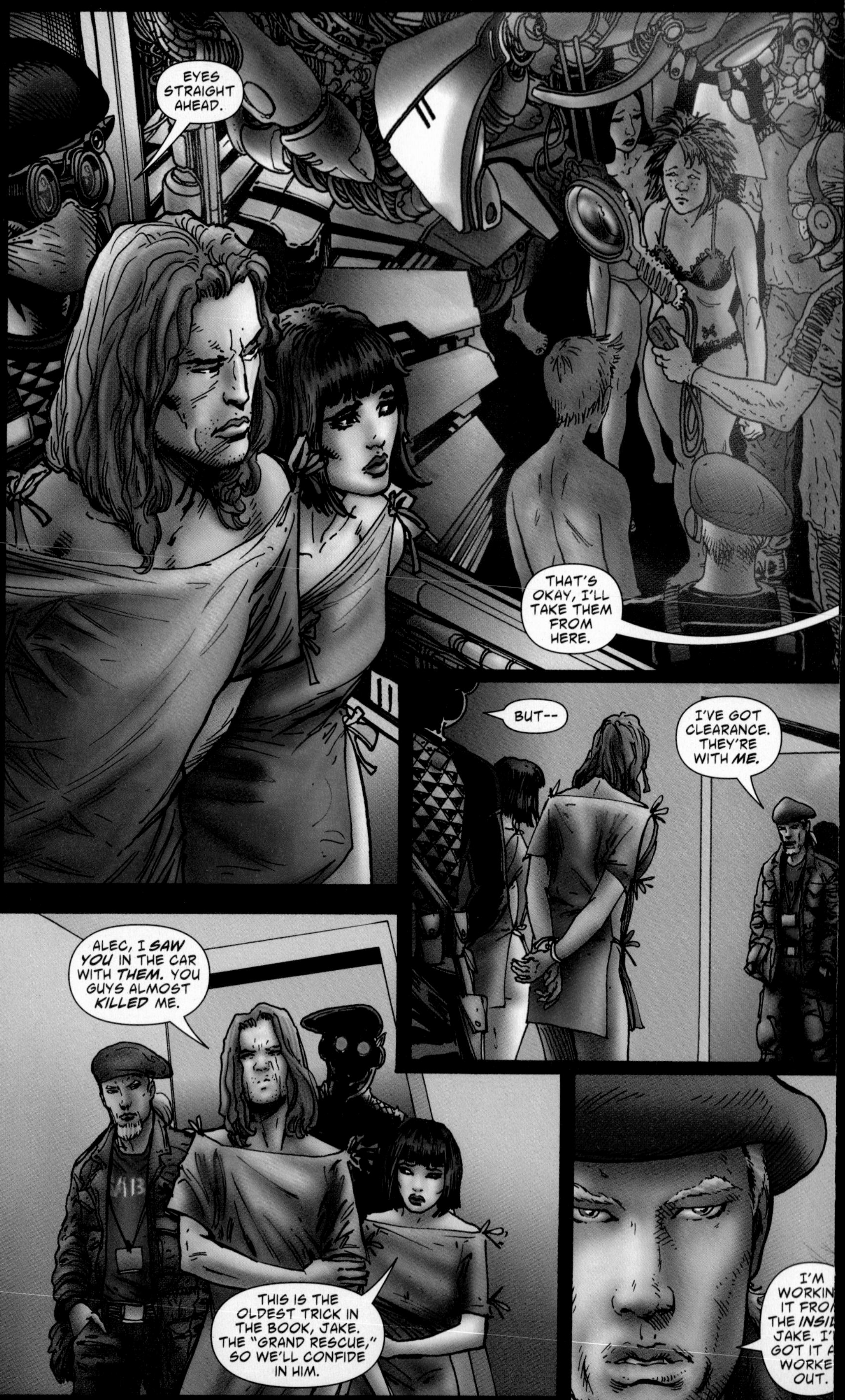

EYES STRAIGHT AHEAD.
THAT'S OKAY, I'LL TAKE THEM FROM HERE.
BUT--
I'VE GOT CLEARANCE. THEY'RE WITH ME.
ALEC, I SAW YOU IN THE CAR WITH THEM. YOU GUYS ALMOST KILLED ME.
THIS IS THE OLDEST TRICK IN THE BOOK, JAKE. THE "GRAND RESCUE," SO WE'LL CONFIDE IN HIM.
I'M WORKIN IT FRO THE INSI JAKE. I' GOT IT A WORKE OUT.

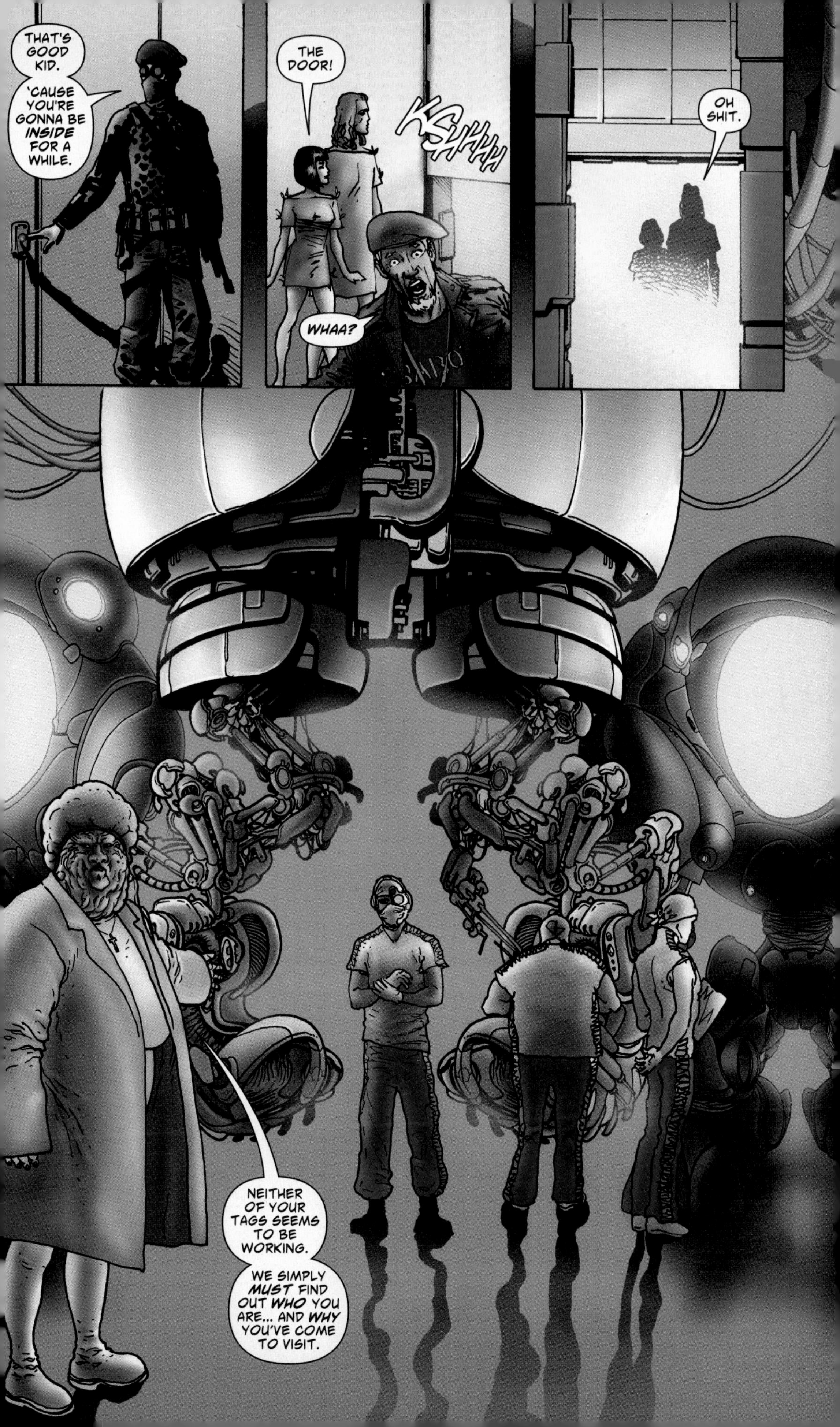
THAT'S GOOD KID.
'CAUSE YOU'RE GONNA BE *INSIDE* FOR A WHILE.
THE DOOR!
KSHHHH
WHAA?
OH SHIT.
NEITHER OF YOUR TAGS SEEMS TO BE WORKING.
WE SIMPLY *MUST* FIND OUT *WHO* YOU ARE... AND *WHY* YOU'VE COME TO VISIT.

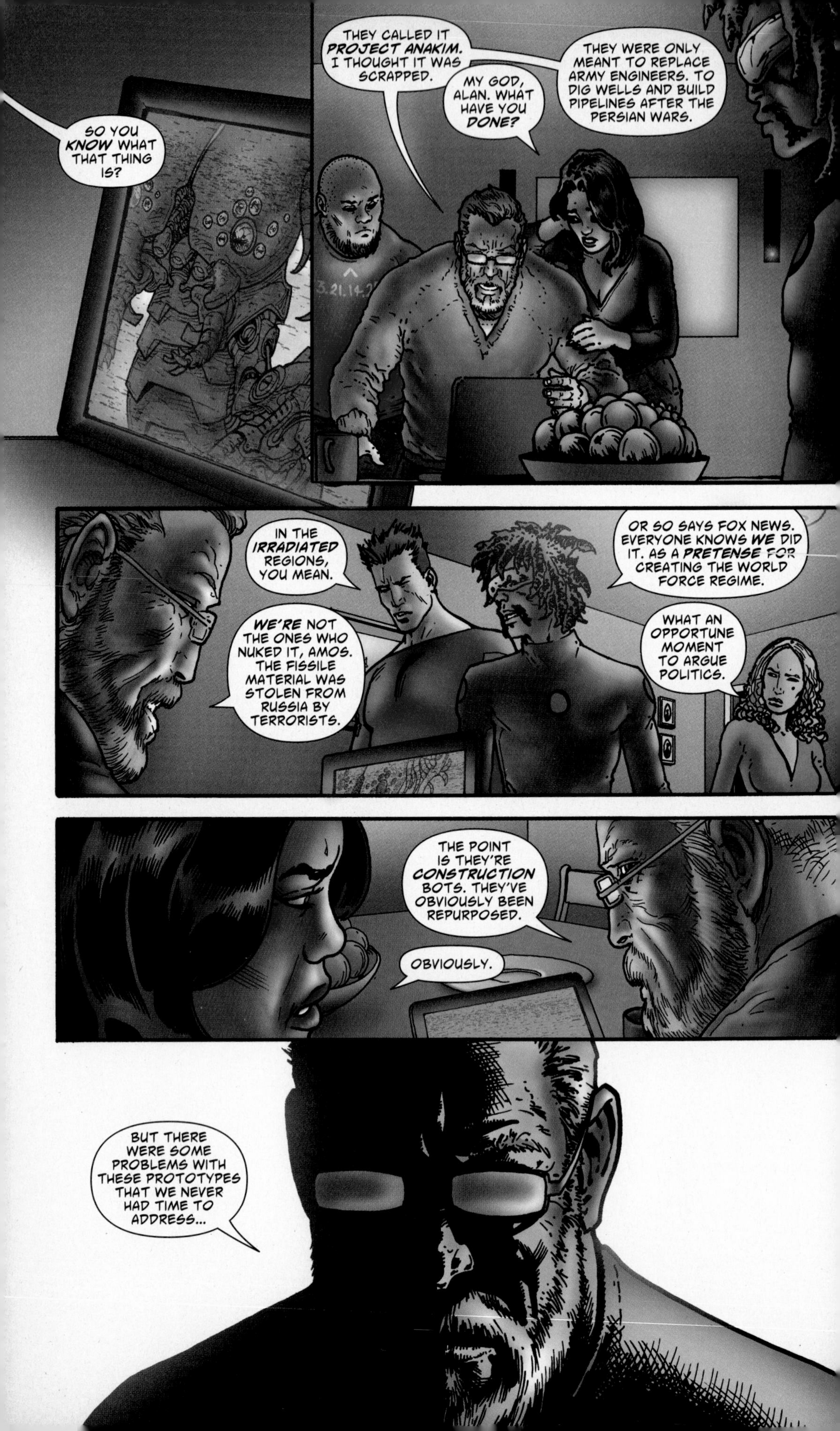
SO YOU KNOW WHAT THAT THING IS?
THEY CALLED IT PROJECT ANAKIM. I THOUGHT IT WAS SCRAPPED.
MY GOD, ALAN. WHAT HAVE YOU DONE?
THEY WERE ONLY MEANT TO REPLACE ARMY ENGINEERS. TO DIG WELLS AND BUILD PIPELINES AFTER THE PERSIAN WARS.
IN THE IRRADIATED REGIONS, YOU MEAN.
WE'RE NOT THE ONES WHO NUKED IT, AMOS. THE FISSILE MATERIAL WAS STOLEN FROM RUSSIA BY TERRORISTS.
OR SO SAYS FOX NEWS. EVERYONE KNOWS WE DID IT. AS A PRETENSE FOR CREATING THE WORLD FORCE REGIME.
WHAT AN OPPORTUNE MOMENT TO ARGUE POLITICS.
THE POINT IS THEY'RE CONSTRUCTION BOTS. THEY'VE OBVIOUSLY BEEN REPURPOSED.
OBVIOUSLY.
BUT THERE WERE SOME PROBLEMS WITH THESE PROTOTYPES THAT WE NEVER HAD TIME TO ADDRESS...

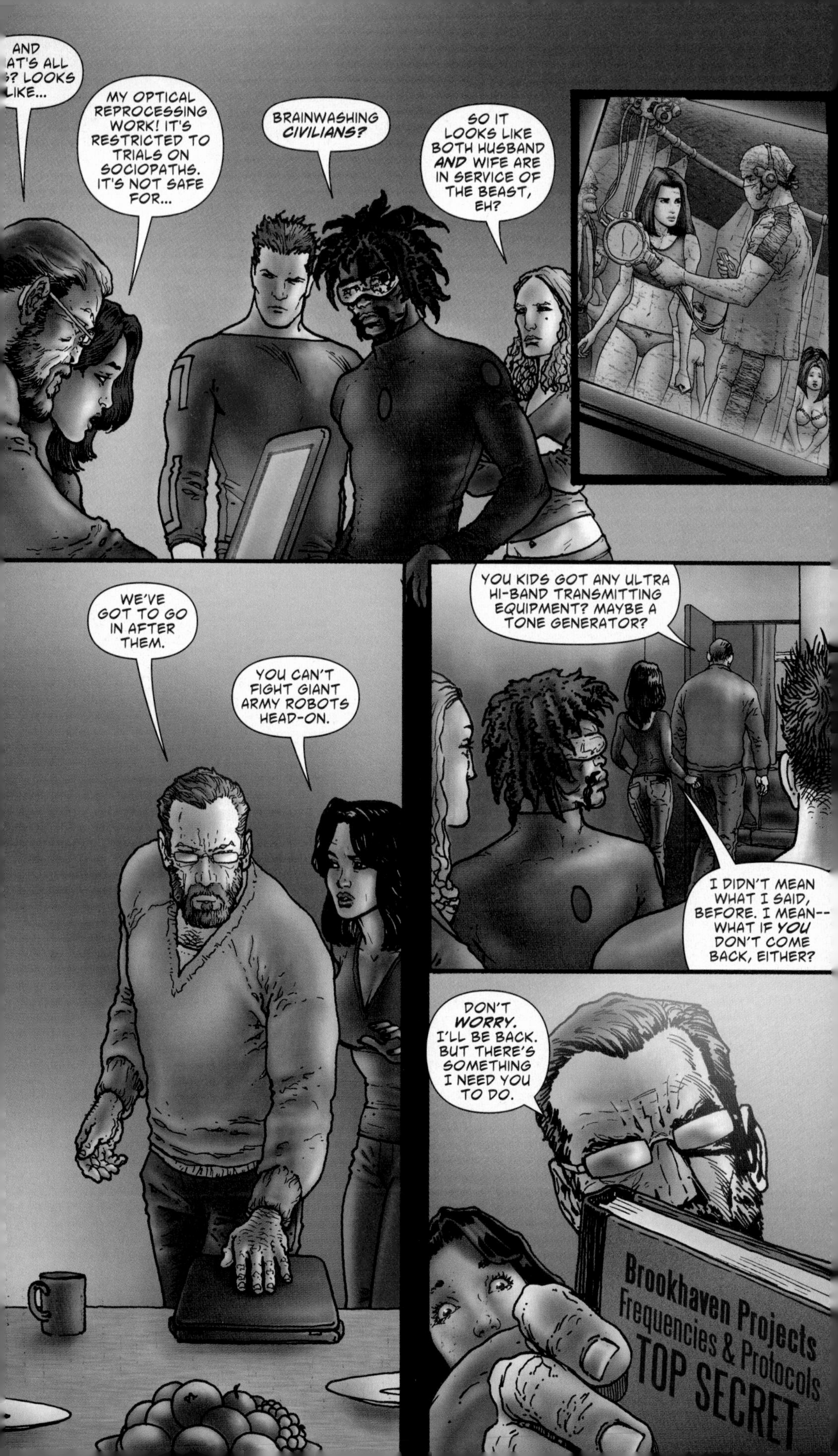
AND AT'S ALL S? LOOKS LIKE...
MY OPTICAL REPROCESSING WORK! IT'S RESTRICTED TO TRIALS ON SOCIOPATHS. IT'S NOT SAFE FOR...
BRAINWASHING *CIVILIANS?*
SO IT LOOKS LIKE BOTH HUSBAND *AND* WIFE ARE IN SERVICE OF THE BEAST, EH?
WE'VE GOT TO GO IN AFTER THEM.
YOU CAN'T FIGHT GIANT ARMY ROBOTS HEAD-ON.
YOU KIDS GOT ANY ULTRA HI-BAND TRANSMITTING EQUIPMENT? MAYBE A TONE GENERATOR?
I DIDN'T MEAN WHAT I SAID, BEFORE. I MEAN-- WHAT IF *YOU* DON'T COME BACK, EITHER?
DON'T *WORRY.* I'LL BE BACK. BUT THERE'S SOMETHING I NEED YOU TO DO.
Brookhaven Projects
Frequencies & Protocols
TOP SECRET

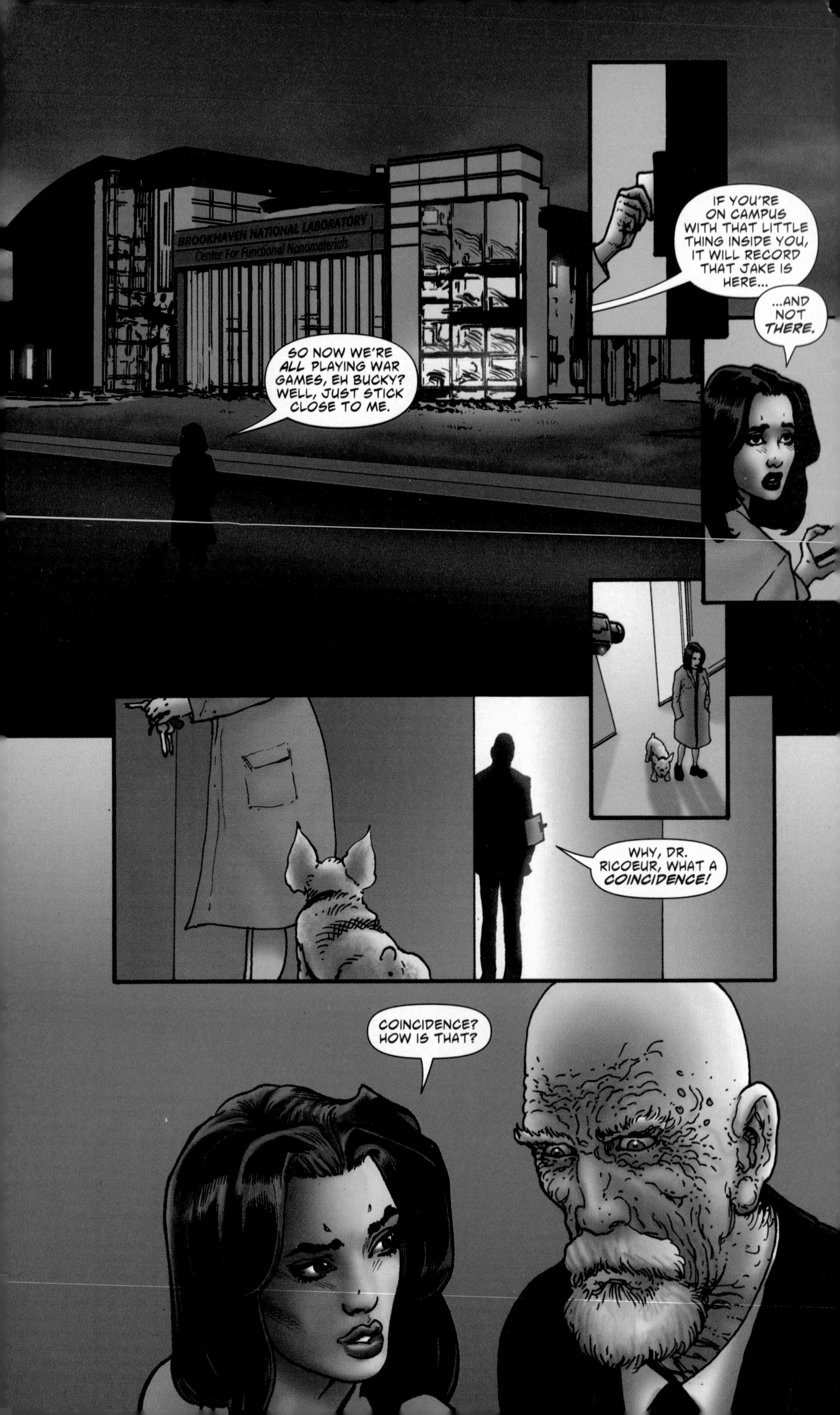
BROOKHAVEN NATIONAL LABORATORY
Center For Functional Nanomaterials
SO NOW WE'RE ALL PLAYING WAR GAMES, EH BUCKY? WELL, JUST STICK CLOSE TO ME.
IF YOU'RE ON CAMPUS WITH THAT LITTLE THING INSIDE YOU, IT WILL RECORD THAT JAKE IS HERE...
...AND NOT THERE.
WHY, DR. RICOEUR, WHAT A COINCIDENCE!
COINCIDENCE? HOW IS THAT?

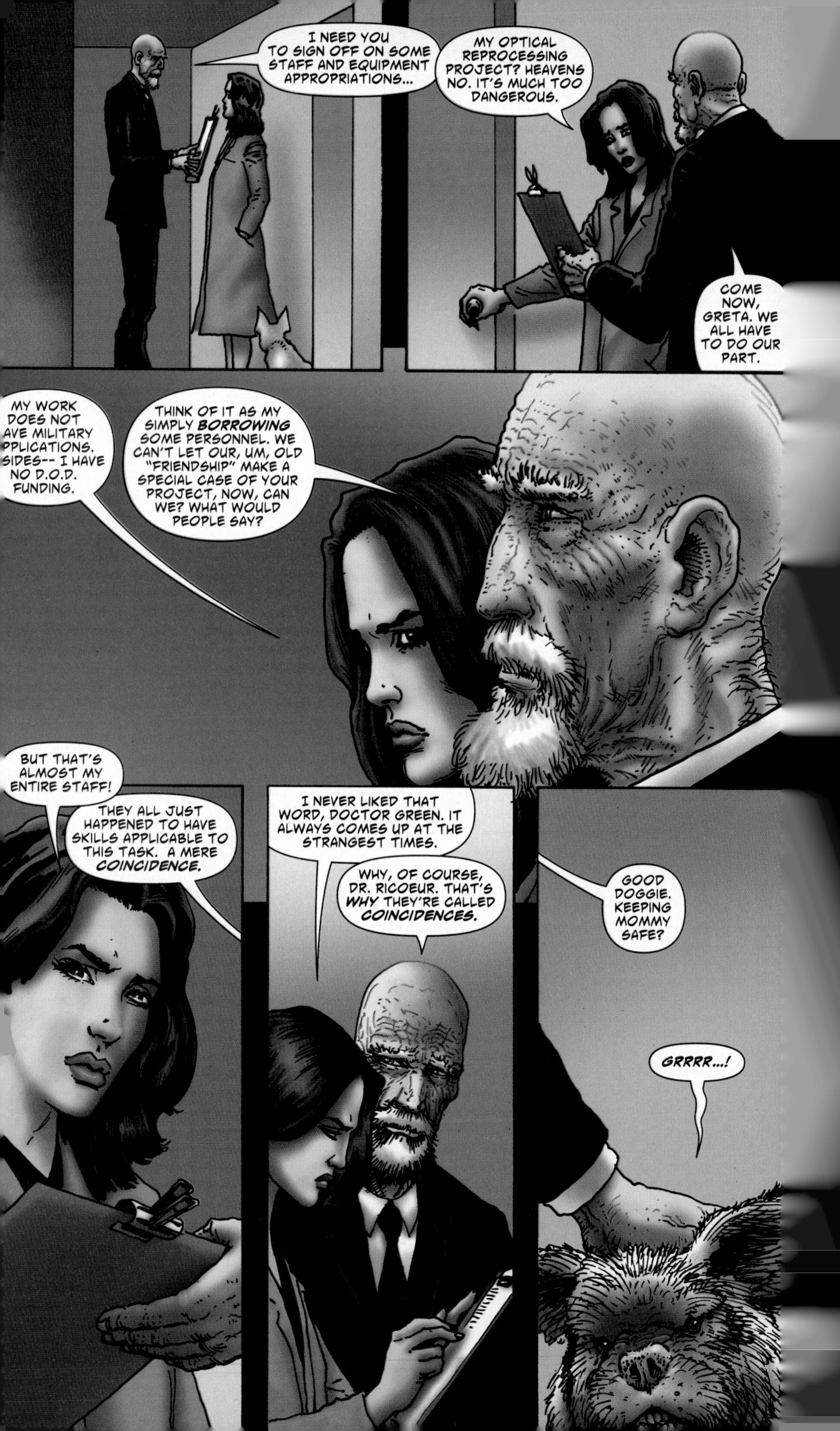
I NEED YOU TO SIGN OFF ON SOME STAFF AND EQUIPMENT APPROPRIATIONS...
MY OPTICAL REPROCESSING PROJECT? HEAVENS NO. IT'S MUCH TOO DANGEROUS.
COME NOW, GRETA. WE ALL HAVE TO DO OUR PART.
MY WORK DOES NOT AVE MILITARY PPLICATIONS. SIDES-- I HAVE NO D.O.D. FUNDING.
THINK OF IT AS MY SIMPLY BORROWING SOME PERSONNEL. WE CAN'T LET OUR, UM, OLD "FRIENDSHIP" MAKE A SPECIAL CASE OF YOUR PROJECT, NOW, CAN WE? WHAT WOULD PEOPLE SAY?
BUT THAT'S ALMOST MY ENTIRE STAFF!
THEY ALL JUST HAPPENED TO HAVE SKILLS APPLICABLE TO THIS TASK. A MERE COINCIDENCE.
I NEVER LIKED THAT WORD, DOCTOR GREEN. IT ALWAYS COMES UP AT THE STRANGEST TIMES.
WHY, OF COURSE, DR. RICOEUR. THAT'S WHY THEY'RE CALLED COINCIDENCES.
GOOD DOGGIE. KEEPING MOMMY SAFE?
GRRRR...!

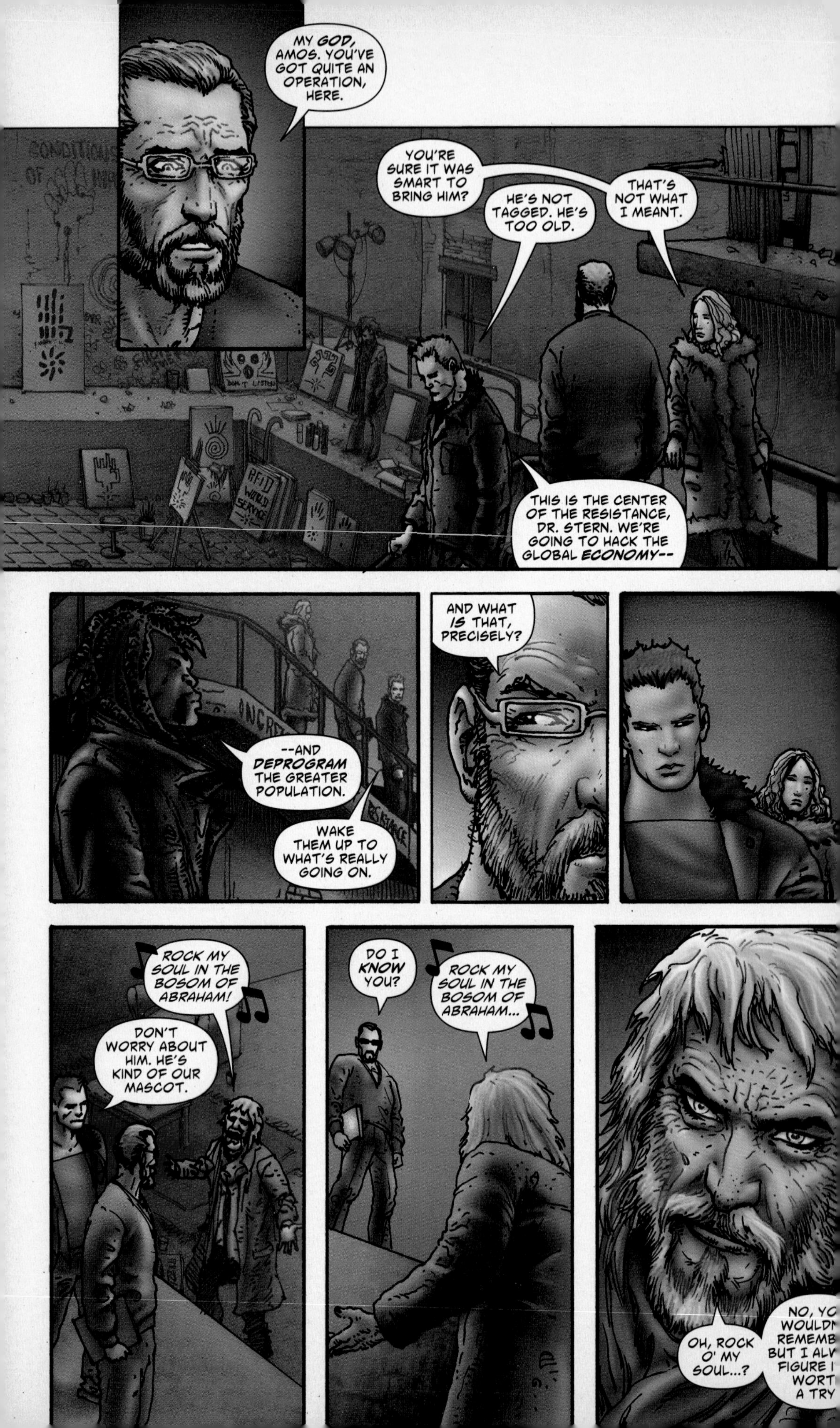
MY GOD, AMOS. YOU'VE GOT QUITE AN OPERATION, HERE.
YOU'RE SURE IT WAS SMART TO BRING HIM?
HE'S NOT TAGGED. HE'S TOO OLD.
THAT'S NOT WHAT I MEANT.
THIS IS THE CENTER OF THE RESISTANCE, DR. STERN. WE'RE GOING TO HACK THE GLOBAL ECONOMY--
--AND DEPROGRAM THE GREATER POPULATION.
WAKE THEM UP TO WHAT'S REALLY GOING ON.
AND WHAT IS THAT, PRECISELY?
ROCK MY SOUL IN THE BOSOM OF ABRAHAM!
DON'T WORRY ABOUT HIM. HE'S KIND OF OUR MASCOT.
DO I KNOW YOU?
ROCK MY SOUL IN THE BOSOM OF ABRAHAM...
OH, ROCK O' MY SOUL...?
NO, YO WOULDN REMEMB BUT I ALW FIGURE I WORT A TRY

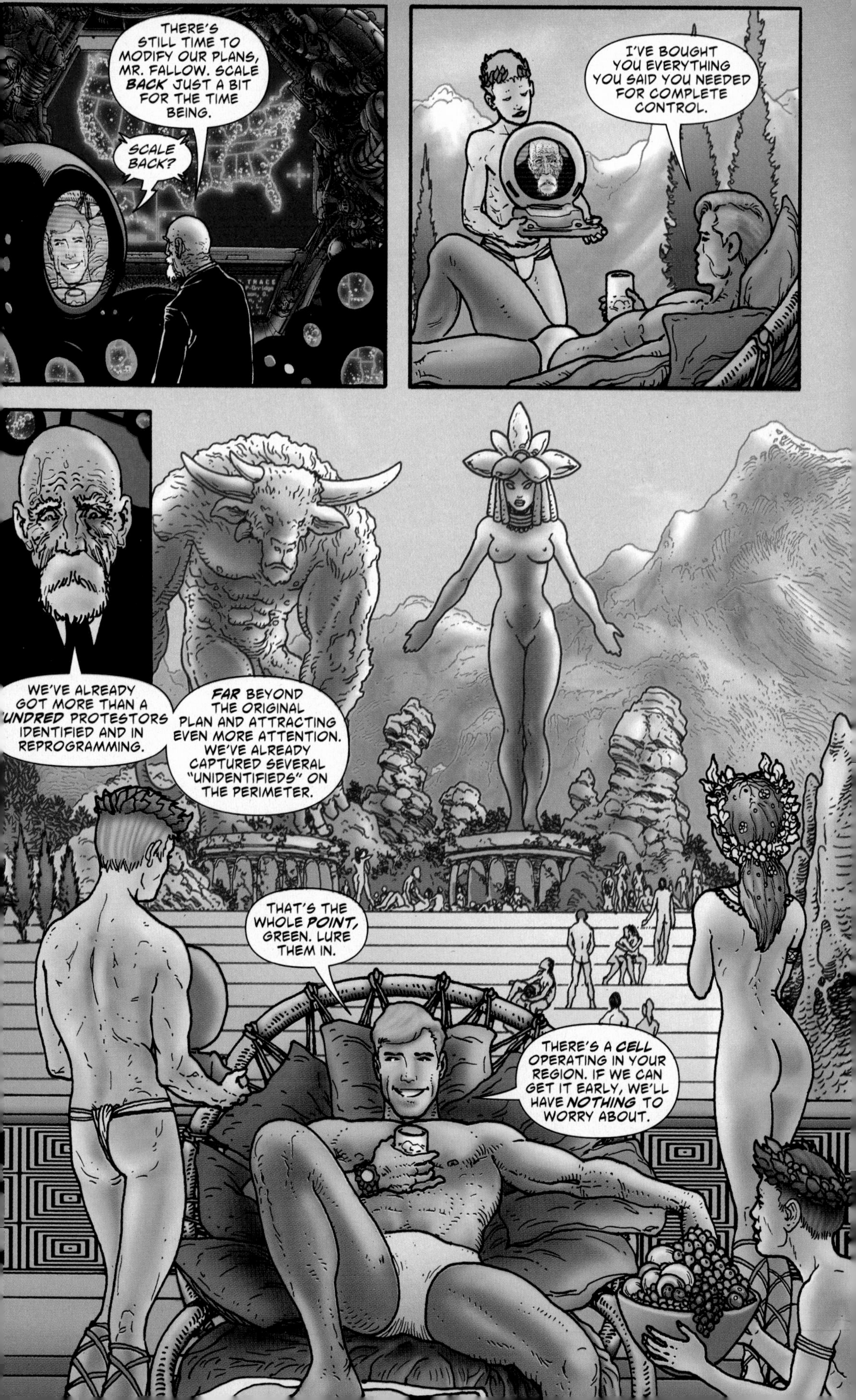
THERE'S STILL TIME TO MODIFY OUR PLANS, MR. FALLOW. SCALE BACK JUST A BIT FOR THE TIME BEING.
SCALE BACK?
I'VE BOUGHT YOU EVERYTHING YOU SAID YOU NEEDED FOR COMPLETE CONTROL.
WE'VE ALREADY GOT MORE THAN A UNDRED PROTESTORS IDENTIFIED AND IN REPROGRAMMING.
FAR BEYOND THE ORIGINAL PLAN AND ATTRACTING EVEN MORE ATTENTION. WE'VE ALREADY CAPTURED SEVERAL "UNIDENTIFIEDS" ON THE PERIMETER.
THAT'S THE WHOLE POINT, GREEN. LURE THEM IN.
THERE'S A CELL OPERATING IN YOUR REGION. IF WE CAN GET IT EARLY, WE'LL HAVE NOTHING TO WORRY ABOUT.

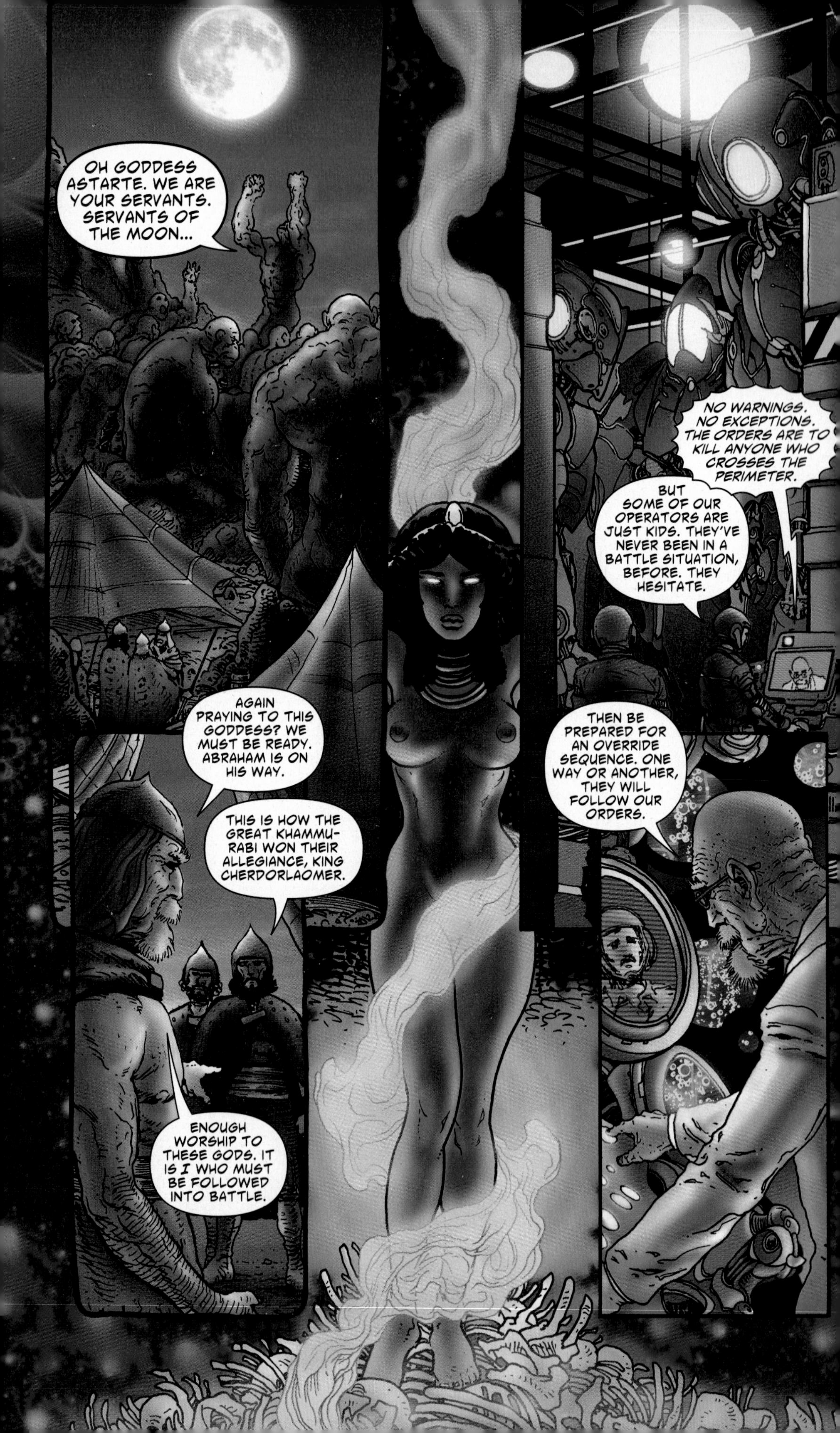
OH GODDESS ASTARTE. WE ARE YOUR SERVANTS. SERVANTS OF THE MOON...
AGAIN PRAYING TO THIS GODDESS? WE MUST BE READY. ABRAHAM IS ON HIS WAY.
THIS IS HOW THE GREAT KHAMMU-RABI WON THEIR ALLEGIANCE, KING CHERDORLAOMER.
ENOUGH WORSHIP TO THESE GODS. IT IS I WHO MUST BE FOLLOWED INTO BATTLE.
NO WARNINGS. NO EXCEPTIONS. THE ORDERS ARE TO KILL ANYONE WHO CROSSES THE PERIMETER.
BUT SOME OF OUR OPERATORS ARE JUST KIDS. THEY'VE NEVER BEEN IN A BATTLE SITUATION, BEFORE. THEY HESITATE.
THEN BE PREPARED FOR AN OVERRIDE SEQUENCE. ONE WAY OR ANOTHER, THEY WILL FOLLOW OUR ORDERS.

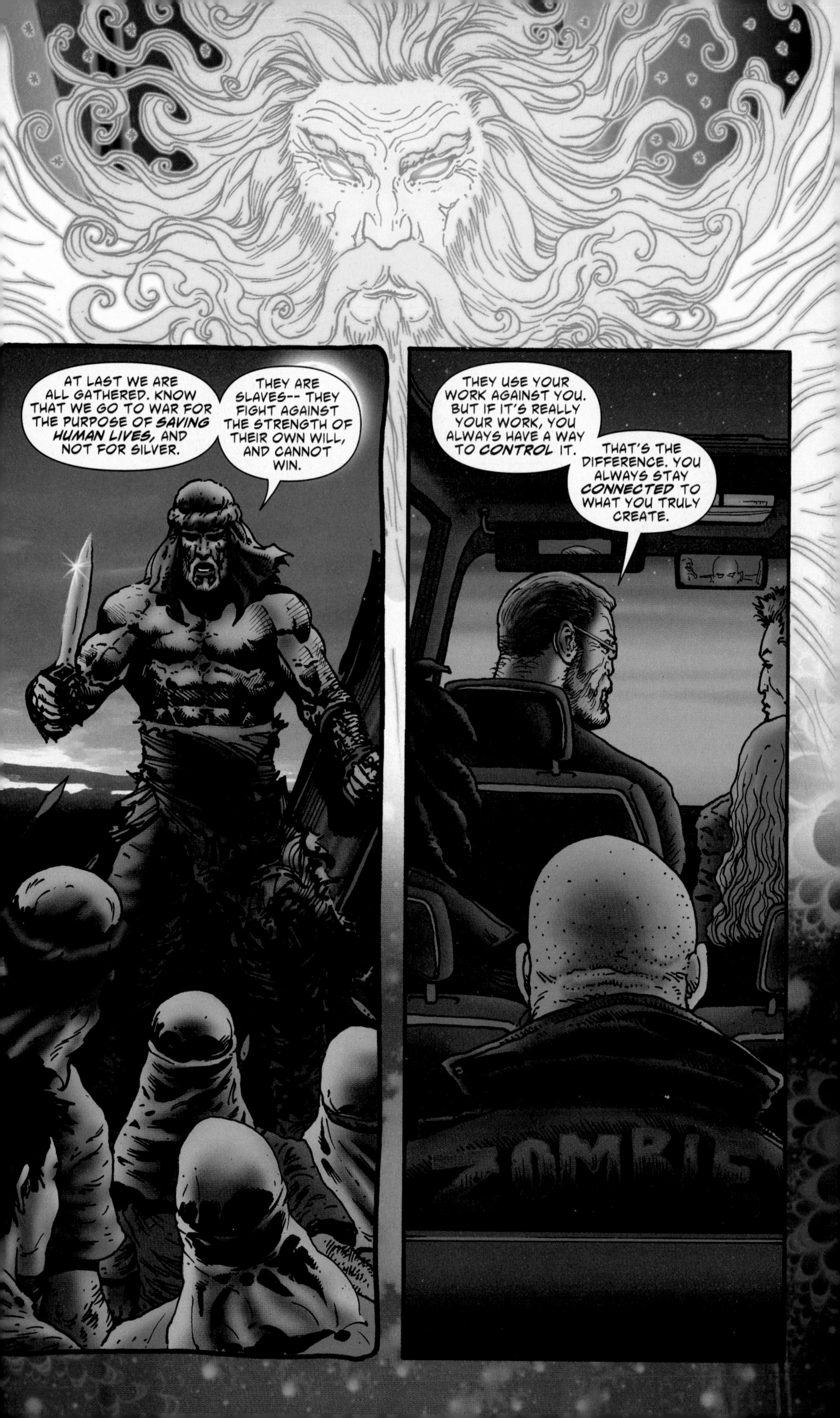
AT LAST WE ARE ALL GATHERED. KNOW THAT WE GO TO WAR FOR THE PURPOSE OF *SAVING HUMAN LIVES,* AND NOT FOR SILVER.
THEY ARE SLAVES-- THEY FIGHT AGAINST THE STRENGTH OF THEIR OWN WILL, AND CANNOT WIN.
THEY USE YOUR WORK AGAINST YOU. BUT IF IT'S REALLY YOUR WORK, YOU ALWAYS HAVE A WAY TO *CONTROL* IT.
THAT'S THE DIFFERENCE. YOU ALWAYS STAY *CONNECTED* TO WHAT YOU TRULY CREATE.
ZOMBIE

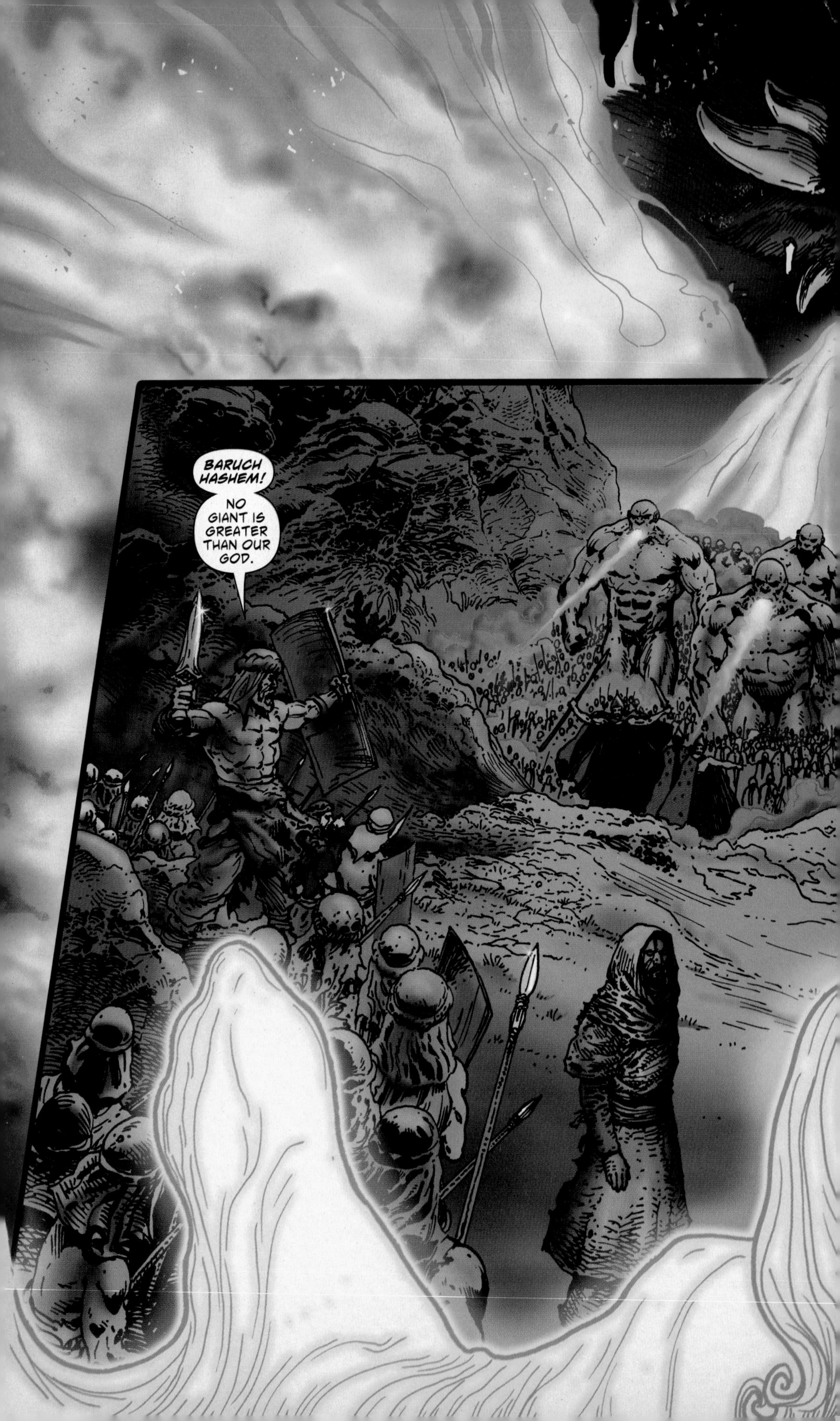
BARUCH HASHEM!
NO GIANT IS GREATER THAN OUR GOD.

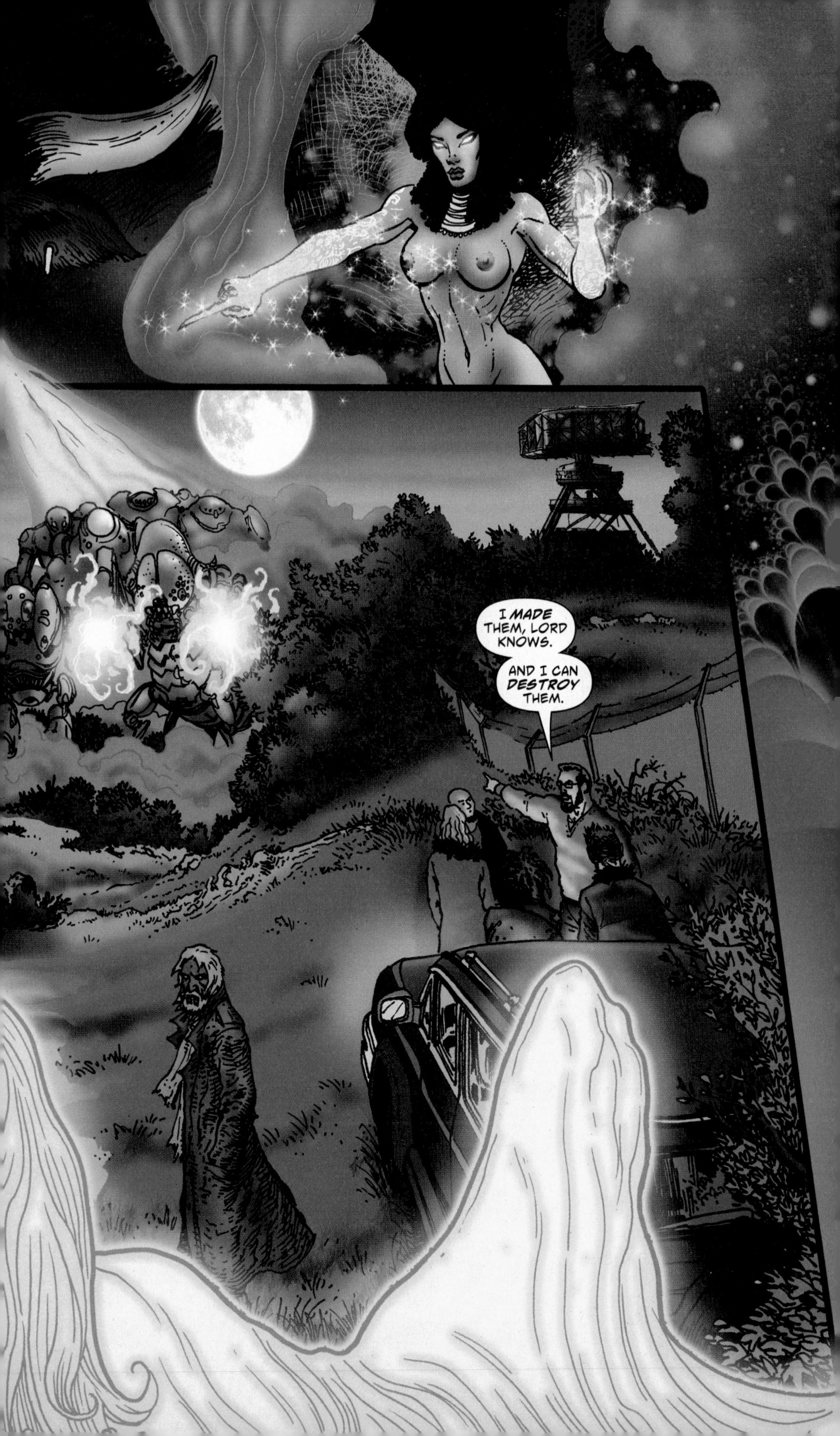
I MADE THEM, LORD KNOWS.
AND I CAN DESTROY THEM.

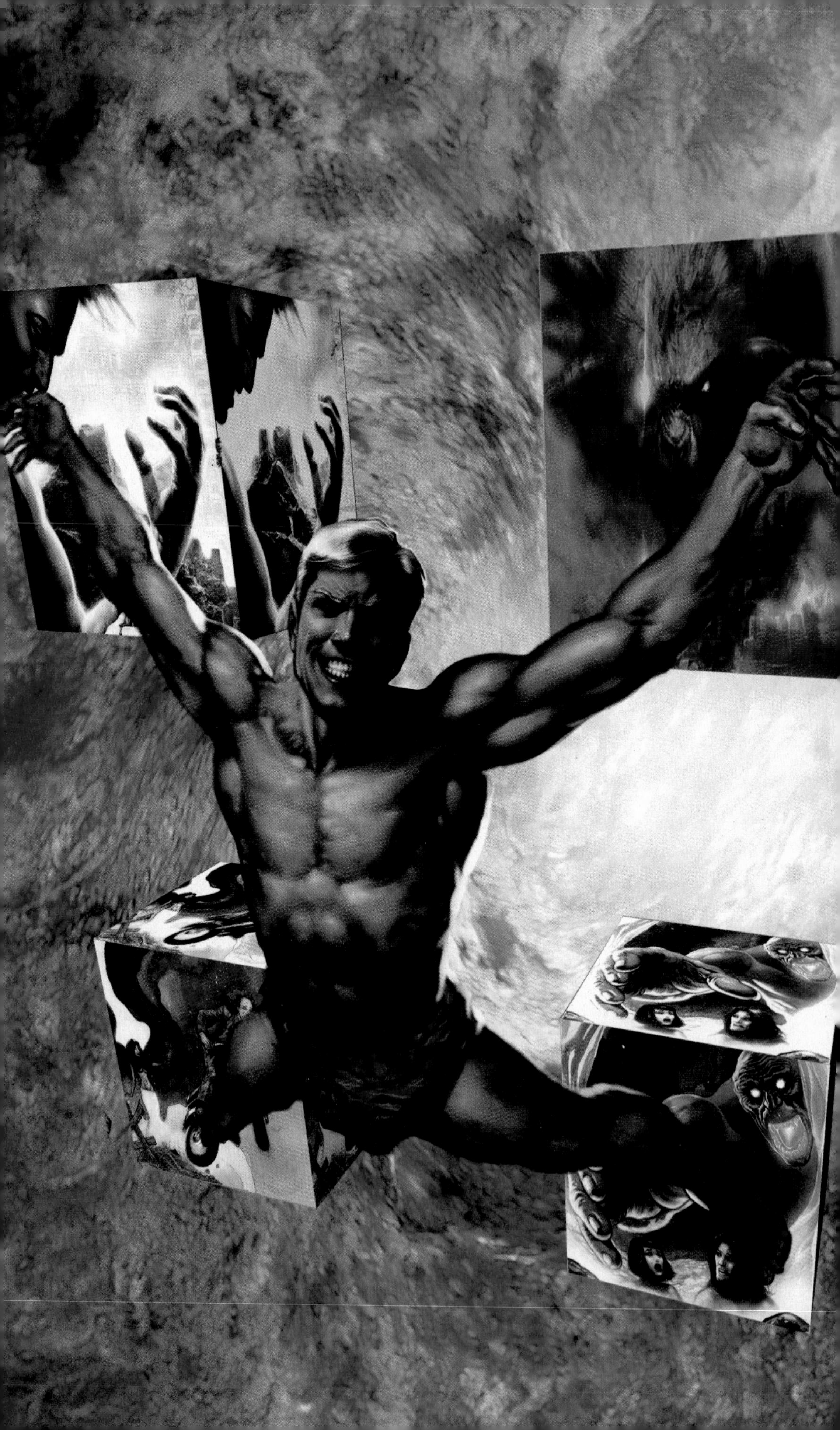

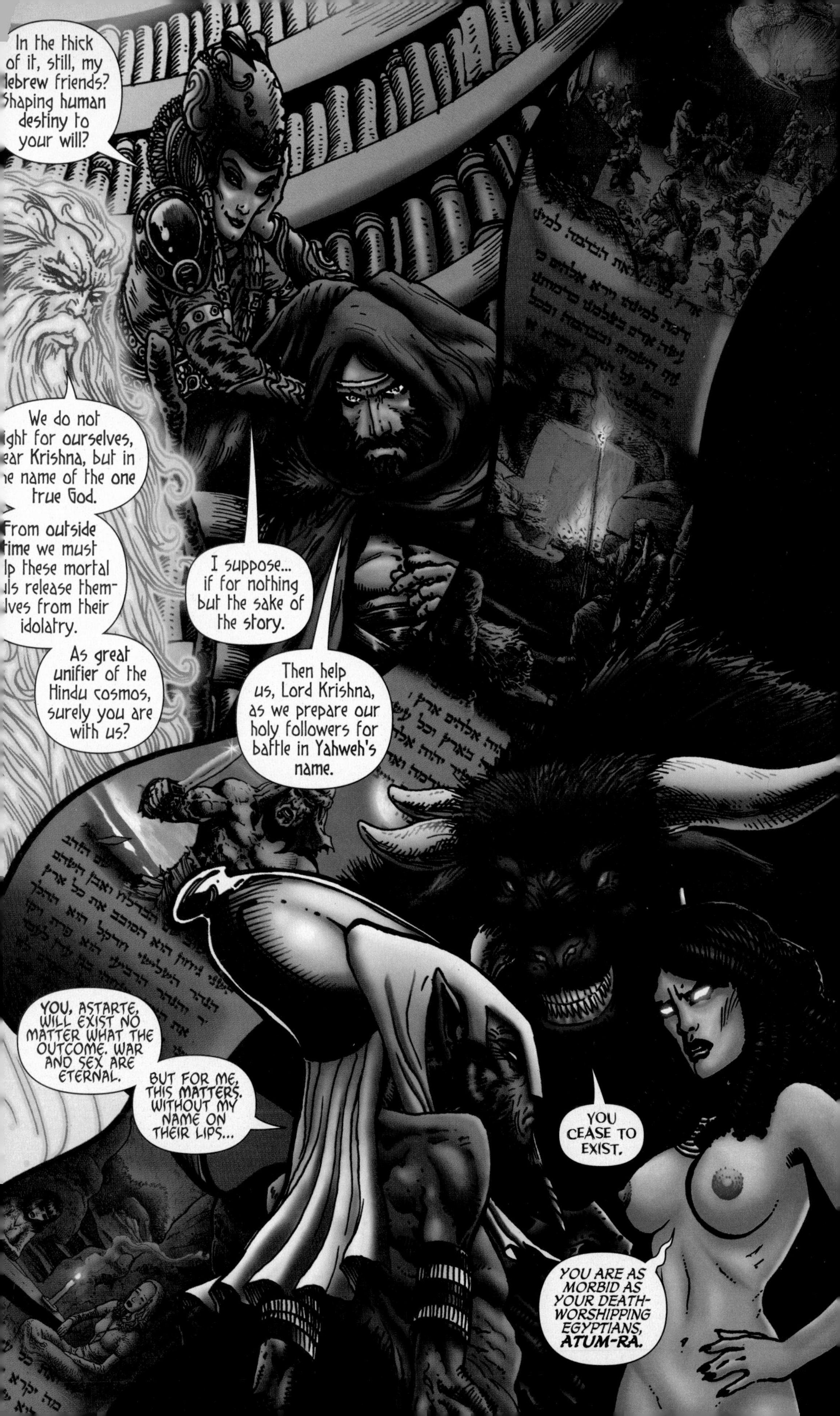
In the thick of it, still, my lebrew friends? Shaping human destiny to your will?
We do not ight for ourselves, ear Krishna, but in he name of the one true God.
From outside time we must lp these mortal uls release them- lves from their idolatry.
I suppose... if for nothing but the sake of the story.
As great unifier of the Hindu cosmos, surely you are with us?
Then help us, Lord Krishna, as we prepare our holy followers for battle in Yahweh's name.
YOU, ASTARTE, WILL EXIST NO MATTER WHAT THE OUTCOME. WAR AND SEX ARE ETERNAL.
BUT FOR ME, THIS MATTERS. WITHOUT MY NAME ON THEIR LIPS...
YOU CEASE TO EXIST.
YOU ARE AS MORBID AS YOUR DEATH-WORSHIPPING EGYPTIANS, **ATUM-RA.**

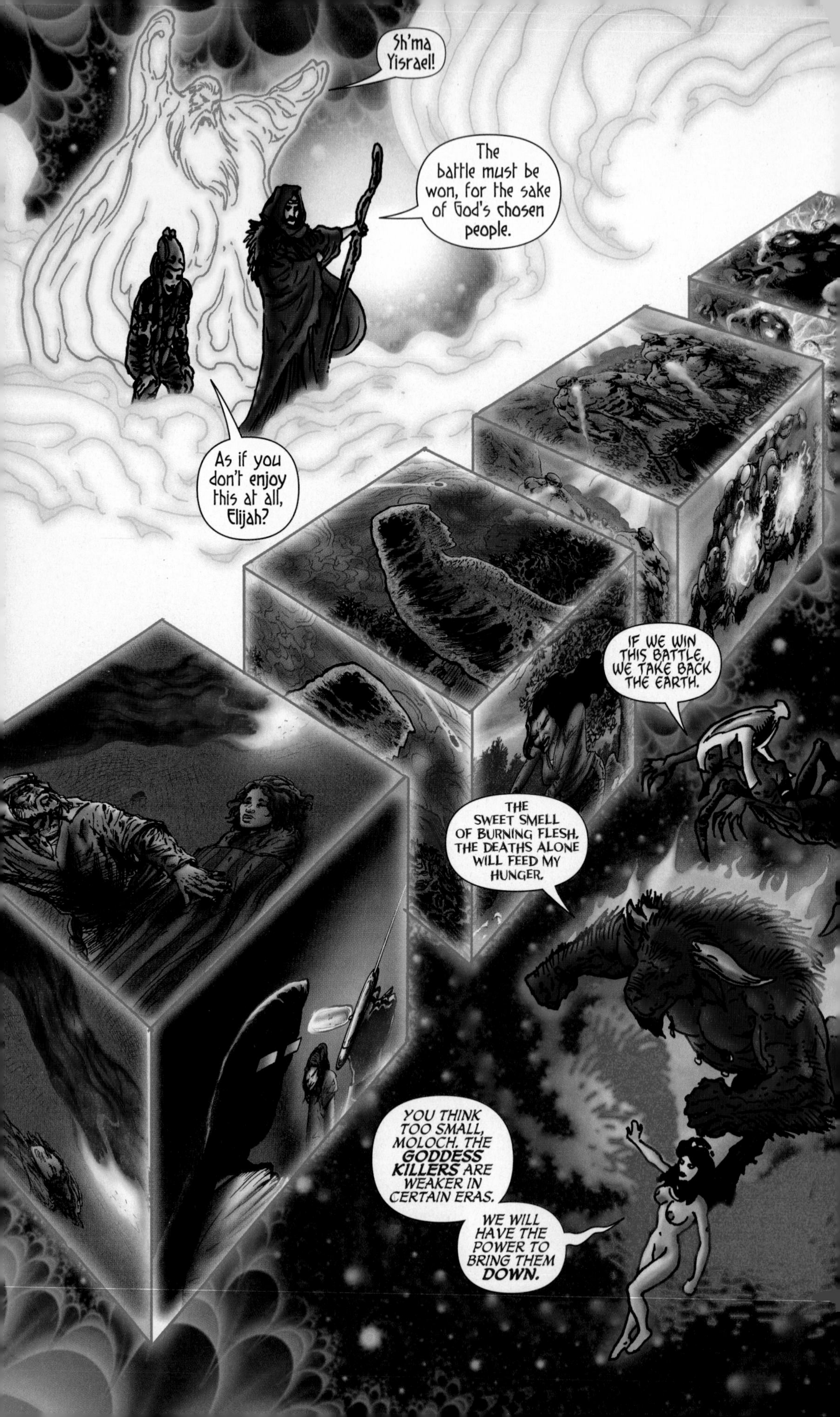

Sh'ma Yisrael!
The battle must be won, for the sake of God's chosen people.
As if you don't enjoy this at all, Elijah?
IF WE WIN THIS BATTLE, WE TAKE BACK THE EARTH.
THE SWEET SMELL OF BURNING FLESH. THE DEATHS ALONE WILL FEED MY HUNGER.
YOU THINK TOO SMALL, MOLOCH. THE **GODDESS KILLERS** ARE WEAKER IN CERTAIN ERAS.
WE WILL HAVE THE POWER TO BRING THEM **DOWN.**

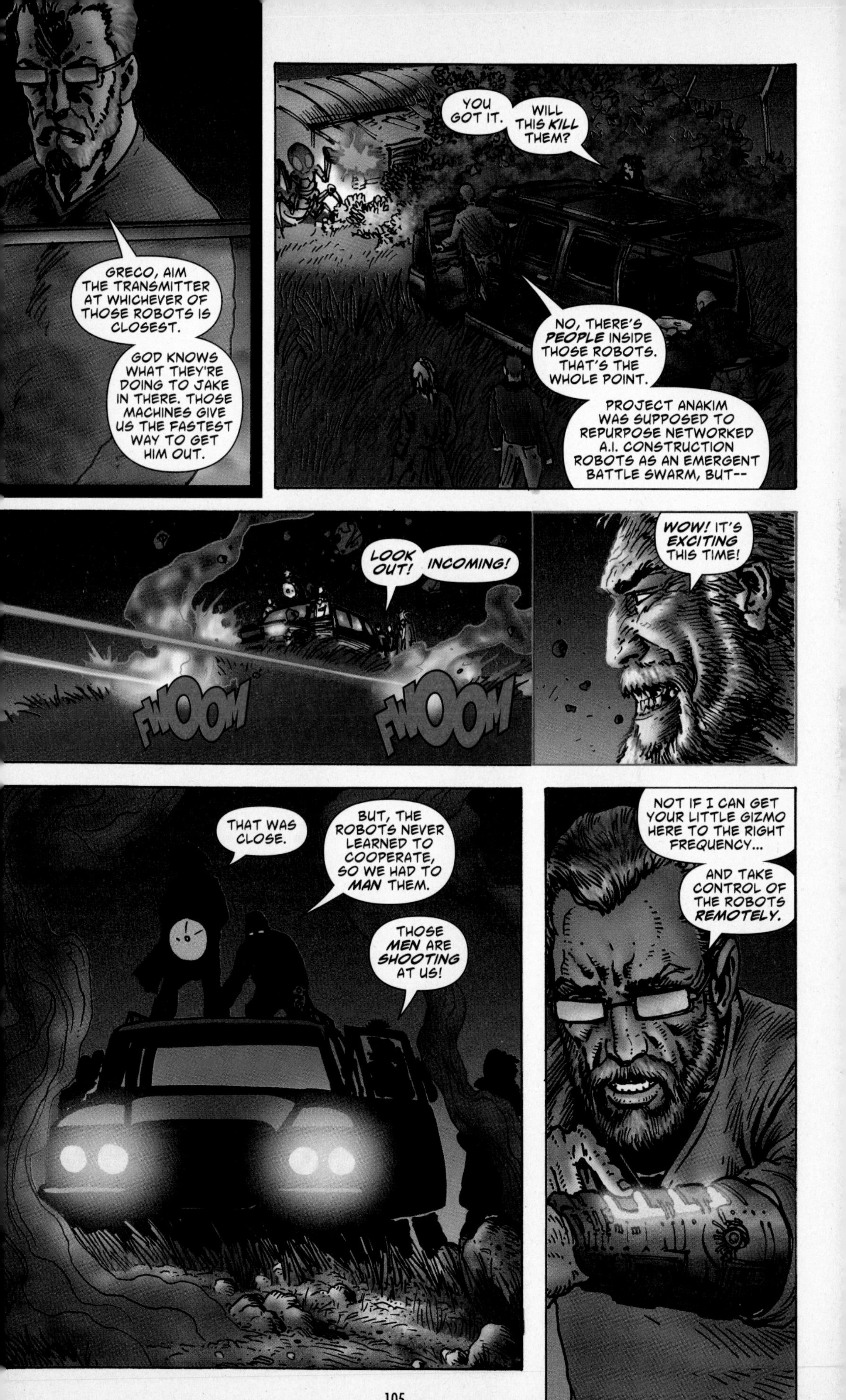
GRECO, AIM THE TRANSMITTER AT WHICHEVER OF THOSE ROBOTS IS CLOSEST.
GOD KNOWS WHAT THEY'RE DOING TO JAKE IN THERE. THOSE MACHINES GIVE US THE FASTEST WAY TO GET HIM OUT.
YOU GOT IT.
WILL THIS KILL THEM?
NO, THERE'S PEOPLE INSIDE THOSE ROBOTS. THAT'S THE WHOLE POINT.
PROJECT ANAKIM WAS SUPPOSED TO REPURPOSE NETWORKED A.I. CONSTRUCTION ROBOTS AS AN EMERGENT BATTLE SWARM, BUT--
LOOK OUT!
INCOMING!
FWOOM
FWOOM
WOW! IT'S EXCITING THIS TIME!
THAT WAS CLOSE.
BUT, THE ROBOTS NEVER LEARNED TO COOPERATE, SO WE HAD TO MAN THEM.
THOSE MEN ARE SHOOTING AT US!
NOT IF I CAN GET YOUR LITTLE GIZMO HERE TO THE RIGHT FREQUENCY...
AND TAKE CONTROL OF THE ROBOTS REMOTELY.

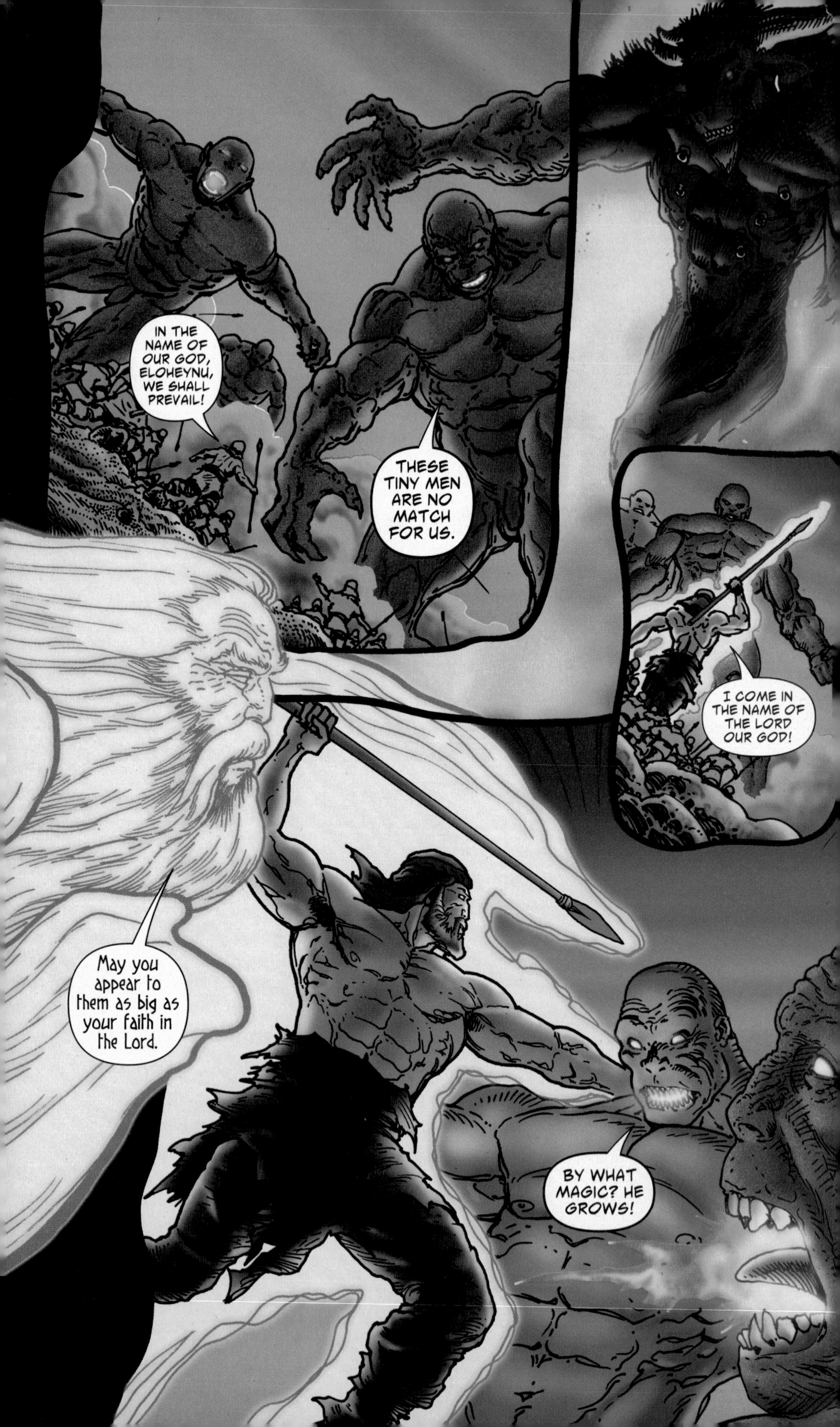
IN THE NAME OF OUR GOD, ELOHEYNU, WE SHALL PREVAIL!
THESE TINY MEN ARE NO MATCH FOR US.
I COME IN THE NAME OF THE LORD OUR GOD!
May you appear to them as big as your faith in the Lord.
BY WHAT MAGIC? HE GROWS!

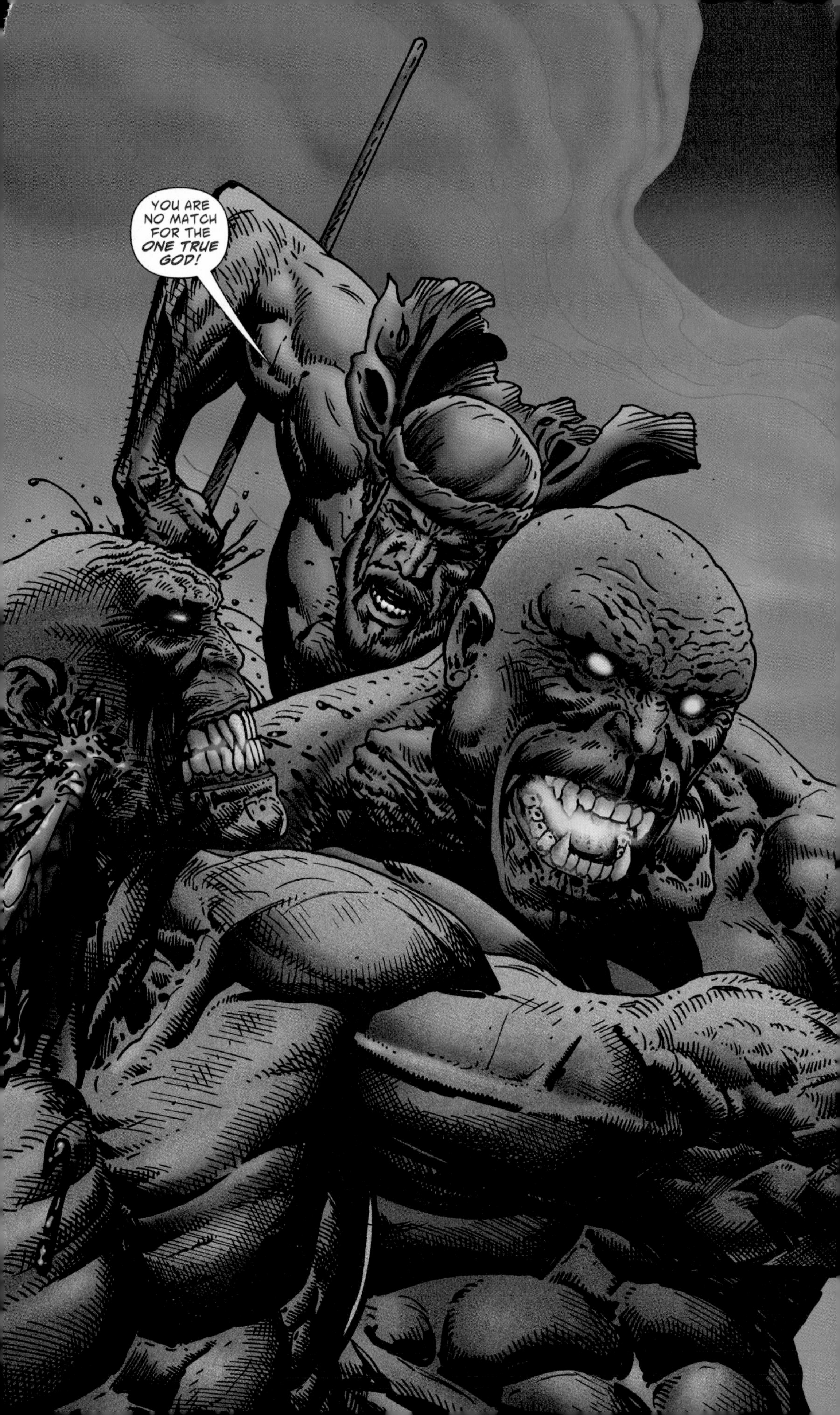
YOU ARE NO MATCH FOR THE ONE TRUE GOD!

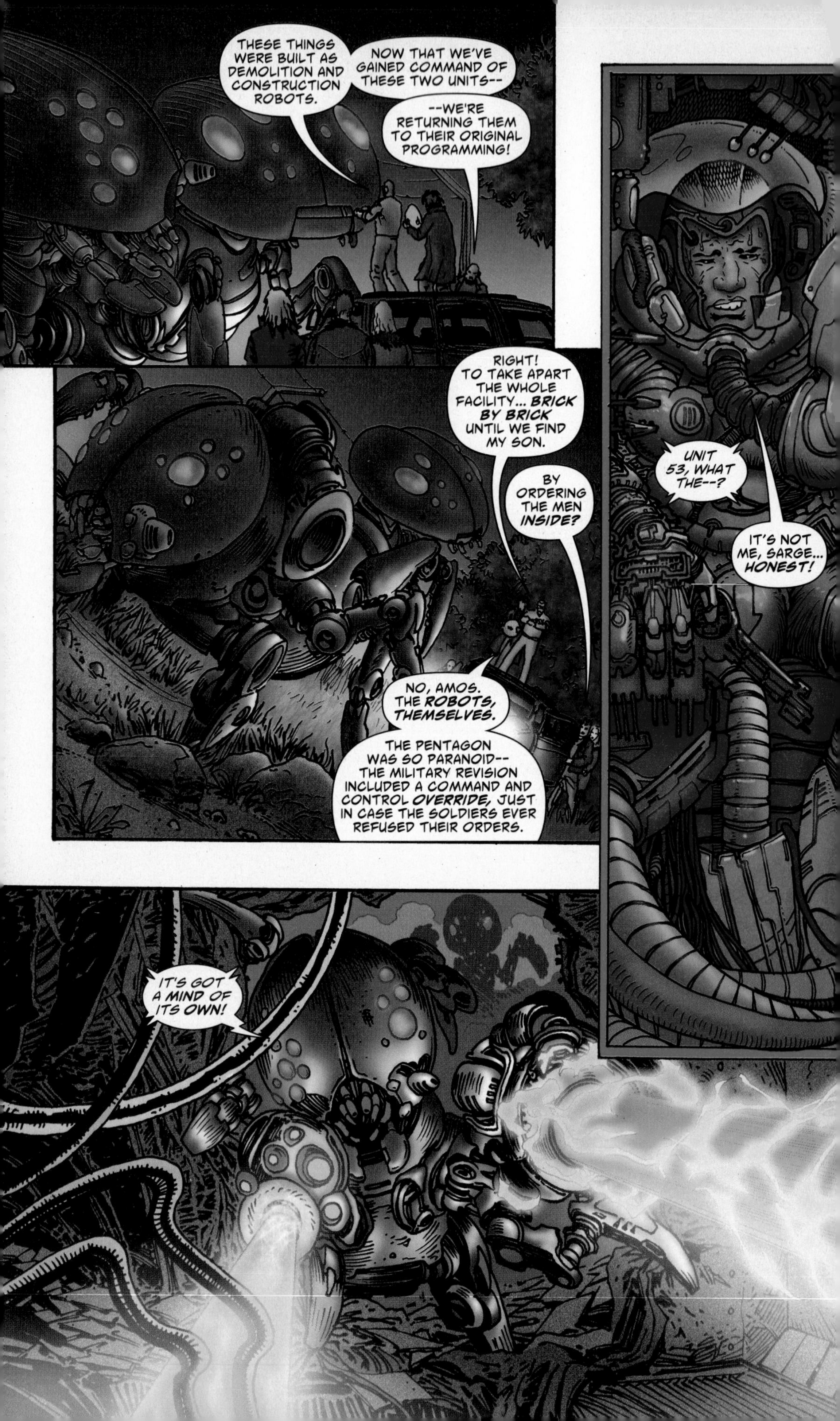
THESE THINGS WERE BUILT AS DEMOLITION AND CONSTRUCTION ROBOTS.
NOW THAT WE'VE GAINED COMMAND OF THESE TWO UNITS--
--WE'RE RETURNING THEM TO THEIR ORIGINAL PROGRAMMING!
RIGHT! TO TAKE APART THE WHOLE FACILITY... ***BRICK BY BRICK*** UNTIL WE FIND MY SON.
BY ORDERING THE MEN *INSIDE?*
NO, AMOS. THE ***ROBOTS, THEMSELVES.***
THE PENTAGON WAS SO PARANOID-- THE MILITARY REVISION INCLUDED A COMMAND AND CONTROL *OVERRIDE,* JUST IN CASE THE SOLDIERS EVER REFUSED THEIR ORDERS.
UNIT 53, WHAT THE--?
IT'S NOT ME, SARGE... ***HONEST!***
IT'S GOT A *MIND* OF ITS *OWN!*

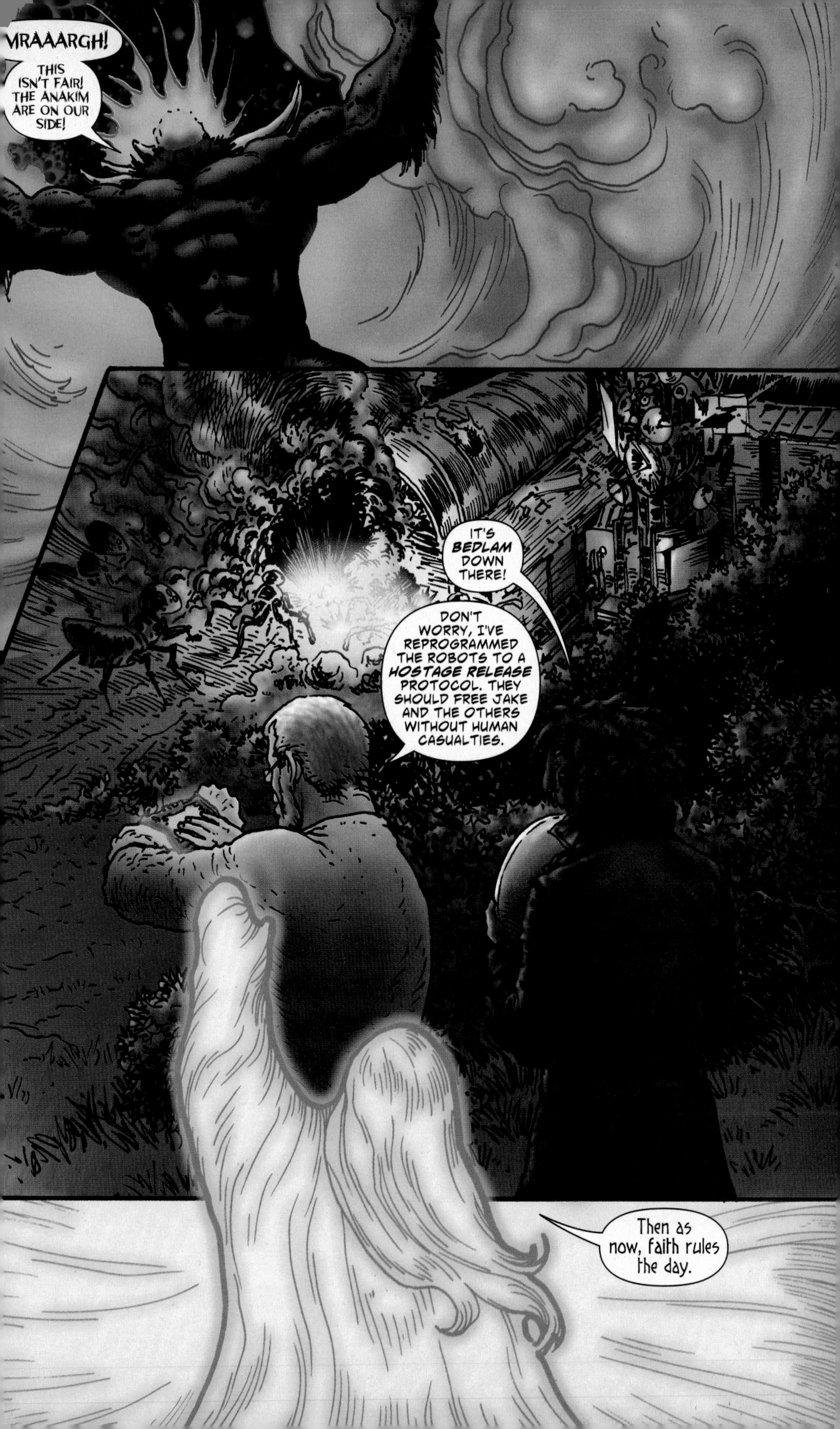
MRAAARGH!
THIS ISN'T FAIR! THE ANAKIM ARE ON OUR SIDE!
IT'S BEDLAM DOWN THERE!
DON'T WORRY, I'VE REPROGRAMMED THE ROBOTS TO A HOSTAGE RELEASE PROTOCOL. THEY SHOULD FREE JAKE AND THE OTHERS WITHOUT HUMAN CASUALTIES.
Then as now, faith rules the day.

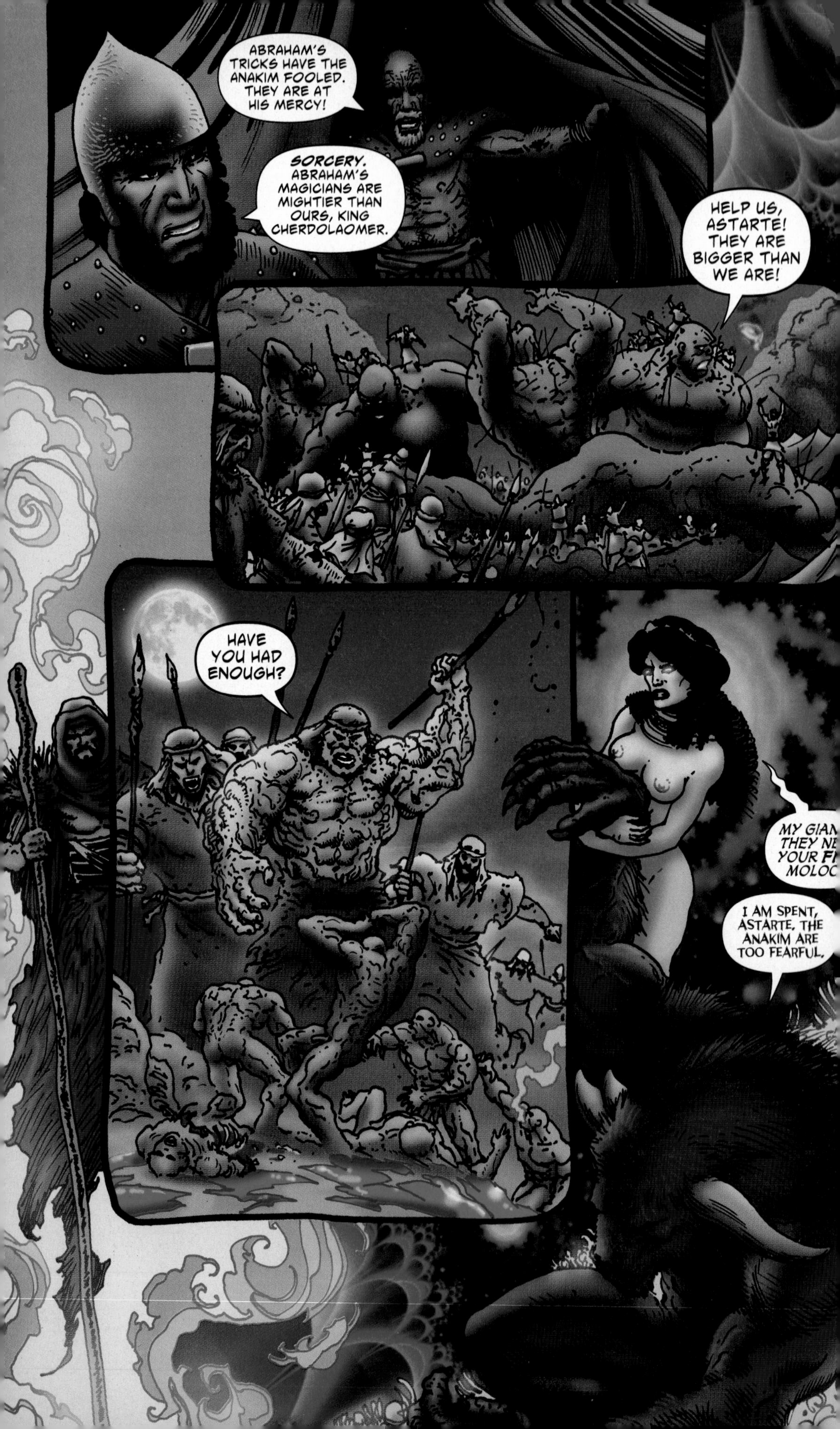
ABRAHAM'S TRICKS HAVE THE ANAKIM FOOLED. THEY ARE AT HIS MERCY!
SORCERY. ABRAHAM'S MAGICIANS ARE MIGHTIER THAN OURS, KING CHERDOLAOMER.
HELP US, ASTARTE! THEY ARE BIGGER THAN WE ARE!
HAVE YOU HAD ENOUGH?
MY GIAN THEY NE YOUR F MOLOC
I AM SPENT, ASTARTE. THE ANAKIM ARE TOO FEARFUL.

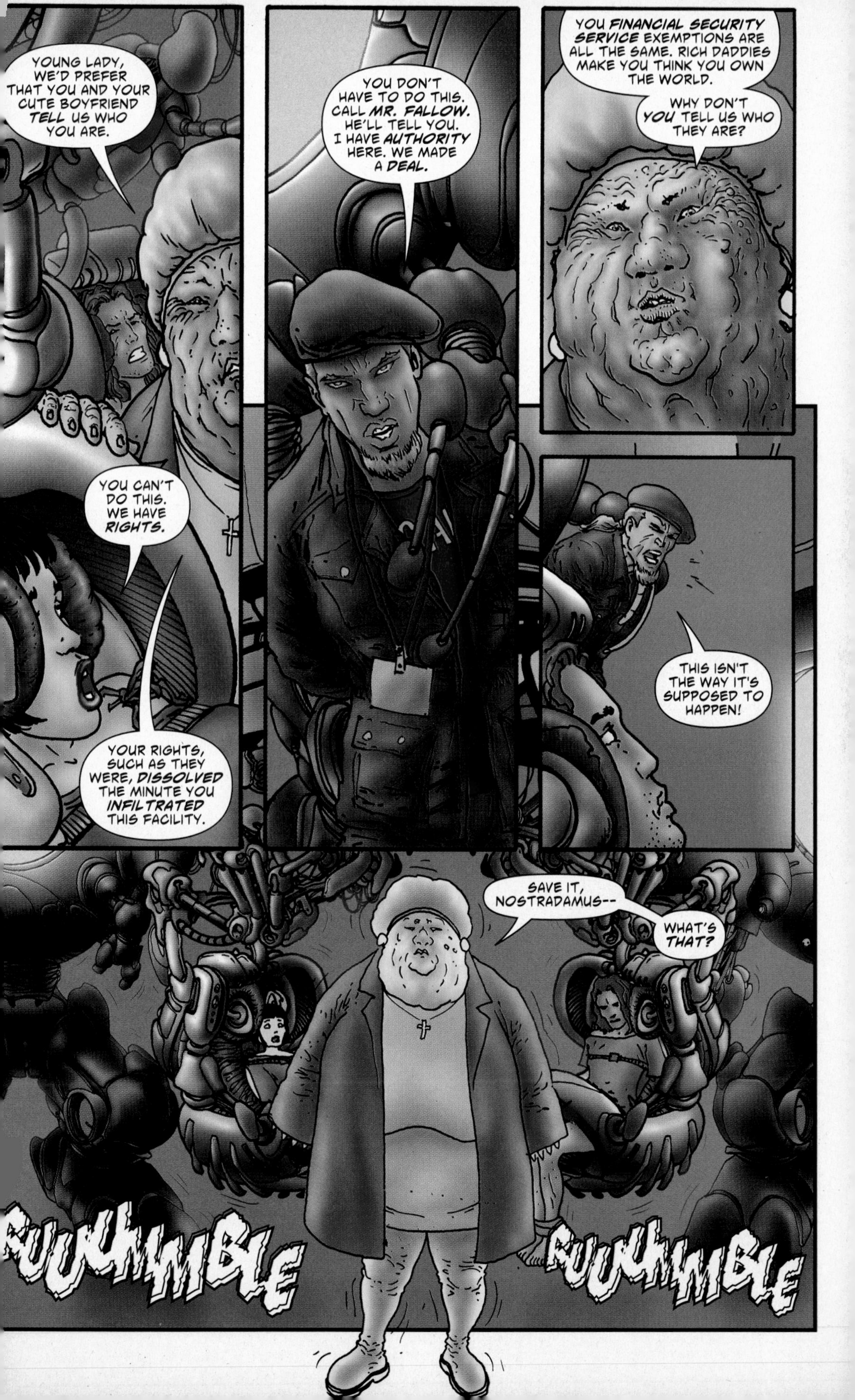
YOUNG LADY, WE'D PREFER THAT YOU AND YOUR CUTE BOYFRIEND TELL US WHO YOU ARE.
YOU CAN'T DO THIS. WE HAVE RIGHTS.
YOUR RIGHTS, SUCH AS THEY WERE, DISSOLVED THE MINUTE YOU INFILTRATED THIS FACILITY.
YOU DON'T HAVE TO DO THIS. CALL MR. FALLOW. HE'LL TELL YOU. I HAVE AUTHORITY HERE. WE MADE A DEAL.
YOU FINANCIAL SECURITY SERVICE EXEMPTIONS ARE ALL THE SAME. RICH DADDIES MAKE YOU THINK YOU OWN THE WORLD.
WHY DON'T YOU TELL US WHO THEY ARE?
THIS ISN'T THE WAY IT'S SUPPOSED TO HAPPEN!
SAVE IT, NOSTRADAMUS--
WHAT'S THAT?
RUUUMMBLE
RUUUMMBLE

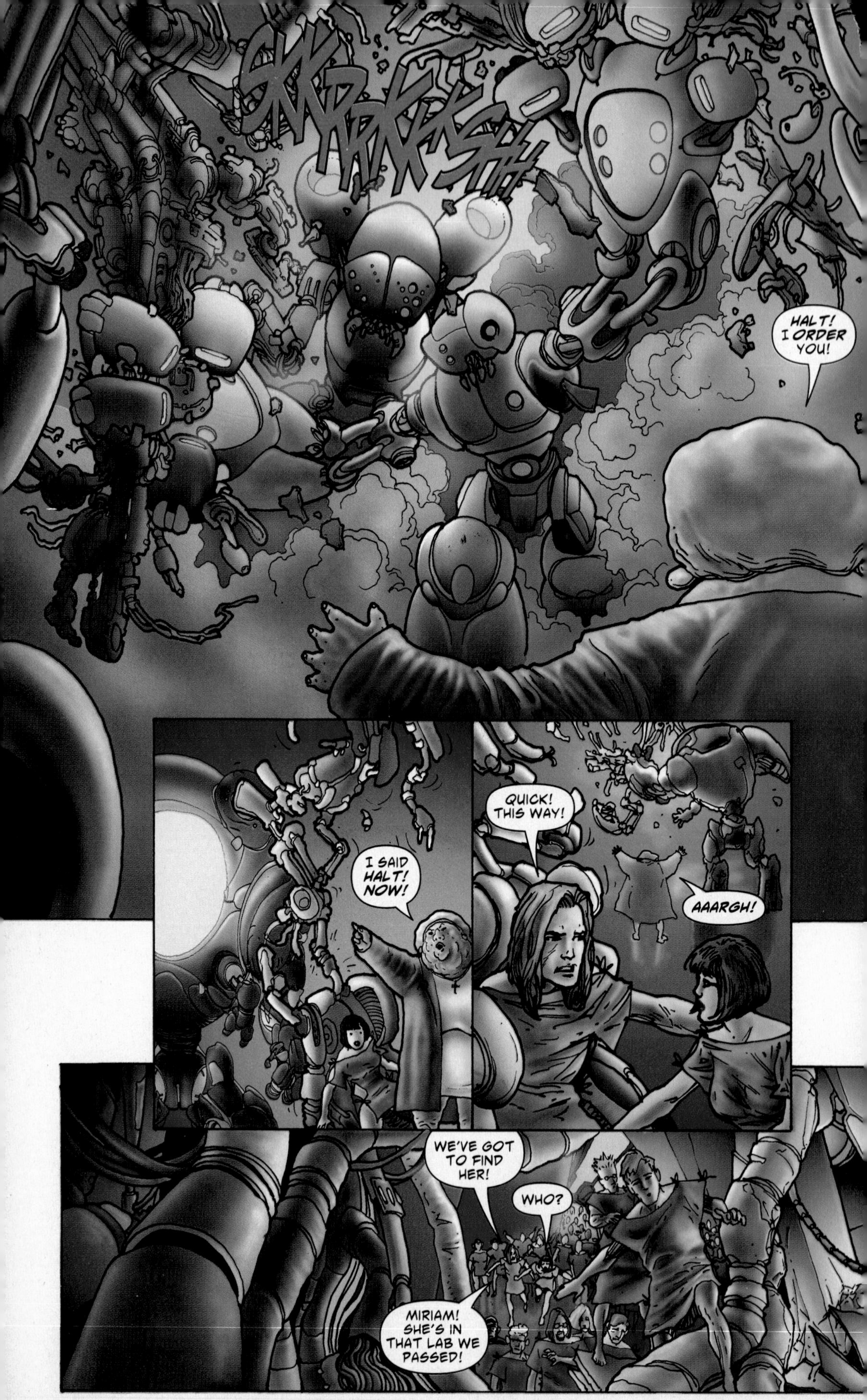
SKKRRKKSHH
HALT! I ORDER YOU!
I SAID HALT! NOW!
QUICK! THIS WAY!
AAARGH!
WE'VE GOT TO FIND HER!
WHO?
MIRIAM! SHE'S IN THAT LAB WE PASSED!

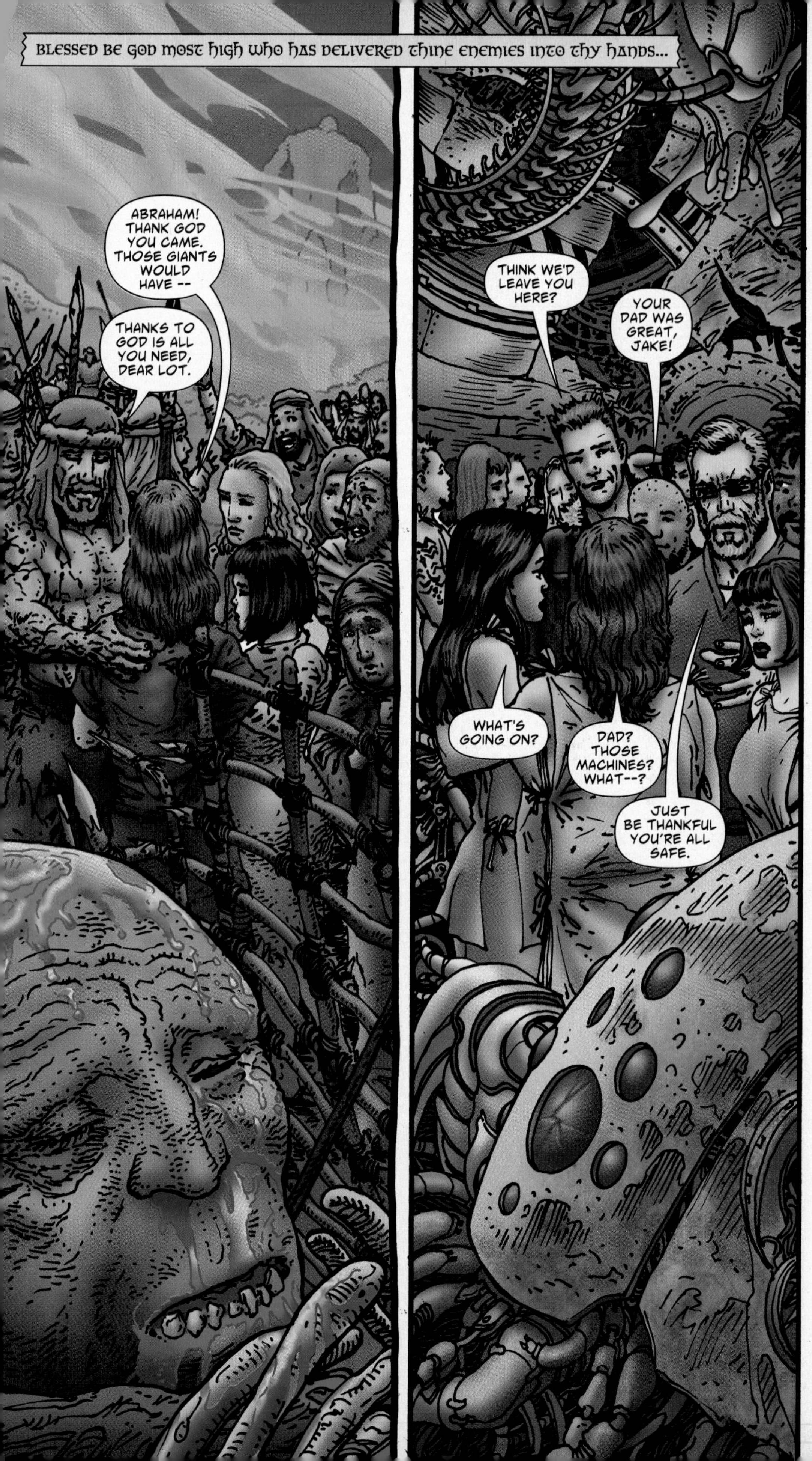
BLESSED BE GOD MOST HIGH WHO HAS DELIVERED THINE ENEMIES INTO THY HANDS...
ABRAHAM! THANK GOD YOU CAME. THOSE GIANTS WOULD HAVE --
THANKS TO GOD IS ALL YOU NEED, DEAR LOT.
THINK WE'D LEAVE YOU HERE?
YOUR DAD WAS GREAT, JAKE!
WHAT'S GOING ON?
DAD? THOSE MACHINES? WHAT--?
JUST BE THANKFUL YOU'RE ALL SAFE.

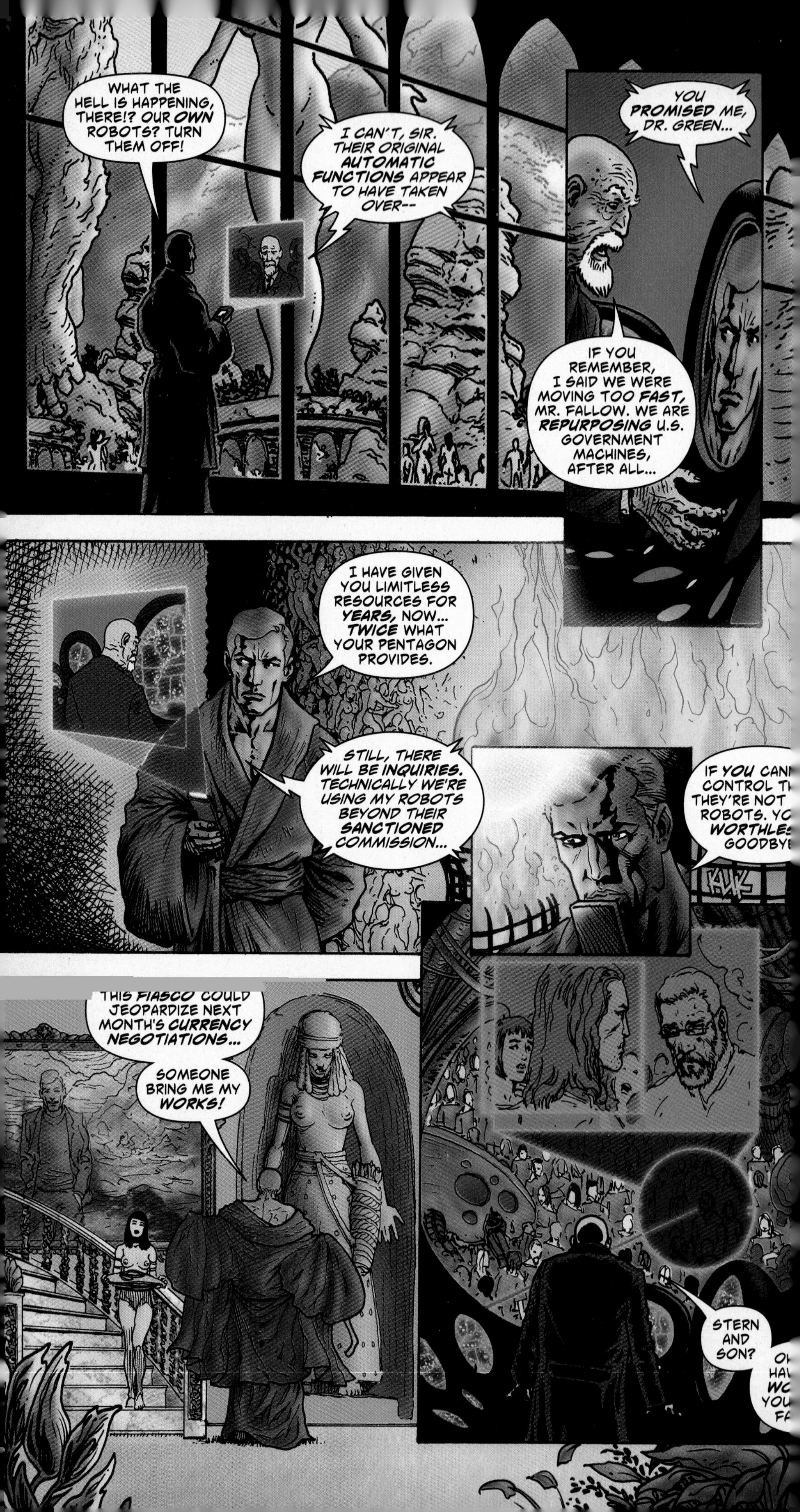
WHAT THE HELL IS HAPPENING, THERE!? OUR OWN ROBOTS? TURN THEM OFF!
I CAN'T, SIR. THEIR ORIGINAL AUTOMATIC FUNCTIONS APPEAR TO HAVE TAKEN OVER--
YOU PROMISED ME, DR. GREEN...
IF YOU REMEMBER, I SAID WE WERE MOVING TOO FAST, MR. FALLOW. WE ARE REPURPOSING U.S. GOVERNMENT MACHINES, AFTER ALL...
I HAVE GIVEN YOU LIMITLESS RESOURCES FOR YEARS, NOW... TWICE WHAT YOUR PENTAGON PROVIDES.
STILL, THERE WILL BE INQUIRIES. TECHNICALLY WE'RE USING MY ROBOTS BEYOND THEIR SANCTIONED COMMISSION...
IF YOU CANN CONTROL TH THEY'RE NOT ROBOTS. YO WORTHLES GOODBYE
THIS FIASCO COULD JEOPARDIZE NEXT MONTH'S CURRENCY NEGOTIATIONS...
SOMEONE BRING ME MY WORKS!
STERN AND SON?
OH HAV WO YOU FA

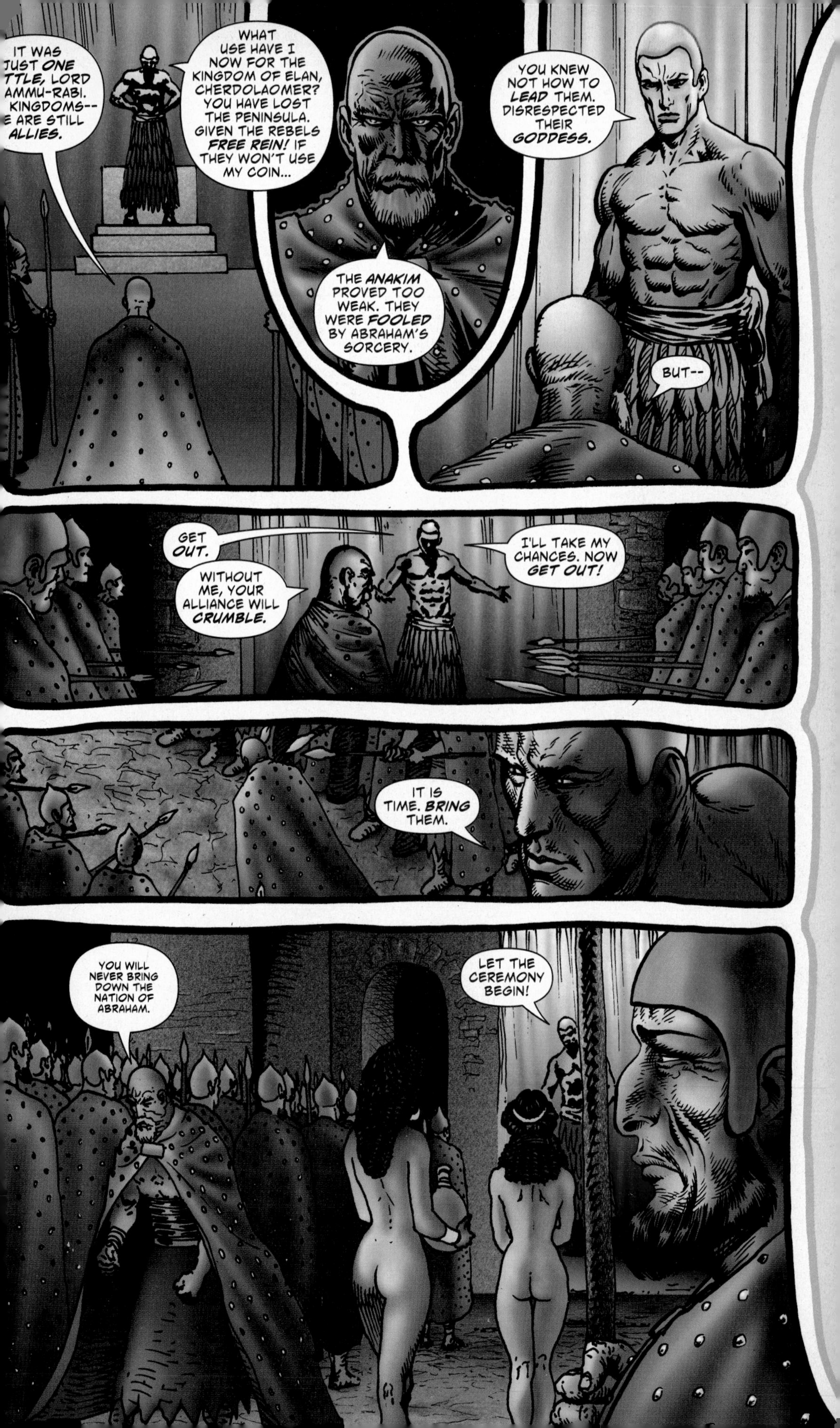

IT WAS JUST ONE TTLE, LORD AMMU-RABI. KINGDOMS-- E ARE STILL ALLIES.
WHAT USE HAVE I NOW FOR THE KINGDOM OF ELAN, CHERDOLAOMER? YOU HAVE LOST THE PENINSULA. GIVEN THE REBELS FREE REIN! IF THEY WON'T USE MY COIN...
THE ANAKIM PROVED TOO WEAK. THEY WERE FOOLED BY ABRAHAM'S SORCERY.
YOU KNEW NOT HOW TO LEAD THEM. DISRESPECTED THEIR GODDESS.
BUT--
GET OUT.
WITHOUT ME, YOUR ALLIANCE WILL CRUMBLE.
I'LL TAKE MY CHANCES. NOW GET OUT!
IT IS TIME. BRING THEM.
YOU WILL NEVER BRING DOWN THE NATION OF ABRAHAM.
LET THE CEREMONY BEGIN!

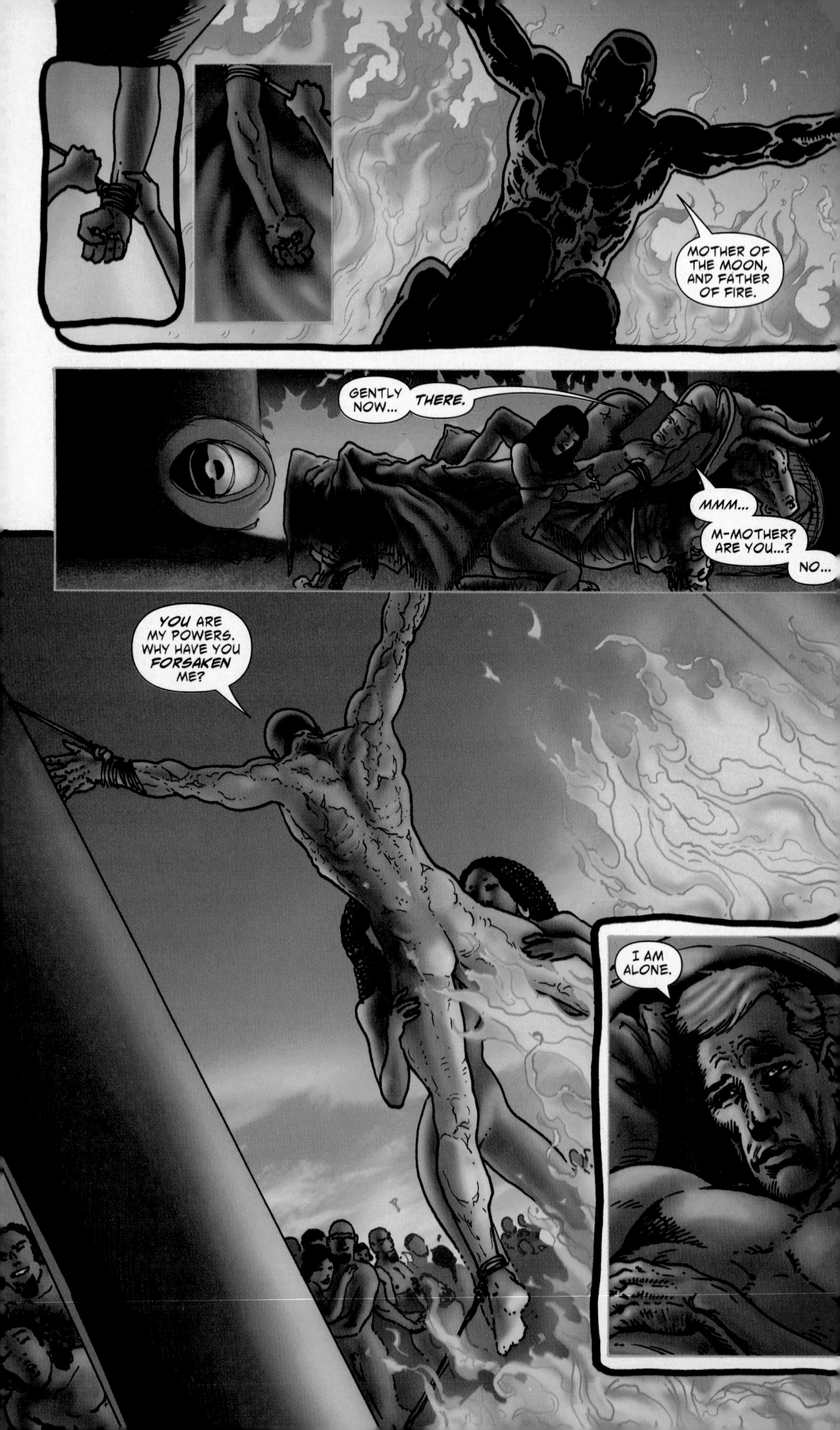
MOTHER OF THE MOON, AND FATHER OF FIRE.
GENTLY NOW...
THERE.
MMM...
M-MOTHER? ARE YOU...?
NO...
YOU ARE MY POWERS. WHY HAVE YOU FORSAKEN ME?
I AM ALONE.

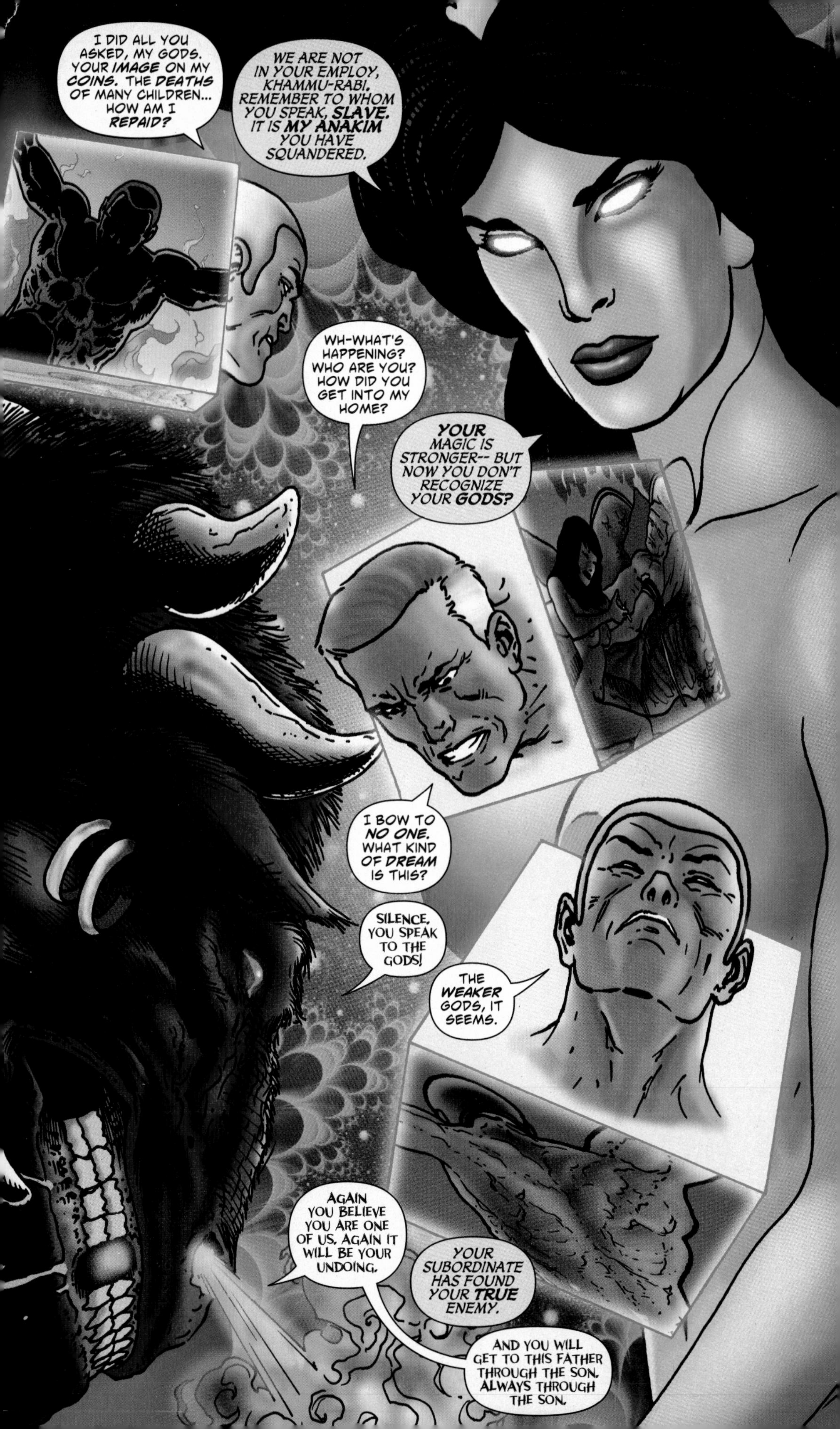
I DID ALL YOU ASKED, MY GODS. YOUR IMAGE ON MY COINS. THE DEATHS OF MANY CHILDREN... HOW AM I REPAID?
WE ARE NOT IN YOUR EMPLOY, KHAMMU-RABI. REMEMBER TO WHOM YOU SPEAK, SLAVE. IT IS MY ANAKIM YOU HAVE SQUANDERED.
WH-WHAT'S HAPPENING? WHO ARE YOU? HOW DID YOU GET INTO MY HOME?
YOUR MAGIC IS STRONGER-- BUT NOW YOU DON'T RECOGNIZE YOUR GODS?
I BOW TO NO ONE. WHAT KIND OF DREAM IS THIS?
SILENCE. YOU SPEAK TO THE GODS!
THE WEAKER GODS, IT SEEMS.
AGAIN YOU BELIEVE YOU ARE ONE OF US. AGAIN IT WILL BE YOUR UNDOING.
YOUR SUBORDINATE HAS FOUND YOUR TRUE ENEMY.
AND YOU WILL GET TO THIS FATHER THROUGH THE SON. ALWAYS THROUGH THE SON.

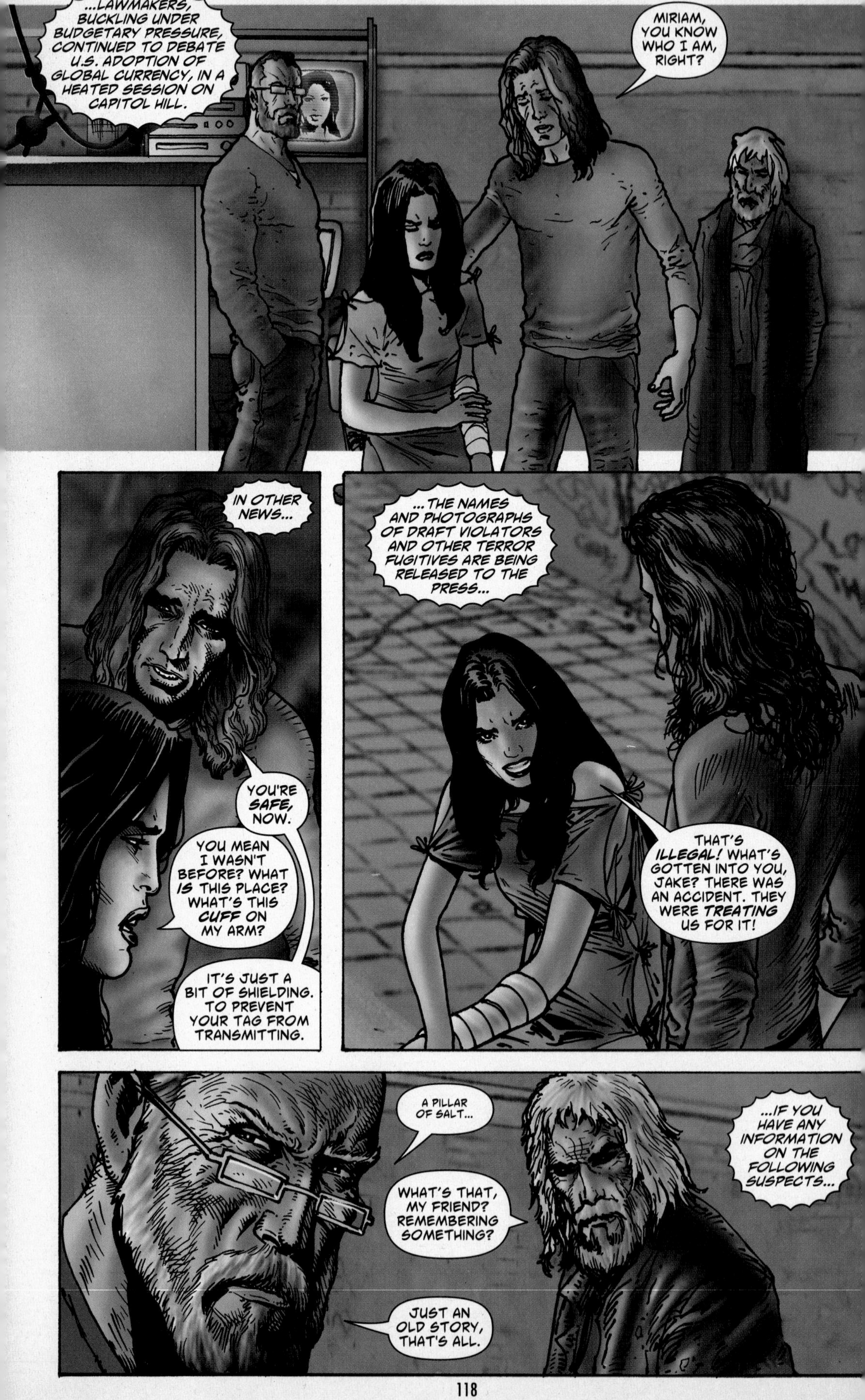
...LAWMAKERS, BUCKLING UNDER BUDGETARY PRESSURE, CONTINUED TO DEBATE U.S. ADOPTION OF GLOBAL CURRENCY, IN A HEATED SESSION ON CAPITOL HILL.
MIRIAM, YOU KNOW WHO I AM, RIGHT?
IN OTHER NEWS...
YOU'RE SAFE, NOW.
YOU MEAN I WASN'T BEFORE? WHAT IS THIS PLACE? WHAT'S THIS CUFF ON MY ARM?
IT'S JUST A BIT OF SHIELDING. TO PREVENT YOUR TAG FROM TRANSMITTING.
...THE NAMES AND PHOTOGRAPHS OF DRAFT VIOLATORS AND OTHER TERROR FUGITIVES ARE BEING RELEASED TO THE PRESS...
THAT'S ILLEGAL! WHAT'S GOTTEN INTO YOU, JAKE? THERE WAS AN ACCIDENT. THEY WERE TREATING US FOR IT!
A PILLAR OF SALT...
WHAT'S THAT, MY FRIEND? REMEMBERING SOMETHING?
JUST AN OLD STORY, THAT'S ALL.
...IF YOU HAVE ANY INFORMATION ON THE FOLLOWING SUSPECTS...

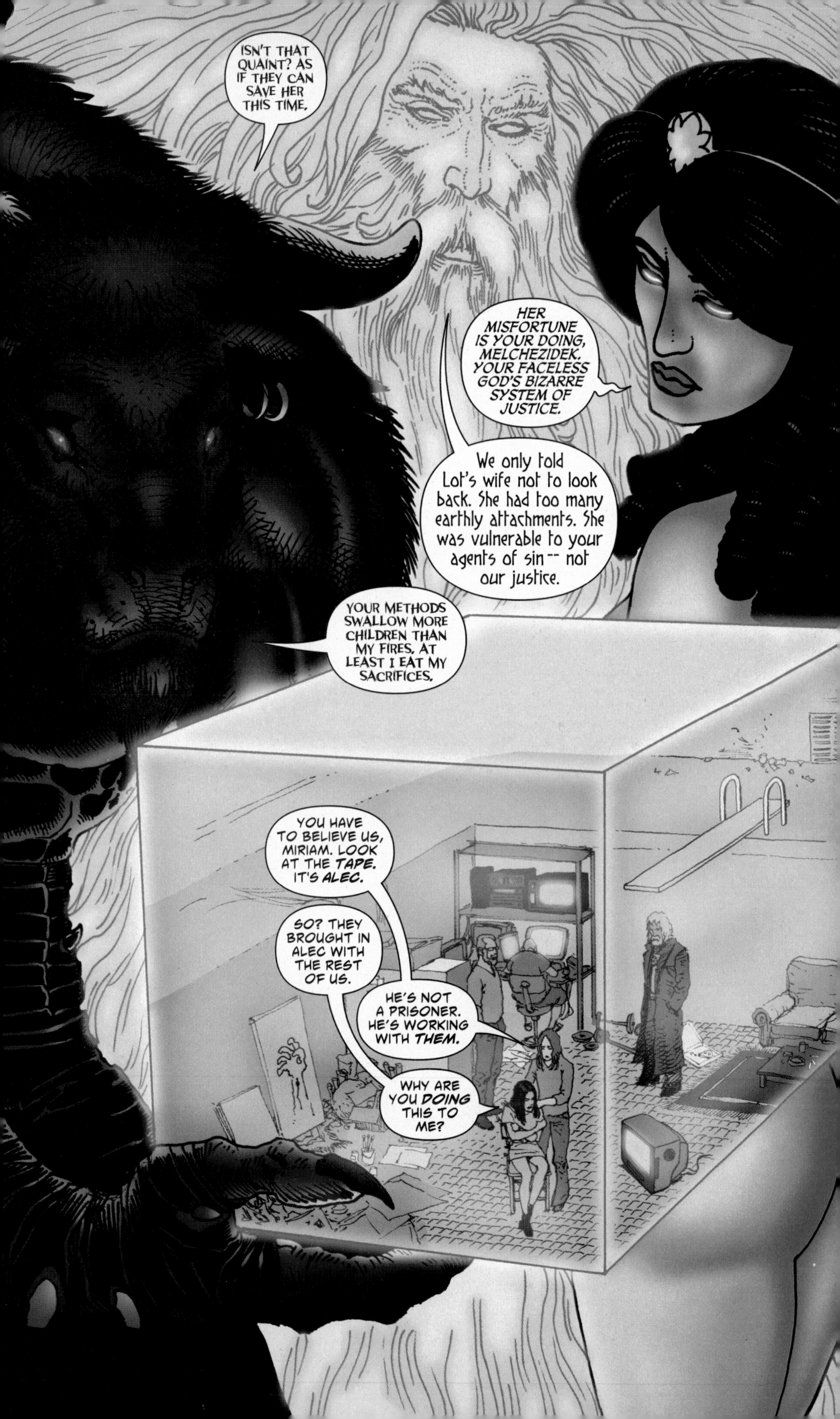
ISN'T THAT QUAINT? AS IF THEY CAN SAVE HER THIS TIME.
HER MISFORTUNE IS YOUR DOING, MELCHEZIDEK. YOUR FACELESS GOD'S BIZARRE SYSTEM OF JUSTICE.
We only told Lot's wife not to look back. She had too many earthly attachments. She was vulnerable to your agents of sin-- not our justice.
YOUR METHODS SWALLOW MORE CHILDREN THAN MY FIRES. AT LEAST I EAT MY SACRIFICES.
YOU HAVE TO BELIEVE US, MIRIAM. LOOK AT THE TAPE. IT'S ALEC.
SO? THEY BROUGHT IN ALEC WITH THE REST OF US.
HE'S NOT A PRISONER. HE'S WORKING WITH THEM.
WHY ARE YOU DOING THIS TO ME?

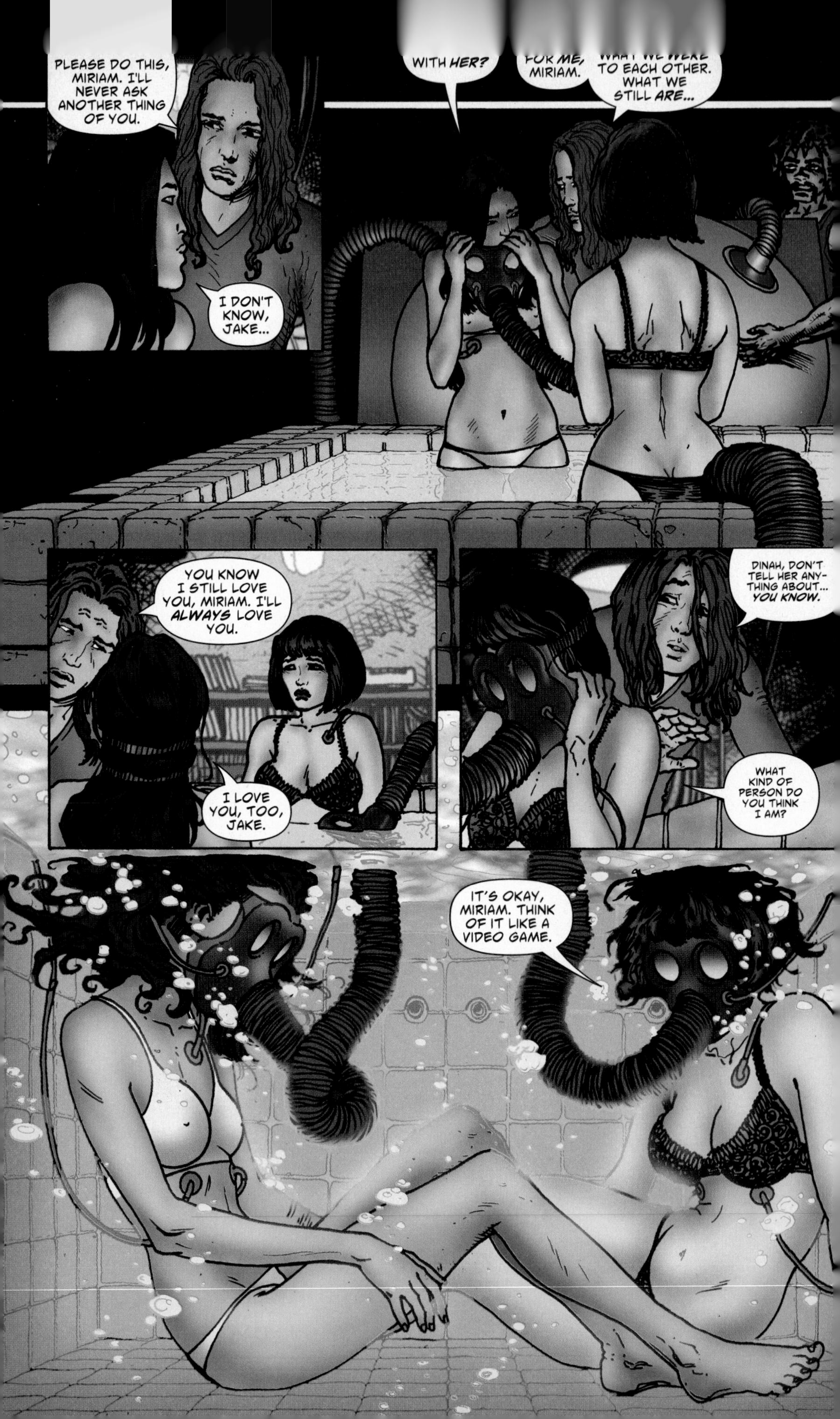
PLEASE DO THIS, MIRIAM. I'LL NEVER ASK ANOTHER THING OF YOU.
I DON'T KNOW, JAKE...
WITH HER?
MIRIAM.
TO EACH OTHER. WHAT WE STILL ARE...
YOU KNOW I STILL LOVE YOU, MIRIAM. I'LL ALWAYS LOVE YOU.
I LOVE YOU, TOO, JAKE.
DINAH, DON'T TELL HER ANY-THING ABOUT... YOU KNOW.
WHAT KIND OF PERSON DO YOU THINK I AM?
IT'S OKAY, MIRIAM. THINK OF IT LIKE A VIDEO GAME.

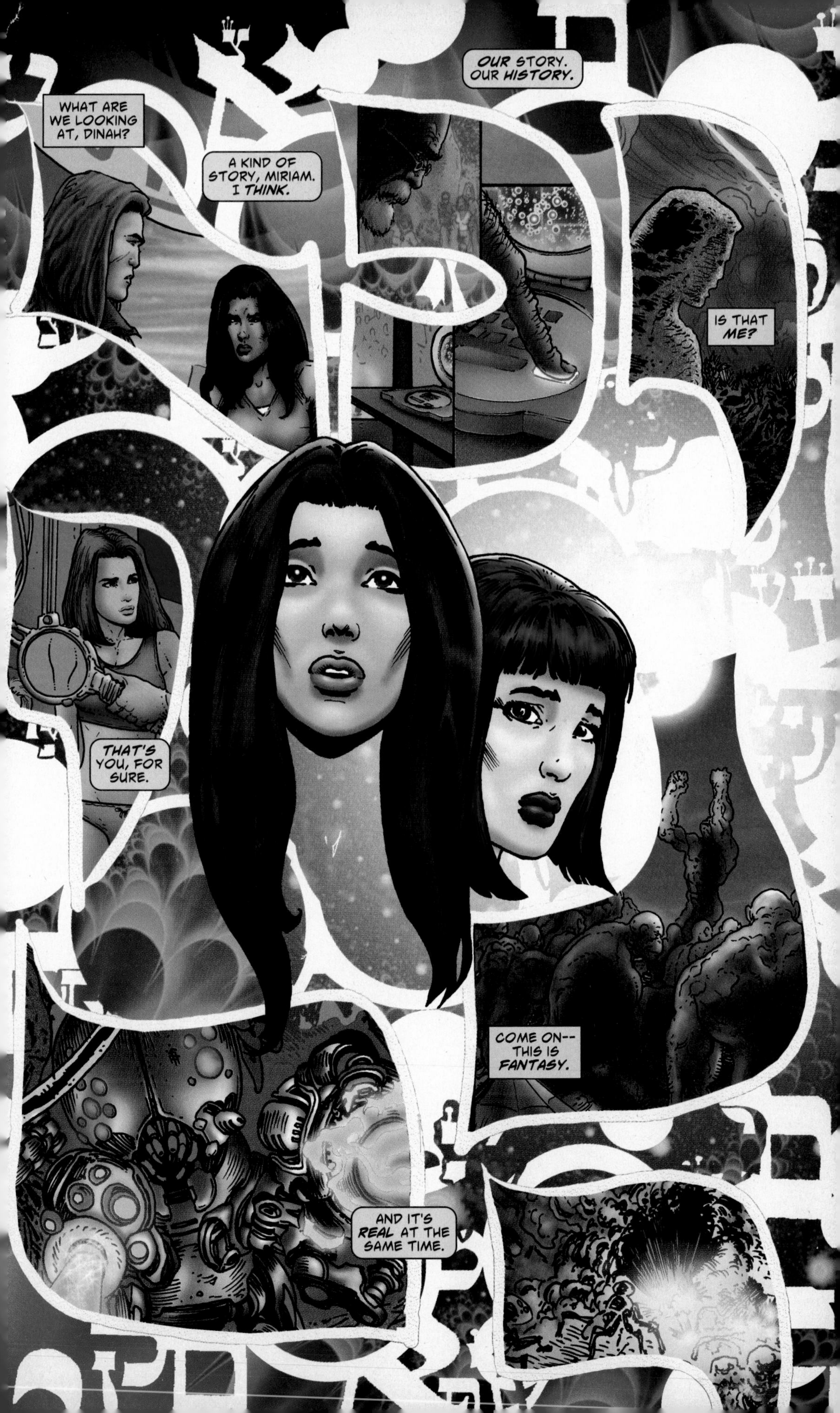
WHAT ARE WE LOOKING AT, DINAH?
A KIND OF STORY, MIRIAM. I THINK.
OUR STORY. OUR HISTORY.
IS THAT ME?
THAT'S YOU, FOR SURE.
COME ON-- THIS IS FANTASY.
AND IT'S REAL AT THE SAME TIME.

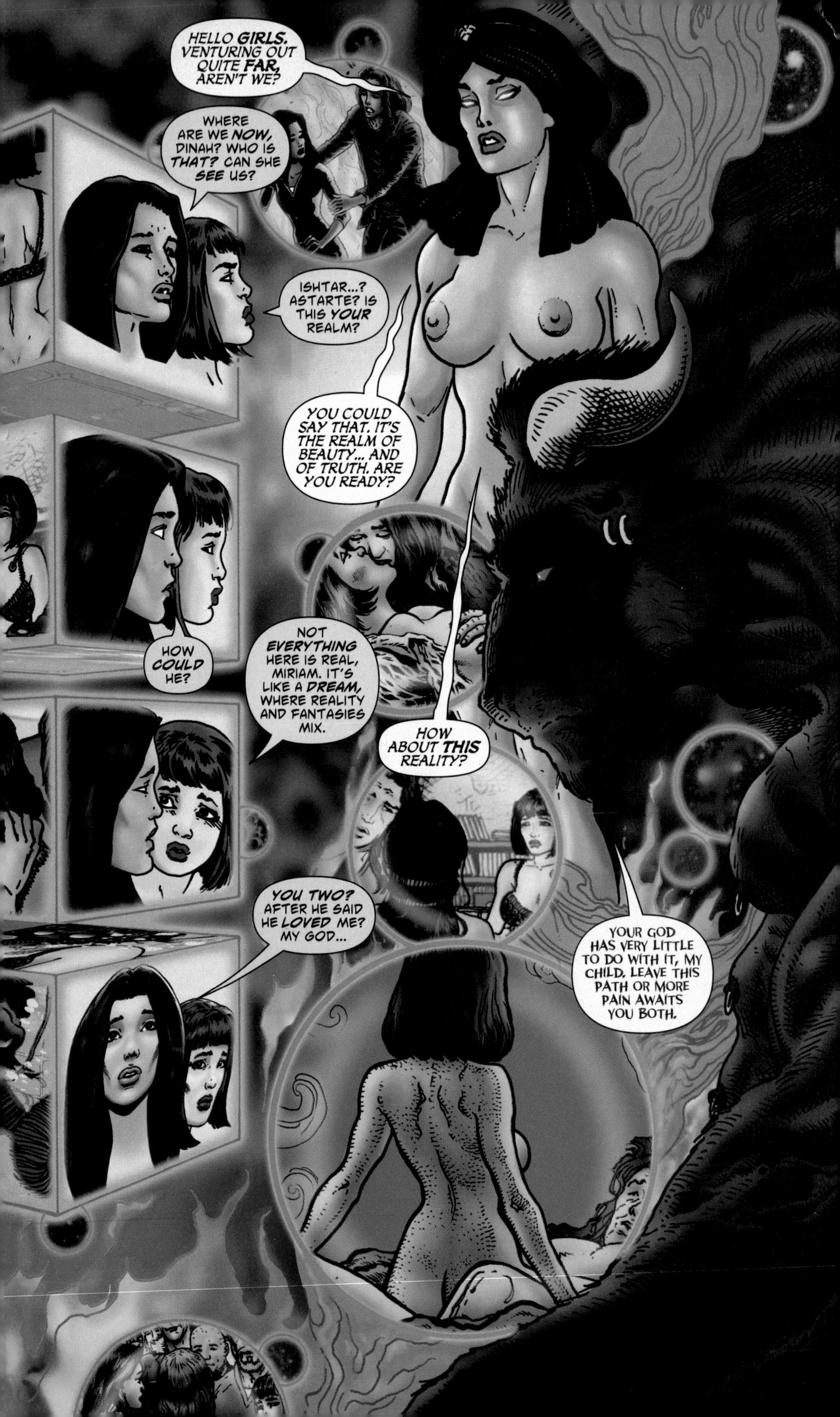
HELLO GIRLS. VENTURING OUT QUITE FAR, AREN'T WE?
WHERE ARE WE NOW, DINAH? WHO IS THAT? CAN SHE SEE US?
ISHTAR...? ASTARTE? IS THIS YOUR REALM?
YOU COULD SAY THAT. IT'S THE REALM OF BEAUTY... AND OF TRUTH. ARE YOU READY?
HOW COULD HE?
NOT EVERYTHING HERE IS REAL, MIRIAM. IT'S LIKE A DREAM, WHERE REALITY AND FANTASIES MIX.
HOW ABOUT THIS REALITY?
YOU TWO? AFTER HE SAID HE LOVED ME? MY GOD...
YOUR GOD HAS VERY LITTLE TO DO WITH IT, MY CHILD. LEAVE THIS PATH OR MORE PAIN AWAITS YOU BOTH.

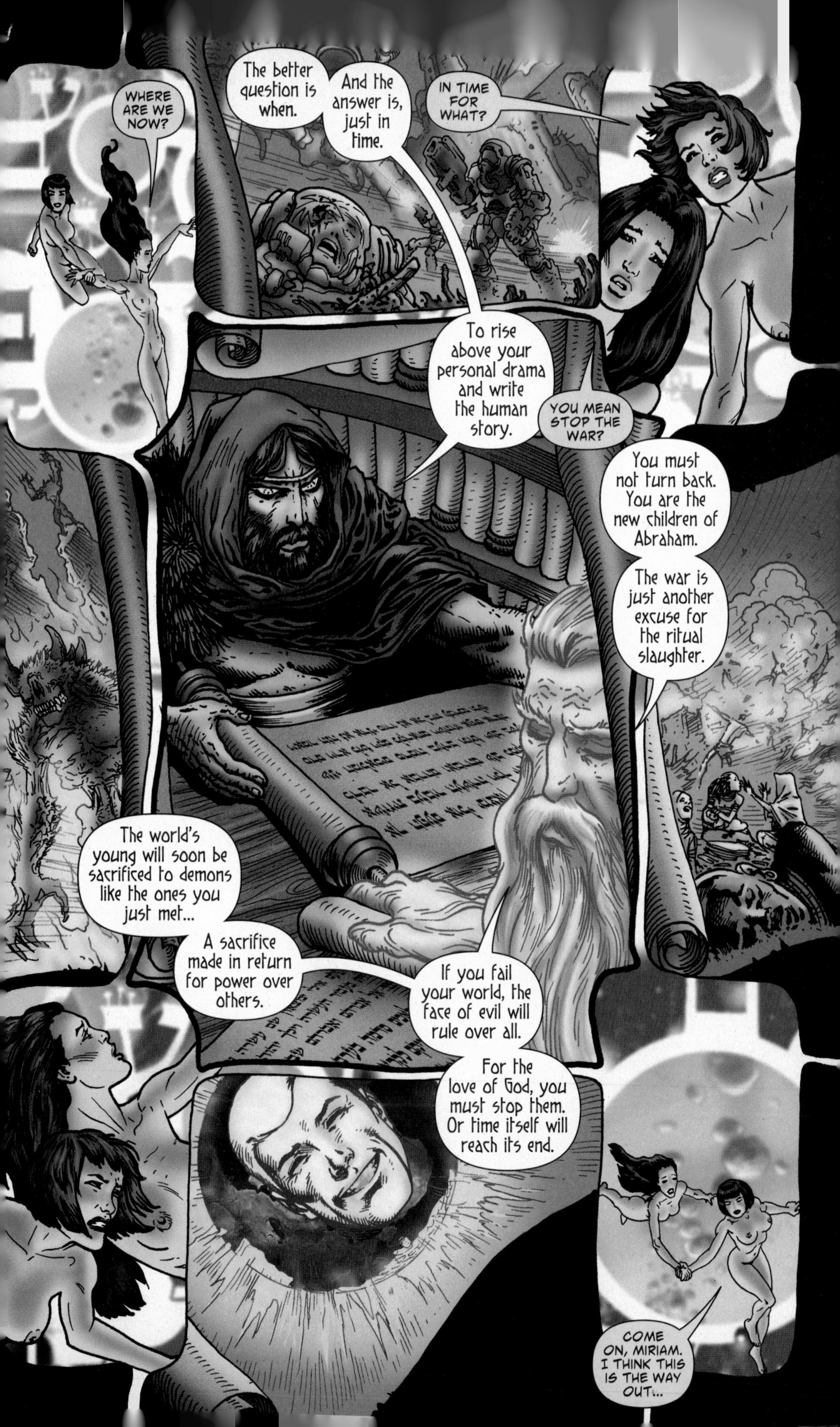
WHERE ARE WE NOW?
The better question is when.
And the answer is, just in time.
IN TIME FOR WHAT?
To rise above your personal drama and write the human story.
YOU MEAN STOP THE WAR?
You must not turn back. You are the new children of Abraham.
The war is just another excuse for the ritual slaughter.
The world's young will soon be sacrificed to demons like the ones you just met...
A sacrifice made in return for power over others.
If you fail your world, the face of evil will rule over all.
For the love of God, you must stop them. Or time itself will reach its end.
COME ON, MIRIAM. I THINK THIS IS THE WAY OUT...

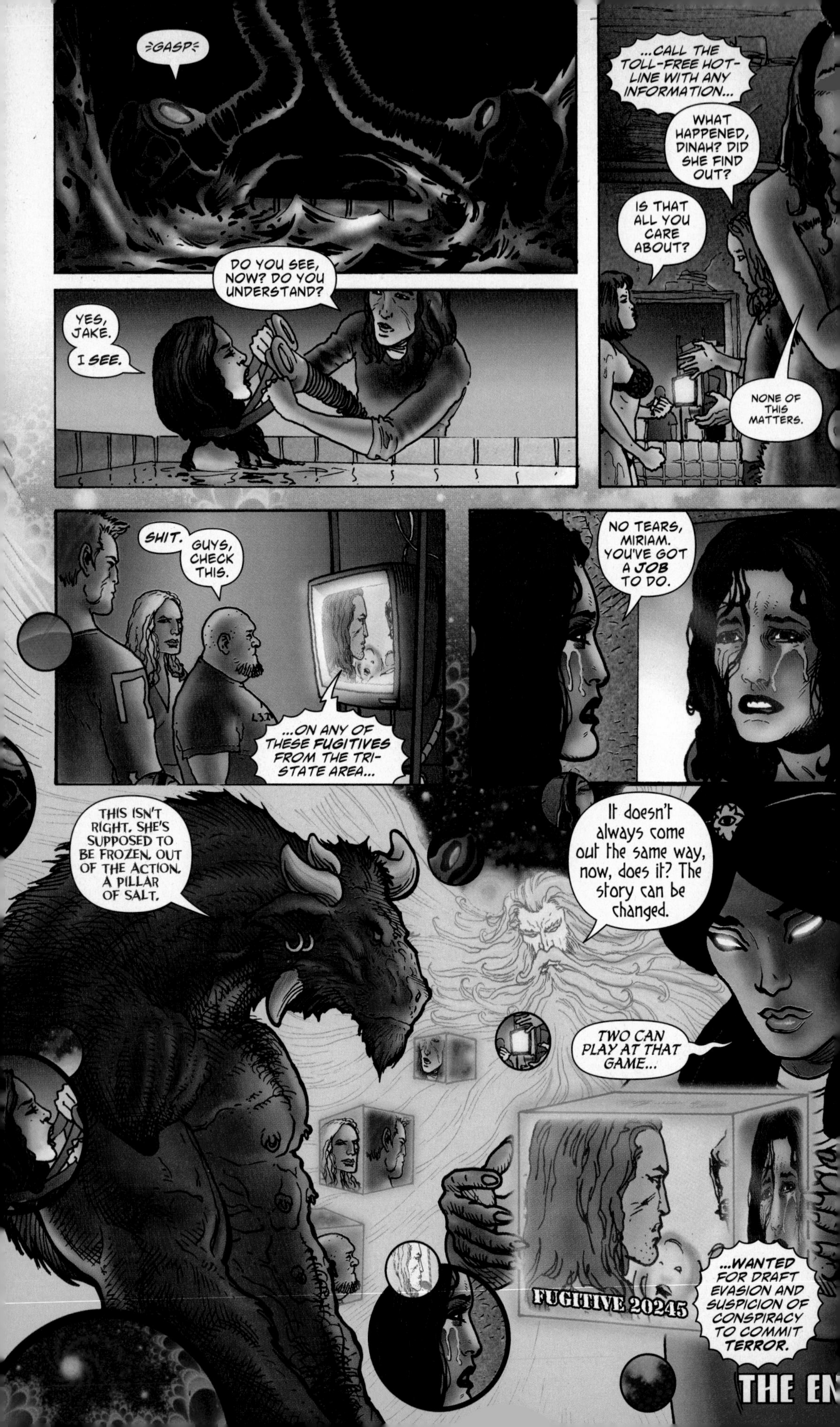
GASP
...CALL THE TOLL-FREE HOT-LINE WITH ANY INFORMATION...
WHAT HAPPENED, DINAH? DID SHE FIND OUT?
IS THAT ALL YOU CARE ABOUT?
DO YOU SEE, NOW? DO YOU UNDERSTAND?
YES, JAKE.
I SEE.
NONE OF THIS MATTERS.
SHIT.
GUYS, CHECK THIS.
...ON ANY OF THESE FUGITIVES FROM THE TRI-STATE AREA...
NO TEARS, MIRIAM. YOU'VE GOT A JOB TO DO.
THIS ISN'T RIGHT. SHE'S SUPPOSED TO BE FROZEN. OUT OF THE ACTION. A PILLAR OF SALT.
It doesn't always come out the same way, now, does it? The story can be changed.
TWO CAN PLAY AT THAT GAME...
FUGITIVE 20245
...WANTED FOR DRAFT EVASION AND SUSPICION OF CONSPIRACY TO COMMIT TERROR.
THE EN

BRIAN K. VAUGHAN AND PIA GUERRA'S COMPELLING TALE OF THE LAST MAN ON EARTH UNFOLDS IN THESE COLLECTIONS FROM VERTIGO:

Y THE LAST MAN

VERTIGO
BOOK 1
"This is why God created comic books."
— RevolutionSF.com
"This book blew us away."
— WIZARD
Brian K. Vaughan Pia Guerra José Marzán, Jr.
Y THE LAST MAN
Unmanned

VOLUME 1: UNMANNED

ALSO AVAILABLE:
- VOL. 2: CYCLES
- VOL. 3: ONE SMALL STEP
- VOL. 4: SAFEWORD
- VOL. 5: RING OF TRUTH
- VOL. 6: GIRL ON GIRL
- VOL. 7: PAPER DOLLS

"COMPLETE AND UTTER COMIC GOLD."
— *PUBLISHERS WEEKLY* (STARRED REVIEW)

ALL TITLES ARE SUGGESTED FOR MATURE READERS.

EX MACHINA
THE FIRST HUNDRED DAYS
BRIAN K. VAUGHAN TONY HARRIS TOM FEISTER

SCI-FI ACTION COLLIDES WITH FAST-PACED DRAMA IN THIS EXPLOSIVE POLITICAL THRILLER FROM WRITER BRIAN K. VAUGHAN AND WILDSTORM:

EX MACHINA

VOLUME 1: THE FIRST HUNDRED DAYS

ALSO AVAILABLE:
- VOL. 2: TAG
- VOL. 3: FACT V. FICTION

"TERRIFICALLY INTRIGUING."
— *ENTERTAINMENT WEEKLY*

SEARCH THE GRAPHIC NOVELS SECTION OF
www.VERTIGOCOMICS.com
FOR ART AND INFORMATION ON ALL OF OUR BOOKS

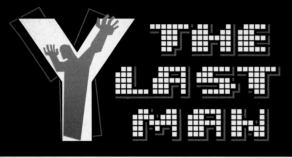

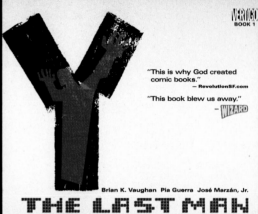

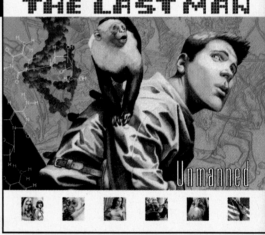

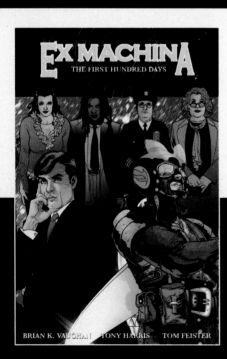

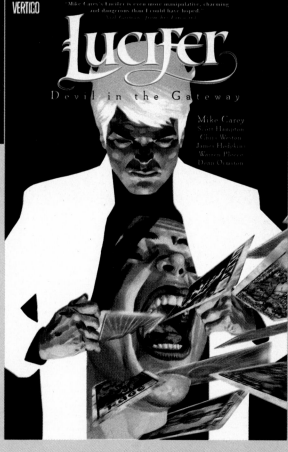
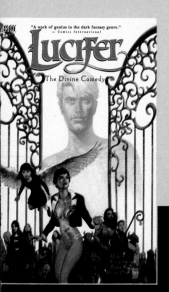

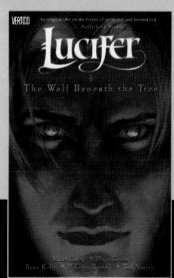